THE EPIC RHETORIC OF TASSO
THEORY AND PRACTICE

THE EUROPEAN HUMANITIES RESEARCH CENTRE

UNIVERSITY OF OXFORD

The European Humanities Research Centre of the University of Oxford organizes a range of academic activities, including conferences and workshops, and publishes scholarly works under its own imprint, LEGENDA, as well as *Oxford German Studies*. Within Oxford, the EHRC bridges, at the research level, the main humanities faculties: Modern Languages, English, Modern History, Literae Humaniores, Music and Theology. The Centre stimulates interdisciplinary research collaboration throughout these subject areas and provides an Oxford base for advanced researchers in the humanities.

The Centre's publications programme focuses on making available the results of advanced research in medieval and modern languages and related interdisciplinary areas. An Editorial Board, whose members are drawn from across the British university system, covers the principal European languages. Titles include works on French, German, Italian, Portuguese, Russian and Spanish literature. In addition, the EHRC publishes Research Monographs in French Studies in association with the Society for French Studies, and Studies in Comparative Literature in association with the British Comparative Literature Association. The Centre has also launched a Special Lecture Series under the LEGENDA imprint.

Enquiries about the Centre's publishing activities should be addressed to:
Professor Malcolm Bowie, Honorary Director (Publications)

Further information:
Kareni Bannister, Senior Publications Officer
European Humanities Research Centre
47 Wellington Square
Oxford OX1 2JF
E-mail: ehrc@modern-languages.ox.ac.uk
www.ehrc.ox.ac.uk

LEGENDA

EUROPEAN HUMANITIES RESEARCH CENTRE
MODERN HUMANITIES RESEARCH ASSOCIATION

The Epic Rhetoric of Tasso
Theory and Practice

MAGGIE GÜNSBERG

LEGENDA

European Humanities Research Centre
Modern Humanities Research Association
1998

Published by the European Humanities Research Centre
of the University of Oxford
47 Wellington Square
Oxford OX1 2JF
in conjunction with the
Modern Humanities Research Association

LEGENDA is the publications imprint of the
European Humanities Research Centre

ISBN 1-900755-05-X

First published 1998

British Cataloguing in Publication Data
A CIP catalogue record for this book is available from the British Library

LEGENDA series designed by Cox Design Partnership, Witney, Oxon
Printed in Great Britain by Information Press, Eynsham, Oxford OX8 1JJ

THIS BOOK IS DEDICATED TO BERTIE

CONTENTS

ACKNOWLEDGEMENTS

This book is a revised version of a doctoral thesis entitled 'Torquato Tasso: Theoretician and Poet', completed in 1985 at the University of Reading. My first supervisor was Luigi Meneghello, who was then succeeded by Giulio Lepschy. I should like to acknowledge their support, both in terms of meticulous critique and encouragement. After a decade I am at last able to incorporate some of Giulio Lepschy's suggestions that did not find their way into the thesis, especially those relating to Chapter 5. Zygmunt Barański, Cesare Segre and Shirley Vinall kindly commented on individual sections of the thesis during the period of its gestation. I also remember the Italian Department at Reading, where I took both undergraduate and graduate degrees, as a very nurturing and sociable environment in which to study. As far as the current revision is concerned, I should like to thank Peter Hainsworth and Martin McLaughlin for their crucial help in spotting the book within the thesis, and for their detailed comments on the manuscript. Peter Brand, whose seminal study on Tasso never left my side during the years when the thesis was taking shape, has provided a multitude of suggestions for this revision, most of which I have incorporated. My thanks also to Diego Zancani for kindly agreeing to read the proofs, to Bonnie Blackburn for her erudite copy-editing, and to Kareni Bannister at the EHRC for all her hard work in seeing this project through to publication.

ABBREVIATIONS

Discorsi	Tasso, *Discorsi dell'arte poetica e del poema eroico*, ed. L. Poma (Bari: Laterza, 1964)
Lettere	Tasso, *Le lettere di Torquato Tasso*, ed. C. Guasti, 5 vols. (Florence: Le Monnier, 1852–5)
Prose	Tasso, *Prose*, ed. E. Mazzali (Milan and Naples: Riccardo Ricciardi, 1959)

INTRODUCTION

Torquato Tasso (1544–95) was both theoretician and practitioner of the art of epic poetry. He lived and worked in an era of Italian cultural history dominated, in the intellectual sphere, by treatises and commentaries on all aspects of composition. Also of mounting importance for all writers and artists in Italy as the sixteenth century wore on was the impact of the authoritarian climate of the Counter-Reformation.[1]

Tasso wrote his first major treatise on *poetica*, the *Discorsi dell'arte poetica*, during his *fanciullezza* in 1561–2, prior to the most severe phase of the Counter-Reformation (*Prose*, letter no. 48, 25 Feb. 1585, p. 913). His *Apologia in difesa della Gerusalemme liberata* appeared in 1585, four years after the publication of the Bonnà edition of the *Gerusalemme liberata* in 1581. A completely rewritten version of the *Liberata* appeared as the less popular *Gerusalemme conquistata* in 1593. The *Arte poetica* also underwent revision and was published as the *Discorsi del poema epico* the following year. During this period Tasso began a critique of his second epic poem, the *Giudizio sovra la Gerusalemme conquistata*, a work left unfinished. His correspondence, especially the *lettere poetiche*, sheds light on the writing process itself, as well as revealing his response to religious and academic censure.

An ever-present consideration for Tasso was the Church censorship of writing that was not considered to uphold the status quo. Such works were subject to inclusion in a series of prohibitive papal indices inaugurated by Paul IV's *Index auctorum et librorum prohibitorum* of 1559. Papal censorship of the printed word had begun on a localized level as early as 1479, mere decades after the invention of printing, with Sixtus IV's breve *Accepimus literas* granting the University of Cologne the right to censor books. Although censorship became progressively more efficient and severe as the printing industry expanded, it did not reach its zenith until the final decades of the sixteenth century. Prohibition affected not only religious, political and scientif-

---

[1] On the life and works of Tasso, see Brand 1965, Donadoni 1967, Solerti 1895.

ic writings, but later also literary works, with Boccaccio, Ariosto and Bembo among the authors to be censored.

Studies of the period emphasize the negative effects of censorship on Italian secular cultural production (Garin 1969, Grendler 1977). The intellectual climate underwent a notable change during the 1560s in response to a progressively harsher enforcement of the Index. This was reflected by the printing industry in the numbers of governmental permissions issued for new titles. Figures for the period 1550–1606 given by Grendler, writing on the Venetian press, suggest that, following a transitional period during the 1560s, secular titles fell by a quarter, from 27 per cent to 20 per cent. Religious titles, on the other hand, doubled in number, comprising 30 per cent of new titles published between 1570 and 1606, compared with 14 per cent during the period 1550–9 (Grendler 1975, 55).

Inclusion in a papal index could lead to a variety of penalties. These ranged from confiscation of goods, house searches and fines to excommunication, imprisonment, torture and capital punishment (Brown 1969, 112, 115, 120–1, 132). Tasso's letters testify to extensive, wearisome and, at times, highly disturbing dealings with the Inquisition regarding the revision of his poem, a procedure that necessarily preceded publication. In one letter he speaks of 'questo benedetto rancore de la proibizione d'infiniti poeti' (*Lettere*, i, no. 25, 15 Apr. 1575). Five years later he talks about visits to the Inquisitor and even mentions having been denounced (ii, no. 133, 17 May 1580). An earlier letter is addressed to the cardinals of the Supreme Inquisition of Rome itself (*Prose*, no. 21, July 1577, p. 818).[2]

The precise nature of the effects of religious and literary authoritarianism on writers is difficult to quantify. However, a certain degree of internalization of dominant values would seem likely. In the case of Tasso, bouts of mental illness further cloud the picture. While issues of censorship are present in his letters, which also show him seeking advice on the composition of the *Gerusalemme liberata*, ultimately much was left in the poem which might remain open to censure. The pressures of the historical and cultural climate on Tasso are mirrored in both his *poetica* and his *poesia*, if in very different ways and to different degrees.

Part I of this study examines his major theoretical works on *poetica* from the point of view of the three central rhetorical faculties of

---

[2] For further discussion of the Counter-Reformation in Italy, see Brown 1969, Eisenstein 1972, Firetto 1933, Garin 1969, Grendler 1977, Tedeschi 1971.

inventio, dispositio and *elocutio*. The changing religious and cultural context affecting the interpretation of these categories is seen in an ongoing comparison between Tasso's earlier and later *poetica*. In order to highlight the significant time lapse between the composition of the *Discorsi dell'arte poetica* and their extensive revision as the *Discorsi del poema eroico* three decades later, the former work will often be referred to as the 'early *Discorsi*' and the latter as the 'later *Discorsi*'. Not included here is the unfinished *Giudizio sovra la Gerusalemme conquistata* (nor, indeed, the *Gerusalemme conquistata* itself).

This study also makes use of twentieth-century theories. Of special interest in Chapter 2 on *dispositio* is the coincidence of ideas on art between Tasso and the Russian Formalists of the 1920s, both traceable to Aristotelian ideas on plot. Part II is devoted to a three-part analysis of the *Gerusalemme liberata* using a range of modern methodologies. Matters of literary precedent and intertextuality are left aside in order to focus on the development of new methods of reading the epic text. Freudian negation, Lacanian socialization of the *I*, and the role of body language in reinforcing the status quo of power relations form focal points of discussion in Chapters 4, 5 and 6 respectively. Attention is also paid to the way in which these covert aspects of the poem function in relation to the progression of the narrative to its conclusion. The two parts of this volume, dealing with Tasso's theory and practice respectively, are intended to offer complementary approaches that together illuminate his epic contribution, achieved despite (or, some might say, because of) the historical period in which he lived and worked.

PART I

❖

Poetica

Tasso's Epic Theory and the
Rhetorical Tradition

CHAPTER 1

Inventio

Tasso opens his *Discorsi dell'arte poetica* (written 1561–2 and published 1587) with a statement of the three classical rhetorical faculties which the epic poet should bear in mind, namely *inventio*, *dispositio* and *elocutio*:

A tre cose deve aver riguardo ciascuno che di scriver poema eroico si prepone: a *sceglier materia* tale che sia atta a ricever in sé quella più eccelente forma che l'artificio del poeta cercarà d'introdurvi; a *darle* questa tal *forma*; ed a *vestirla* ultimamente con que' più esquisiti ornamenti, ch'a la natura di lei siano convenevoli (*Discorsi*, 3).[1]

Inventio, or the choice of *materia*, is the first of the rhetorical faculties, providing the basis for the following two. Selection of appropriate *materia*, or *argomento*, is essential to the next stage of the poetic process, namely its shaping or ordering (*dispositio*), after which it can be 'exquisitely clothed' with words (*elocutio*). That Tasso followed this procedure in composing the *Gerusalemme liberata* appears to be borne out by his correspondence. Writing to Scipio Gonzaga on 20 May 1575, he says: 'ho cominciato a distendere l'argomento de la favola e de gli episodi interseritivi, così in prosa' (*Lettere*, i. 77). Almost a year later, Tasso has in mind a concerted effort to be spent on the final stage of the poetic process, namely *elocutio*, as he informs Gonzaga on 11 February 1576: 'ma io per ancora non ho avuto alcun diligente riguardo a le voci ed a la lingua' (i. 129). (However, the transition from *dispositio* to *elocutio* is not as straightforward in temporal terms as that from *inventio* to *dispositio*; this will be explored in Ch. 3.)

In his treatment of *inventio*, Tasso discusses the choice of *materia*, using the term *invenzione* itself predominantly in the sense of 'fiction',

[1] 1561–2 is the date of composition of the early *Discorsi* proposed by Poma in the edition used in this study (cited hereafter as *Discorsi*). A translation into English can be found in Tasso, *Discourses on the Heroic Poem*. All italics are my own, unless otherwise indicated.

as in the following passages from the *Discorsi*: 'La materia ... o si finge, e allora par che il poeta abbia parte non solo nella scelta, ma nella invenzione ancora, o si toglie dall'istorie' and 'la finzione è riputata invenzione' (*Discorsi*, 4, 80). The term *invenzione* is used for the rhetorical faculty in the later *Discorsi del poema epico* (1594): 'or debbiam considerare in qual luogo ella [materia] debba ricercarsi; il che appertiene in qualche modo a l'invenzione' (*Discorsi*, 83). However, the final clause (in particular the phrase *in qualche modo*) seems to indicate that Tasso does not associate the term *invenzione* as readily with the first rhetorical faculty of *inventio* as he does with *finzione*.

Classical meanings of *materia*

Materia denotes not only the subject-matter to be used by the poet or orator, but also matter in general. As well as occurring in the rhetorical faculties, it is therefore also to be found in philosophical categorizations. The most fundamental of these is the *materia–forma* division.[2] Based on this was the *res–verba* distinction (with *res* corresponding to *materia*).[3] *Res* originated in philosophy, while *verba* enters the distinction from rhetoric and grammar.[4] All discourse, such as a speech or poem, was divided into *res* and *verba*.[5] In its Renaissance manifestation as *materia/cose–forma/parole/voci*, the distinction became coupled, as a result of the revival of Aristotle's *Poetics*, with two of the qualitative

---

[2] The *materia–forma* division is discussed by Aristotle in the *Physics*. He examines the relationship between the two parts as follows: 'the conception of *materia* is relative, for it is different material that is suited to receive the several forms' and 'one way of regarding "nature"—as the ultimately underlying material of all things that have in themselves the principle of movement and change. But from another point of view we may think of the nature of a thing as residing rather in its form, that is to say in the "kind" of thing it is by definition' (194^b II. ii. 9, 193^a II. i. 28–30). All translations from classical sources are taken from the edition listed in the Bibliography unless otherwise stated.

[3] *Res* can be seen to correspond to *materia* in Geoffroi de Vinsauf's *Poetria nova*: 'When, in the recesses of the mind, order has arranged the matter [*rem*], let the art of poetry come to clothe the matter [*materiam*] with words' (p. 17). See also Titi's use of *materia* and *verba* in his *Locorum controversorum* of 1583 (Weinberg 1961, 210).

[4] According to Badius, for example, in his commentary on Horace's *Ars poetica*: 'Res autem ex philosophia originem trahit ut praecepta contineat. Oratio in grammatica & rhetorica dicitur' (with *oratio* corresponding to *verba*) (Weinberg 1961, 84).

[5] Speech was divided into *res* and *verba* by Quintilian in his *Institutio oratoria*: 'But all speech expressive of purpose involves ... a subject [*rem*] and words [*verba*]' (III. iii. 1),

parts of tragedy and the epic (plot and diction respectively).[6]

Castelvetro formulates this distinction in an interesting way in his *Poetica d'Aristotele vulgarizzata, et sposta* (1570) by placing plot (together with character and thought) under the heading of what he calls *capo interno*, and speech (together with dance, sound and song) under that of *capo forestiero*. He explains the first heading as 'imaginevole, ciò è ha per soggetto le cose sottoposte all'imaginativa', and the second as 'udevole, & vedevole, ciò è ha per soggetto le cose sottoposte alla veduta, & all'udita'. The *capo interno* appears to relate to *materia* ('la favola, e 'l costume & la sententia si deono alla materia rappresentativa attribuire'), while the *capo forestiero* is concerned with how this is presented to the senses of sight and hearing, in other words, the form given to *materia* (pp. 67–8). This distinction is already inherent in Aristotle's tripartite division of the qualitative parts of representation into objects (relating to *materia*), means and manner (both relating to *forma*). However, Castelvetro's grouping of these under two *capi* helps polarize Aristotle's parts into what can be interpreted essentially as the *materia–forma* distinction, thereby characterizing the way in which the Renaissance attempted to clarify a rather terse, and possibly even incomplete, text.[7]

and the oration similarly divided by Cicero in his *De oratore*: 'Every speech consists of matter [*re*] and words [*verbis*]' (III. v. 19). Badius applied this division to poetry:'Poema enim constat ex re & oratione' (Weinberg 1961, 84). Correa divided both the oration and the poem into *res* and *verba* in his *In librum de arte poetica Q. Horatij Flacci explanationes* of 1587: 'since a poem, like a speech, consists of things [*rebus*] and of words [*verbis*]' (Weinberg 1961, 216 n. 26).

   [6] Tasso formulates this distinction as follows in his *Discorsi*: 'Ogni poesia è composta di parole e di cose' (*Discorsi*, 136). Other 16th-c. expressions of the distinction are as follows: Lapini, in his *Letione nella quale si ragiona in universale del fine della poesia* (1567), says: 'Conchiudiamo adunque che sendo la *materia* del Poeta la Favola … & la *forma* sendo la imitazione' (Weinberg 1961, 502 n. 55); Sassetti, *Sposizione della Poetica* (1576): 'cose naturali, le quali sono composte di *materia* e di *forma*' (Weinberg 1961, 577 n. 24); Muzio, *Dell'arte poetica* (1551): 'Gli scrittori d'Atene e quei di Roma / Daranno al vostro dir *materia* e *forma*' (Weinberg 1970–4, ii. 166); B. Tasso, *Ragionamento della poesia* (1562): 'Non sapete voi che la poesia è composta di *parole* e di *cose*, e che la filosofia è fecondissima madre d'esse cose?' (Weinberg 1970–4, ii. 575); Daniello, *Della poetica* (1536): 'Della quale "convenevolezza" chiunque poca o niuna cognizione avesse, non solamente nelle *cose* ma potrebbe eziandio errare nelle *parole*' (Weinberg, 1970–4, i. 250); Giraldi, *Discorso intorno al comporre de i romanzi, delle comedie, e delle tragedie* (1554): 'non movendo le *cose* da sé gli affetti senza le *voci* acconciamente e numerosamente insieme giunte' (p. 177).

   [7] The precise manner in which Castelvetro's regrouping takes place is as follows: he

The *materia/cosa/res–forma/parole/verba* distinction was also linked
to the dual function of utility (produced by *materia*) and pleasure
(evoked by *parole*). These functions had been extrapolated by Horace
for poetry from Cicero's trio of rhetorical functions, *docere*, *delectare*
and *movere*.[8] Giraldi states in his *Discorso intorno al comporre dei romanzi*
(1554) that 'come il *giovare* è delle sentenze, et delle *cose*, che si trattano, così le *voci* oltre l'espressione del concetto sono tutte del *piacere*
et della vaghezza' (Weinberg 1961, 439 n. 37). Varchi, invoking the
further duality of body and mind in his *Lezzioni della poetica* (1553–4),
believes that harmonious words please the body, while useful subject-
matter pleases the mind: 'l'armonia delle *parole*, che s'odono ... *diletta* propriamente il corpo, e l'*utilità* delle *cose*, che s'intendono, *diletta*
propriamente l'animo' (Weinberg 1961, 136 n. 36). The
materia/res–forma/verba pair, moreover, also encapsulated all the
resources (*vis*) brought to bear by the orator, according to Cicero's *De
partitione oratoria*: 'In what do the speaker's personal resources [*vis*]
consist? In matter [*rebus*] and in language [*verbis*]' (I. 3).

Materia is a basic component in each of the five categories into
which classical treatises divided rhetoric: the facultative, qualitative,
quantitative, functional and causal. *Materia*, *res*, or *inventio* (translated
in the following definitions by Cicero in his *De inventione* as argu-

---

acknowledges and interprets Aristotle's tripartite division of *materia* (objects) as *favola*,
costume and *sentenza*, of *stormento* (means) as 'la melodia, che sono il ballo, il canto e
'l suono ... insieme con la favella', and of *modo* (manner) as 'la vista sola' (spectacle).
In his bipartite redistribution, the three elements of *materia* form the first group ('tre
parti di qualità ciò è, favola, costume, & sententia si contengono nel capo interno o
imaginevole'), while *stormento* and *modo* fuse to make up the second ('Hora passiamo
a favellare del capo forestiero, che habbiamo detto essere doppio ciò è vedevole, &
udevole, dico che il vedevole contiene in sé il ballo, & l'ornamento della vista, &
l'udevole contiene in sé la favella, il canto, e 'l suono') (pp. 67–8).

[8] 'Aut prodesse volunt aut delectare poetae / aut simul et iucunda et idonea
dicere vitae' (*Ars poetica* 333). Cicero defines the three rhetorical functions as follows in his *De optimo genere oratorum*: 'The supreme orator, then, is the one whose
speech instructs, delights and moves the minds of his audience. The orator is in
duty bound to instruct; giving pleasure is a free gift to the audience, to move
them is indispensable' (I. 3). In the *Brutus* he says: 'Now there are three things in
my opinion which the orator should effect: instruct his listener, give him pleasure, stir his emotions' (xlix. 185). Both his *De oratore* and *Orator* contain similar
passages: 'those commonplaces from which may be drawn a speech such as to
attain those three things which alone can carry conviction; I mean the winning
over, the instructing and the stirring of men's minds' (I. xxviii. 121) and 'To
prove is the first necessity, to please is charm, to sway is victory' (xxi. 69).

ments, matter, or subject-matter) can be seen to run through each of the five facultative divisions (disposition, elocution, memory and delivery, as well as invention):

Invention is the discovery of valid or seemingly valid *arguments* [*rerum*] to render one's cause plausible … arrangement is the distribution of *arguments* [*rerum*] thus discovered in the proper order … expression is the fitting of the proper language to the invented *matter* [*inventionem*] … memory is the firm mental grasp of *matter* [*rerum*] and words … and delivery is the control of voice and body in a manner suitable to the dignity of the *subject-matter* [*rerum*] and the style (*De optimo genere oratorum* I. vii. 9).[9]

In the *De partitione oratoria*, however, Cicero emphasizes matter (as part of the *res–verba* distinction) particularly in relation to invention, while also intimating its centrality to disposition:

But both matter [*res*] and language have to be found, and have to be arranged—although the term 'invention' is used specially of the matter and 'delivery' of the language, but arrangement, though belonging to both, nevertheless is applied to invention (I. 3).

Matter is assigned to both invention and disposition by Pigna in his *Poetica Horatiana* (1561): 'To the matter [*rei*] belong invention and disposition' (Weinberg 1961, 157 n. 2).

Consideration of *materia* was also introduced into the qualitative method of dividing the poetic composition. This type of division appears to have originated in poetics with Aristotle, with no apparent equivalent as regards the oration. In the words of Aristotle summarizing the qualitative parts of tragedy:

Necessarily then every tragedy has six constituent parts, and on these its quality depends. These are plot, character, diction, thought, spectacle, and song. Two of these are the means of representation [diction and music]: one is the manner [spectacle]: three are the objects represented [plot, character and thought] (1450[a] vi. 9–10, trans. Hamilton Fyfe).

The term *materia* was used in the Renaissance to translate the Aristotelian objects of plot, character and thought. Sigonio says in his *Emendationum libri duo* (1557): 'Nam tragici imitantur fabulam, mores, & sententiam, ut *materiam*' (Weinberg 1961, 457 n. 74). Castelvetro, in

---

[9] This Ciceronian group of five *partes* was the format finally given to the faculties of the orator, while Aristotle appears to have been the first before Cicero to classify the first three faculties (*Rhetoric*, 1403[b] III. 1) and to add delivery (*Rhetoric*, 1403[b] III. 1) (see Caplan's translation of the *Rhetorica ad Herennium*, 6 n. a).

the same context, says in his *Poetica d'Aristotele vulgarizzata, et sposta* (1570): 'la favola, e 'l costume, & la sententia si deono alla *materia* rappresentativa attribuire' (p. 68). And Riccoboni, also commenting on this section of the *Poetics*, relates *materia* to the same qualitative parts in his *Poetica Aristotelis latine conversa* (1587): 'Duae enim ad instrumentum referuntur melopoeia, & dictio: tres ad *materiam*, fabula, mores, sententia; una ad modum, quae est apparatus' (p. 32).

This was, however, not the only method of dividing up the qualitative parts. Robortello, for instance, assigned diction, character and thought to *materia*, attributing plot to manner in his *In librum Aristotelis de arte poetica explicationes* (1548): 'per tertiam differentiam scilicet quae subiectam *materie* significat ... ex tertia [differentia], tres partes. DICTIO, MORES, SENTENTIA' (p. 57). Grifoli follows the same arrangement, two years later, using the term *res* for *materia* in his *In artem poeticam Horatii interpretatio* (1550): 'dictio verò, mores sententiae *res* sunt, quae ad imitandum sunt propositae' (Weinberg 1961, 418 n. 115).

Classical rhetoric divided the oration into six quantitative parts: introduction, statement of facts or narration, division, proof or demonstration, refutation and conclusion.[10] This division was then extended in a variety of ways to poetic composition, with *materia* inevitably present, in diverse forms, in all the parts in their varying combinations, such as invocation, proposition and narration. For example, Campanella says in his *Poetica italiana* (1596): 'Fa dunque tre parti il poeta: l'invocazione, la proposizione e la narrazione' (p. 411). A different set of quantitative divisions was introduced by Aristotle in the *Poetics* as specific to tragedy alone: 'The separable members into which it [tragedy] is quantitatively divided are these: Prologue, Episode, Exode, Choral Song, the last being divided into Parode and Stasimon' (1452^b xi. 12, trans. Hamilton Fyfe).

These quantitative divisions were actually called 'material parts' by, for instance, Pellegrino in *Il Carrafa, o vero della epica poesia* (1584) ('parti di quantità o materiali'), and were extended from tragedy to the epic, there being no equivalent set for the latter genre. As Pellegrino comments: 'Delle parti di quantità, o materiali, dell'e-

---

[10] These parts are enumerated in the *Rhetorica ad Herennium* (I. iii. 4). Plato's Socrates, speaking to Phaedrus in *Phaedrus*, lists the following: introduction, narration, proofs, probabilities and confirmation (266D–E). Aristotle in his *Rhetoric* gives only exordium, statement, proof and epilogue (1414^b III. xiii. 4).

popea Aristotile non ragiona' (Weinberg 1970–4, iii. 321, 342). *Materia* is thus 'quantified' in combinations such as that of prologue, episode and epilogue. Tasso himself uses these three divisions in his comparison between the epic form and the *canzone* in his *Considerazioni sopra tre canzoni di M. Gio. Battista Pigna intitolate Le tre sorelle* (1568) (Weinberg 1961, 184). This particular group of divisions was applied to the *Gerusalemme liberata* by Guastavini in his *Discorsi et annotationi* (1592). He groups Cantos I–III together as the prologue, IV–XVIII as the episode, and XIX–XXI as the epilogue (Weinberg 1961, 1053). Oddi also compares Tasso and Ariosto on the basis of these three quantitative parts in his *Dialogo in difesa di Camillo Pellegrini contra gli Academici della Crusca* (1587) (Weinberg 1961, 1034).

As far as the functional divisions of the oration were concerned, *materia*, as has already been indicated, was frequently associated with utility, while words were regarded as giving rise to pleasure. Lastly, *materia* occupies an important position in the causal rhetorical divisions as one of the four causes (material, formal, efficient and final) taken from philosophy (in particular, Aristotle's *Physics* and *Metaphysics*), where they are applied to things in general, and brought to bear on poetics (*Physics* 194^b–195^a II. iii; *Metaphysics* 1013^a V. ii. 1–1013^b V. ii. 6). These philosophical causes were not used by Latin theorists of rhetoric (such as Cicero or Quintilian) and poetics (Horace), or indeed by Aristotle himself in his own *Rhetoric* and *Poetics*, and appear to have entered the rhetorical domain only in the late Middle Ages, when they occur in works by the Modistae. The *Summa grammatica*, or *Grammatica speculativa* by John of Dacia (fl. 1280) makes use of the four causes with reference to modes of signification (Murphy 1974, 155). The *Grammatica speculativa* (1300–10) by Thomas of Erfurt applies them to the principles of construction, with direct reference to Aristotle's *Metaphysics* (p. 275).

The causal divisions predominate, however, in connection with the art of preaching. The application of these causes in the *artes praedicandi* was notably inconsistent, a characteristic that was to be continued in Renaissance poetics. Thus the material cause of the sermon was defined variously as *thema* by John of Wales (*c.*1275), as the form of preaching by Robert of Basevorn (1322) and as *verba casta* by Ranulph Higden (*c.*1340) (Jennings 1978, 116). As far as the art of poetry in the Middle Ages is concerned, the four causes are to be found in only one of the major treatises, namely the *Poetria* by John of Garland (fl. 1250)

(Faral 1962, 379). They can also be seen employed in a practical way in the first commentary on Cavalcanti's 'Donna me prega' by the 'grandissimo dottore in fisica e in più scienze naturali e filosofiche', Dino del Garbo (d. 1327). He declares the material cause of the poem to be the subject-matter, in other words, spiritual love (the formal cause being scientific expression, the efficient cause, a lady, and the final cause, that of satisfying a worthy person) (Corti 1983, 13).[11]

Renaissance theorists tended, rather typically, to fuse Aristotle's generic discussion of the four causes in the *Physics* and the *Metaphysics* with his ideas on the origins of poetry in the *Poetics*. In the *Poetics* he discusses two causes for poetry (namely, man's instinct for representation and imitation, and the enjoyment he derives from the learning process that results from representation), without, however, referring to any of the four causes in his *Physics* (1448^b III. 4). Nevertheless, all the four causes were widely posited for poetry during the Renaissance. The actual definition of these causes, furthermore, shows the same lack of consistency that was observed in the medieval *artes praedicandi*. This is particularly the case as far as the material cause is concerned, a feature that is further reflected in definitions of *materia* itself.

The material cause of poetry was variously defined by Maggi and Lombardi in their *In Aristotelis librum de poetica communes explanationes* (1550) as 'the human mind, which it [poetry] proposes to refine with the best principles of conduct' (Weinberg 1961, 48 n. 14); as 'il verso' by Sassetti in his marginalia to Piccolomini's *Annotationi nel Libro della Poetica d'Aristotele* (1575) (Weinberg 1961, 48 n. 16); as 'il parlare' by Giacomini in *De la purgazione de la tragedia* (1586) (Weinberg 1970–4, iii. 352); as actions by Piccolomini in his *Annotationi* (1575) (Weinberg 1961, 555); as 'la Favola' by Lapini in his *Letione nella quale si ragiona in universale del fine della poesia* (1567) (Weinberg 1961, 502 n. 55); as 'la cosa proposta' by Lionardi in *Dialogi della inventione poetica* (1554) (Weinberg 1961, 48); and as the subject-matter by Caburacci in *Breve discorso in difesa dell'Orlando Furioso di M. Lodovico Ariosto* (1580) (Weinberg 1961, 981).

[11] See Corti also on Cavalcanti and his commentators, and on connections between Cavalcanti and the speculative grammarian Boethius of Dacia. It is possible that the Renaissance use of the four causes is connected with the works of the Modistae, as well as relating directly to Aristotle's *Physics* and *Metaphysics*. See also Murphy 1978, 77.

The final cause is perhaps the one most consistently defined by Renaissance theorists, regularly constituting either pleasure or utility, or both. Pleasure and utility themselves clearly correspond to the Horatian functions of poetry, thereby showing the typical way in which various philosophical and rhetorical categories merge and interlink in Renaissance theory. The fusion of initially separate categories seems to be a particular feature of Renaissance theory, perhaps showing a reaction to the sheer abundance of classical source material that had surfaced and accumulated by that time, and a consequent desire to rationalize the whole by means of synthesis.

Interlinking can be observed taking place between most of the categories: the faculties of the orator or poet, the qualitative and quantitative parts of the speech or poem, and its functions, or ends, of pleasure and utility. Thus the *materia/res–forma/verba* distinction is linked to the facultative category by, for example, Pigna in his *Poetica Horatiana* (1561): 'To the matter belong invention and disposition, and the same two also to words' (Weinberg 1961, 157); to the qualitative category by Maranta in *Lucullianae quaestiones* (1564): 'the words produce the diction and the things themselves the sententiae' (Weinberg 1961, 173); to the functional by Varchi in *Lezzioni della poetica* (1554): 'percioche l'armonia delle parole, che s'odono ... diletta propriamente il corpo, e l'utilità delle cose, che s'intendono diletta propriamente l'animo' (Weinberg 1961, 136 n. 36); to the qualitative and the functional by Maggi in *In Q. Horatii Flacci de arte poetica librum ad Pisones, Interpretatio* (1550) (*res* is linked to the qualitative part of plot and to the function of utility, and *verba* to the qualitative part of diction and to the function of pleasure) (Weinberg 1961, 119–22, 417).

The distinction is linked to the facultative and functional categories by Parrasio in *In Q. Horatii Flacci artem poeticam commentaria* (1531) (*res* is linked to the faculty of invention and the function of utility, and *verba* is linked to the faculty of elocution and to the function of pleasure) (Weinberg 1961, 98); to the facultative, qualitative and functional by Giraldi in *Discorso intorno al comporre dei romanzi* (1554) (*res* is linked to the faculties of invention and disposition, to the qualitative parts of plot, character and thought, and to the function of utility, and *verba* is linked to the faculty of elocution, to the qualitative part of diction, and to the function of pleasure) (Weinberg 1961, 439); and to the facultative, the qualitative, the quantitative and the functional by Minturno in his *De poeta* (1559) (*res* is linked to the faculty of invention, to the qualitative parts of plot and character, and to the function of *docere*, while *verba* is linked to the faculty of elocution, to the qualitative parts of diction and thought, and to the functions of *delectare* and *movere*) (Weinberg 1961, 741).

The facultative category is linked to the qualitative by Speroni in *Dialogo sopra Virgilio* (1563–4) (the faculty of invention is linked to the qualitative parts of plot and character; the faculty of elocution is linked to the qualitative parts of thought and diction) (Weinberg 1961, 169, 199); to the quantitative by San Martino in *Osservazioni grammaticali e poetiche della lingua italiana* (1555) (he considers invention to be made up of exordium, narration, division, confirmation, confutation and conclusion) (Weinberg 1961, 139–40); and to the qualitative and the quantitative by Ceruti in *Paraphrasis in Q. Horatii Flacci librum de arte poetica* (1588) (the faculty of invention is linked to the qualitative parts of plot and episode; the faculty of disposition is linked to the qualitative part of plot and to the quantitative exordium; the faculty of elocution is linked to the qualitative part of diction) (Weinberg 1961, 22). Finally, the qualitative distinction of plot is linked to the quantitative one of episode by Maranta in his lectures on the *Ars poetica* in 1561, when he says that the episode 'non fa altro che dilatare et accrescere la favola' and 'Favola è ... tutto l'aggregato della universale e delli episodij' (Weinberg 1961, 471–2).

Bearing in mind what has been said concerning the ubiquitous presence of *materia* in all these categories, the further phenomenon of the interlinking of these categories adds yet another dimension to the role of *materia* in Renaissance theory. *Materia* is, moreover, often equated with the material cause, so that their definitions are frequently identical. Consequently all the definitions that have been listed for the material cause will reappear in the following survey of definitions of *materia*. This study is ultimately concerned with *materia* in the sense of subject-matter, and its function within the faculty of invention. However, it may also be of interest to note other meanings and associations which *materia* would have had for Tasso, and for the rhetorical tradition of which he was a part.

Materia vs. *forma*

Definitions of the material cause of poetry use a variety of terms. These fall mainly into two groups, one relating to things (for example, 'la cosa proposta', 'favola' and 'il verisimile'), and the other to words (for example, 'il verso' and 'parole'), in other words, the terms of the fundamental rhetorical *res–verba* distinction. Salviati, for instance, uses both types of definition in *Della poetica lezion prima* (1564). He first of all defines the material cause of poetry in terms of words: 'Materia sono, addunque, della poesia le parole; la forma, l'invenzione e le cose' and 'sono dunque le parole ... secondo l'autorità d'Aristotile, materia generalissima di tutta la Poesia' (the formal cause being the *invenzione*, the efficient cause, the *intelletto* of the poet, and the final cause, 'il giovare a gli animi con diletto') (Weinberg 1970–4, ii. 608, 609). On the other hand, in his later *Parafrasi e commento della Poetica d'Aristotile* (1585–6) language is subordinated to considerations of content, in particular the verisimilar, in the definition of the material cause: 'La materia del medesimo poema si è il verisimile espresso col favellar condito.' The formal cause has now become the disposition ('La forma è la disposizione senza fallo'), the efficient cause remains the mind of the poet ('La cagione del poema, la cagione dico, la quale agente, o vero efficiente è chiamata, è l'anima del poeta'), while the final cause also remains the same, in other words, 'giovare e dilettare' (Weinberg 1961, 49 n. 18).

The same dualistic approach applies to definitions of *materia*, some of which concern subject-matter, while others are expressed solely in terms of language. Tasso himself produces the latter type of definition for *materia*, in addition to his treatment of it as subject-matter in the *Discorsi*, in his *Lezione sopra un sonetto di Monsignor Della Casa* of 1565: 'chiara cosa è, che i concetti siano il fine e conseguentemente la forma dell'orazione; e le parole, e la composizione del verso, la materia o l'instromento' (Weinberg 1961, 176 n. 42). Here the basic philosophical matter–form division is applied to the rhetorical *res–verba* distinction in a converse manner, that is, to words and concepts respectively.

The interpretation of the *materia/res* of discourse as language is present in various Renaissance treatises on poetics. San Martino states in his *Osservazioni grammaticali e poetiche della lingua italiana* (1555) that words constitute the *materia* of poetry (Weinberg 1961, 140). Grifoli, referring in *In artem poeticam Horatii interpretatio* (1550) to Aristotle's qualitative parts, posits diction along with character and thought as matter to be imitated: 'In truth, diction and character and thought are the materials which are proposed for imitation' (Weinberg 1961, 418 n. 115). For Giacomini, applying the *materia–forma* distinction to the composition of tragedy in *De la purgazione de la tragedia* (1583), imitation provides the form, while speech is the material, in a definition that echoes the four Aristotelian causes:

l'imitazione di azione umana è la forma ... Il parlare è la materia, ne la guisa che il colore è al pittore et il marmo a lo scultore. La cagione facitrice è l'arte poetica de l'uomo. I fini secondo Aristotele saranno la purgazione, l'ammaestramento, il riposo da le molestie e da' negozii de la vita, e finalmente il diporto de l'animo ne l'uomo intendente (Weinberg 1970–4, iii. 351–2).

For Torelli, also using the *materia–forma* division in his lectures (*c.*1597) on Aristotle's *Poetics*, the proper material of poetry, namely verse, has similar plastic connotations: 'Ma perché ogni forma par che habbia la propria materia, con la qual'opera, pare, che la Poesia si sia impressa come in materia propria nel verso' (Weinberg 1961, 704 n. 128). At the beginning of the lectures, however, Torelli uses *materia* to signify the subject-matter he is about to discuss: 'la materia, o soggetto del libro' (Weinberg 1961, 700 n. 119). Elsewhere in the lectures, *materia* is also used to refer to the subject of poetry, rather than to its diction.

Salviati is clearly aware of these two types of *materia* in *Parafrasi e commento della Poetica d'Aristotile* (1586). Again invoking the *materia–forma* distinction, and, like Torelli, using the term *propria*, he differentiates between extrinsic and intrinsic matter: 'percioche a fare il composto non è la forma da per se stessa sofficiente, ma vi vuol la materia, e non ogni materia, ma la materia propria, la qual (parlando dell'estrinseca) nella poesia si è 'l verso' (Weinberg 1961, 614 n. 88). Tasso himself not only indicates his awareness of these two definitions of *materia* in the *Discorsi*, but shows that his preference lies with *materia* defined as subject-matter: 'non voglio chiamar materia della poesia le lettere, le sillabe, le parole, come chiamò lo Scaligero ... ma la materia della poesia mi pare che si possa convenevolmente dire il soggetto ch'ella prende a trattare' (*Discorsi*, 75).

The interpretation of material as language appears to stem from a variety of sources. It is already present as the object with which the skill of rhetoric is concerned in the discussion on rhetoric in Plato's *Gorgias*, and in a remark illustrating the opposite view of that held by Plato: '*Socrates*: Come now, answer me in the same way about rhetoric: with what particular thing is its skill concerned? *Gorgias*: With speech' (449D). It is also inherent in Aristotle's *Rhetoric*: 'But in proportion as anyone endeavours to make of Dialectic or Rhetoric, not what they are, faculties, but sciences, to that extent he will, without knowing it, destroy their real nature, in thus altering their character, by crossing over into the domain of sciences, whose subjects are certain definite things, not merely words' (1359^b I. iv. 6). Quintilian lists various definitions of the material of oratory, beginning with one stating this to be speech, and including a reference to the aforementioned passage in Plato's *Gorgias*: 'As to the material of oratory, some have asserted that it is speech, as for instance Gorgias in the dialogue of Plato' (II. xxi. 1).

An important part was also played by Renaissance awareness of the classification by Averroës of poetry together with the discursive sciences, such as dialectic, rhetoric and sophistic, on the grounds that their common subject-matter was discourse itself.[12] The early 'explanations' of the *Poetics* by Robortello and Maggi clearly show this. Robortello says in his *In librum Aristotelis de arte poetica explicationes* (1548): 'Discourse [*oratio*] is placed under the poetic faculty as its material [*materies*], as it is placed under all the others which concern themselves with discourse. These are five in number, demonstrative, dialectic, rhetoric, sophistic, poetic ... All these have discourse [*orationem*] as their matter [*subiectam*]' (Weinberg 1961, 6 n. 6). Maggi and Lombardi mention Averroës by name in *In Aristotelis librum de poetica communes explanationes* (1550), in connection with this classification, and go on to state, regarding poetry, demonstrative logic, dialectic, sophistic and rhetoric, that 'neither do they have a specific thing as their subject-matter [*materiae loco res*], but only words and discourse ('verba tantum & orationem')' (p. 8).

When Tasso says in his *Lezione sopra un sonetto di Monsignor Della Casa*: 'chiara cosa è, che i concetti siano il fine e conseguentemente la forma dell'orazione; e le parole, e la composizione del verso, la materia o l'instromento', he creates a further equation of *materia* with *instromento* (Weinberg 1961, 176 n. 42). This particular link appears to derive ultimately from Renaissance translations of Aristotle's 'means of representation' as 'instrument', and would seem to have occurred in the following manner. Aristotle classifies language in the *Poetics* as one of the three means of representation, along with rhythm and melody, which help to differentiate various art forms from each other: 'But they differ one from another in three ways: either in using means generically different ... in the arts which we have men-

---

[12] See Weinberg 1961, Peters 1968 and Renan 1947.

tioned, they all make their representations in rhythm and language and tune, using these means either separately or in combination' (1447^a I. 3–5, trans. Hamilton Fyfe). Although some translators and commentators translated Aristotle's 'means of representation' with the term *genus*, as did Maggi and Lombardi in *In Aristotelis librum de poetica communes explanationes* (1550), others, like Robortello in *In librum Aristotelis de arte poetica explicationes* (1548) and Vettori in *Commentarii in primum librum Aristotelis de arte poetarum* (1560), used both *genus* and *instrumentum*, and it is the latter translation that appears in Tasso's definition (Maggi and Lombardi, 19; Robortello, 9, 57; Vettori, 26, 62).

Other examples of this use of *instrumentum* can be found in the influential translation of Aristotle into the vernacular by Castelvetro in 1570: 'rassomiglianza per istormento' (p. 7), while Salviati in *Il lasca* (1584) chooses *stromento* (Weinberg 1961, 16). Riccoboni makes use of both *genus* and *instrumentum*; in the first part of *Poetica Aristotelis latine conversa* (1587), he speaks of *genus* and *instrumentum*, and in the second part, concerning the art of comedy, he uses *instrumentum* (pp. 1, 32, 140). In his later compendium of Aristotle's *Poetics*, entitled *Compendium artis poeticae Aristotelis* (1591), the term *instrumentum* again appears in this context (p. 8). Tasso shows an awareness of both terms, with a preference for *instrumentum*, in his *Discorsi* (pp. 11, 101).

Materia as subject-matter

Against the background of this contextualization of the concept of *materia* and its various associations, the major definition of *materia* as subject-matter can now be addressed. The discussion of what should constitute the subject-matter of epic poetry closely resembles debates in classical rhetorical theory concerning the subject-matter of the oration. Quintilian in his *Institutio oratoria* believed all subjects to be suitable: 'I hold that the material of rhetoric is composed of everything that may be placed before it as a subject for speech' (II. xxi. 4). This view survived in Renaissance treatises on rhetoric. Denores, for example, defines subject-matter in his *Breve trattato dell'oratore* (1574) as 'ogni occorrente materia che sia atta ad essere spiegata con parole' (Weinberg 1970–4, iii. 105).

Aristotle had stated in his *Rhetoric* that: 'Rhetoric then may be defined as the faculty of discovering the possible means of persuasion in reference to any subject whatever' (1355^b I. ii. 2). He then goes on to say: 'The function of Rhetoric, then, is to deal with things about which we deliberate', specifying, in particular, that it is 'human actions which are the subject of our deliberation and examination' (1357^a I. ii. 12, 14). The link between the rhetorical and the poetic subject is already discernible. In the *Poetics* Aristotle defines the objects of representation as 'men doing or experiencing something', and explains that 'tragedy is not a representation of men but of a piece of action' (1450^a VI. 12, trans. Hamilton Fyfe, 9 n. d, 25). In a similar way, considerations of the general and the probable, discussed in the *Poetics*, and consequently in Renaissance poetic theory, are already explicit in his *Rhetoric*: 'further, no art has the particular in view ... therefore, Rhetoric will not consider what seems probable in each individual case ... but that which seems probable to this or that class of persons' (1356^b I. ii. 11). The notion of the plausible continued in rhetoric. Thus the *Rhetorica ad Herennium* says: 'Invention is the devising of matter, true or plausible, that would make the case convincing' (I. ii. 3).

Tasso's theoretical treatment of *materia* as subject-matter can be approached from the point of view of both content and structure. Tasso often deals with ideas concerning content in terms of interrelated pairs of opposites, whose relative advantages and disadvantages form the basis for discussion. These pairs are as follows: instruction vs. delight as the functions of poetry, false/invented vs. true/historical material, recent vs. remote history, history of false vs. true religion, the sacred vs. the profane/secular, verisimilitude vs. the marvellous. He also discusses the nobility and illustriousness of epic subject-matter and the specific topics that fall into this category, as well as subjects that should be excluded. The most important of these will be examined here. As regards structural considerations, Tasso discusses the presence or absence of structure in *materia* as an entity preceding the rhetorical stage of disposition. He also deliberates on the issue of which parts of the structure of *materia* (the beginning, middle, and end) may be altered by the poet.

Tasso's theory does not constitute a fixed, unchanging body of opinions. From the *Discorsi dell'arte poetica*, written in 1561–2, when he was in his late teens, and published unchanged, without his approval, in 1587, to the revised version entitled *Discorsi del poema epico* of 1594 (and indeed the *Apologia in difesa della Gerusalemme liber-*

ata of 1585), one can detect some changes. Enthusiasm and certainty, resulting in clarity and simplicity in the earlier *Discorsi*, give way in the later elaboration to diffuseness, emphasis on self-justification, perpetual recourse to authorities for the purpose either of attack or defence, and even contradictions.[13] Nevertheless, the basic ideas, apart from certain shifts in emphasis, tend to remain the same.

One example illustrating several of these points concerns Tasso's open disagreement, in the early *Discorsi*, with the view that tragedy and epic portray the same type of object: 'è stato creduto il tragico e l'epico in tutto conformarsi nelle cose imitate; la quale opinione, benchè commune e universale, vera da me non è giudicata' (*Discorsi*, 11). In the later *Discorsi*, he first of all agrees with this common view: 'In due condizioni dunque sono differente, nelle cose con le quali s'imita e nel modo dell'imitare; *in una concorde, nelle cose imitate*, perché la tragedia ancora, come dice Aristotele ne' *Problemi*, simula l'azioni de gli eroi' (*Discorsi*, 71). Further on, however, he contradicts this by returning to his former position of dissent, which he now expresses in a more attenuated fashion by leaving out the clause 'vera da me non è giudicata', and replacing it with 'si può nondimeno considerare più esquisitamente' (p. 102). His conclusion remains the same as in the early *Discorsi*, except that in this passage, too, the tone is less emphatic and more subdued. The following quotation is from the early work, with brackets around the words that were omitted, significantly, in the revised version:

Da le cose dette può esser manifesto che la differenza ch'è fra la tragedia e l'epopeia non nasce solamente dalla diversità de gli istrumenti e del modo dello imitare, ma [molto più e molto] prima dalla diversità delle cose imitate; la qual differenza è molto più propria [e più intrinseca e più essenzial] dell'altre (*Discorsi*, 13, 103).

Tasso has thus maintained the basic idea outlined in the early *Discorsi*, but only after various detours of contradiction and attenuation, as well as some reworking of the explanation used to justify his opinion. Seven additional examples, all classical, are introduced into the later *Discorsi* (Eteocles, Agamemnon, Ajax, Pyrrhus, Thersites, the Cyclops and the Laestrygones), while four of those present in the early *Discorsi* (all, interestingly enough, from the sixteenth century) are omitted (Marganorre and Bradamante from Ariosto's *Orlando*

---

13 In a letter to Curzio Ardizio, dated 25 Feb. 1585, Tasso writes: 'Ed io scrissi già ne la mia fanciullezza alcuni discorsi in questo subietto' (*Prose*, 913).

furioso, Amadigi and Archeloro from his father's *Amadigi*). Moreover, from his earlier definition of the *illustre* ('l'illustre dell'eroico è fondato sovra l'imprese d'una eccelsa virtù bellica, sovra i fatti di cortesia, di generosità, di pietà, di religione'), he has now left out the lighter elements of *cortesia* and *generosità*, and added the somewhat lugubrious 'magnanimo proponimento di morire' (*Discorsi*, 12, 102).

His attitude towards *materia* itself also reveals a dramatic change of mood: *materia* has now become uncontrollable, boundless and uncertain, with threatening overtones. Immediately before what constituted the opening sentence of his treatment of *materia* in the early *Discorsi* (and of the entire work itself), he now speaks, in Dantesque terms, of 'le tenebre che fanno oscura la grandissima selva della materia poetica':

Ma qual è più incerta, quale più instabile, quale più inconstante della materia? ... dove è tanta mutazione e tanta incostanza di cose; e la materia è simile ad una selva oscura, tenebrosa e priva d'ogni luce ... La materia poetica adunque pare amplissima oltre tutte l'altre (*Discorsi*, 78–9).

Another addition to his earlier treatment of *materia* is a long list of subjects to be excluded, heightening the prescriptive and generally negative tone of the later work. The list includes things that are 'troppo rozze ... le male ordinate ... le materie troppo asciutte e troppo aride ... quelle che sono noiose e rincrescevoli soverchiamente, e l'infelici ... Non s'invaghisca il poeta delle materie troppo sottili ...' (*Discorsi*, 109). The poet should leave aside 'le necessarie, come il mangiare e l'apparecchiar le vivande, o le descriva brevemente', and disdain 'tutte le cose basse, tutte le populari, tutte le disoneste' (pp. 112–13).

The list of matters to be included is expanded and minutely detailed in the later *Discorsi*, together with precise instructions on how not to portray them:

si compiaccia nella descrizione delle battaglie terrestri e maritime, de gli assalti delle città, dell'ordinanza dell'essercito, e del modo di alloggiare; ma in questo schivi il soverchio e temperi il rincrescimento di troppa esquisita dottrina ... Non sia troppo lungo ne gli ammaestramenti dell'arte militare ... Simile avertimento potrebbe mostrare ove descrive la fame, la sete, la peste, il nascer dell'aurora, il cader del sole, il mezzo giorno, la mezza notte, le stagioni dell'anno, la qualità de' mesi o di giorni o piovosi o sereni o tranquilli o tempestosi ... nel descriver l'arme, l'imprese, i cavalli, le navi, i tempii, i palagi, i padiglioni, le tende, le pitture e le statue e l'altre cose somiglianti, abbia sempre riguardo a quel che conviene, e schivi la noia che porta seco la soverchia lunghezza. Nelle morti cerchi la varietà, l'efficacia, l'affetto, nell'incontri di lancia e ne' colpi di spada la verisimilitudine, non passando troppo quel ch'è avvenuto, o che può avvenire, o che si crede, o che si racconta (*Discorsi*, 111).

Love

One particular subject, that of love, interestingly receives increasing emphasis in Tasso's theory. In the early *Discorsi*, love is treated as secondary. It is considered less magnificent and illustrious, for instance, than the subject of Aeneas going to Italy:

> bench'io non nieghi che poema eroico non si potesse formare di accidenti meno magnifici, quali sono gli amori di Florio, e quelli di Teagene e di Cariclea … fa mestieri che la materia sia in se stessa nel primo grado di nobiltà e di eccellenza. In questo grado è la venuta d'Enea in Italia: ch'oltra che l'argomento è per se stesso grande e illustre, grandissimo e illustrissimo è poi avendo riguardo all'Imperio de' Romani che da quella venuta ebbe origine (*Discorsi*, 13).

Love is not regarded as fundamental, historical epic material, but as belonging to the *finto* which is introduced by the poet during the second stage of composition, that of disposition. At that point, in order to create 'più del verisimile o più del mirabile' and produce 'maggior diletto', the poet should proceed in such a way that 'senza rispetto alcuno di vero o di istoria a sua voglia muti e rimuti, e riduca gli accidenti delle cose a quel modo ch'egli giudica migliore, co 'l vero alterato il tutto finto accompagnando'. This precept was ably followed by Virgil: 'Questo precetto molto bene seppe porre in opra il divino Virgilio … perché non solo è falso l'amore e la morte di Didone …' (*Discorsi*, 17). Love therefore appears as one of the *invenzioni* added by the poet: 'nel *Furioso* si leggono amori, cavallerie, venture e incanti, e in somma invenzioni più vaghe e più accomodate alle nostre orecchie che quelle del Trissino non sono' (p. 34). Love is included particularly for the purpose of pleasure, and the poet is advised to 'mescolare fra la severità dell'altre materie i piacevolissimi ragionamenti d'amore' (p. 18).

The suitability of love in the epic poem receives much greater emphasis in the later *Discorsi*. Tasso says: 'l'amore senza fallo dee esser cantato dal poema eroico' and even posits love as a fundamental subject: 'Concedasi dunque che 'l poema epico si possa formar di soggetto amoroso' (*Discorsi*, 107–8). He justifies its inclusion on the basis of its great beauty, thereby taking up a position contrary to that of others ('alcuni') writing on the subject: 'Assegnavano dunque l'amore più tosto alla comedia. Ma io fui sempre di contrario parere, parendomi ch'al poema eroico fossero convenienti le cose bellissime; ma bellissimo è l'amore' (p. 104). As one of the two passions attributable to heroes, *amor*, he maintains, calling on the authority of a Platonic philosopher, is just as suitable as *ira* in the epic poem: 'Ma non si può negare che l'amor non sia passione propria de gli eroi, perché a duo affetti furono principalmente sottoposti, come stima Proclo, gran filosofo nella setta de' platonici: all'ira e all'amore; e se l'uno è convenevole nel poema eroico, l'altro non dee esser disdicevole in modo alcuno' (p. 104). He concludes, citing Thomas Aquinas, that 'se l'amore è non solo una passione e un movimento dell'appetito sensitivo, ma uno abito nobilissimo della volontà, come volle san Tomaso, l'amore sarà più lodevole ne gli eroi, e per conseguente nel poema eroico' (p. 106).

Tasso specifies precisely how love is to be treated by the epic poet. Considerations of class and gender are involved, in that the poet should not portray the 'vil amor d'ancille', but, on the contrary, that of knights: 'ma noi parliamo dell'amor di cavaliero' (p. 105). Moreover, since the ultimate function of the poet is one of instruction that is *onesto*, his subordinate function of pleasure, which involves the subject of love, must correspond by similarly dealing with chaste material: 'ma riguardando in quel che è suo proprio [pleasure], dee guardarsi di non traboccare nel contrario, perché gli onesti piaceri sono contrari a' disonesti' (p. 68). Advocating the euphemistic *onesto* in the portrayal of love for the purpose of instruction was not uncommon in Renaissance treatises, and not only as far as the high style of epic and tragedy was concerned. Pino da Cagli, for instance, writing on comedy in his *Breve considerazione intorno al componimento de la comedia de' nostri tempi* (1572), suggests the choice of 'materie non disoneste; ché le quali, ancor che siano amorose, pure si possono sì gentilmente trattare', so that the author 's'allontanerà da ogni poco lodevole fatto che potesse dare male essempio allo spettatore' (Weinberg 1970–4, ii. 647). Conti's *Orationes et praefationes* (1582) similarly considers the treatment of love from the point of view of instruction, concluding that Virgil's portrayal of love is designed to highlight its negative qualities in opposition to the virtues of piety and fortitude (Weinberg 1961, 269).

Tasso compares the treatment of love in the *Amadigi*, the *Orlando furioso* and *L'Italia liberata dai Goti* on this basis, judging the first work (his father's) as superior to the latter two:

Laonde non meritano lode alcuna coloro c'hanno descritti gli abbracciamenti amorosi in quella guisa che l'Ariosto descrisse quel di Ruggiero con Alcina, o di Ricciardetto con Fiordispina; e per aventura il Trissino ancora avrebbe potuto tacere molte cose quando ci pone quasi innanzi agli occhi l'amoroso diletto che prese l'imperator Giustiniano della moglie (*Discorsi*, 68).

This contrasts with 'Tasso ne l'*Amadigi*, quand'egli descrive l'abbracciamento di Mirinda e di Alidoro, quasi volendoci accennare che l'altre cose deono essere ricoperte sotto le tenebre del silenzio, oltre tutte l'altre' (p. 68).

A similar comparison takes place in the dialogue he wrote in defence of his own poem, the *Apologia in difesa della Gerusalemme liberata* (1585). Tasso here chooses to compare the *Orlando furioso* with the *Amadigi* in the sphere of love:

Nondimeno, paragonandosi una sola parte fra l'uno e l'altro poema, si potrà conoscere agevolmente quel che intorno a l'altro si potesse dimostrare. E 'l paragone sarà tra l'amor di Ruggiero e di Bradamante, e quel d'Alidoro e di Mirinda (*Prose*, 421).

He bases his comparison on a variety of criteria. First, on considerations of equality of class, in other words, the *scambievole*, which both poets observe: 'Dico, adunque, che l'uno e l'altro amore è scambievole, come debbono essere i perfetti amori: l'uno e l'altro di guerriero e di guerriera: l'uno e l'altro di persone d'alto affare'. Second, on the grounds of decorum, which involves class and gender-based conceptions (the 'lover' should be male, and the 'beloved' female, particularly in the case of regal lovers):

senza dubbio sarà più convenevole al maschio quella [persona] dell'amante, ed a la donna, quella dell'amata ... E quantunque ciò sia conveniente in tutti gli amori fra l'uno e l'altro sesso, nondimeno questo decoro è proprio delle persone reali, oltra tutti gli altri (*Prose*, 421).

In this respect the *Amadigi* is superior to the *Orlando furioso*: 'Convenevolmente, dunque, nell'*Amadigi* Alidoro è l'amante, e Mirinda l'amata. Ma questa convenevolezza non si ritrova nel *Furioso*, nel quale Ruggiero è amato più che amante, e Bradamante ama più che non è amata' (*Prose*, 421). Ariosto's portrayal of Ruggiero and Bradamante is considered particularly *sconvenevole* because their marriage was to herald the founding of the Este line. Third, the position of love in the hierarchy of honourable obligations should be strictly observed: 'prima siano obligati a Dio; poi al re; nel terzo luogo a la moglie o a l'amante che ama di casto amore; nel quarto, a l'amico che ha per fine l'utilità e l'ambizione' (p. 425). Tasso concludes that the portrayal of Alidoro conforms to this order, whereas that of Ruggiero does not.

Pleasure vs. instruction

The close relationship between the representation of love and the function of the poet raises another area of interest in Tasso's theory, namely that of the functions themselves. Earlier in this chapter the functions were traced back to rhetoric (Cicero) and poetics (Horace). Both functions of pleasure and instruction are already present, however, in Aristotle's discussion of the causes of poetry in his *Poetics* (1448^a III. 4–1448^b 6). There they are, moreover, closely linked, rather than opposed to each other, as they were sometimes to become in later times. Pleasure is seen by Aristotle to derive from instruction (itself the result of the perception of a successfully imitative representation). In his *Rhetoric* he similarly says: 'And learning and admiring are as a rule pleasant' (1371^a I. xi. 21). In the *Poetics* he states that pleasure derives from the marvellous: 'But that the marvellous causes pleasure is shown by the fact that people always tell a piece of news with additions by way of being agreeable' (1460^a xxiv. 17, trans. Hamilton Fyfe). From his comment that the marvellous is especially appropriate to the epic poem, it can be inferred that he believes pleasure to be intrinsic to the function of the epic poet: 'Now the marvellous should certainly be portrayed in tragedy, but epic affords greater scope for the inexplicable (which is the chief element in what is marvellous), because we do not actually see the persons of the story' (1460^a xxiv. 15).

In Tasso's early *Discorsi, giovamento* is explicitly referred to only once as an important consideration for the poet, not, notably, in his capacity as poet, but as *uomo civile*:

Taccio per ora che, dovendo il poeta aver molto riguardo al giovamento, se non in quanto egli è poeta (ché ciò come poeta non ha per fine), almeno in quanto è uomo civile e parte della republica, molto meglio accenderà l'animo de' nostri uomini con l'essempio de' cavalieri fedeli che d'infedeli (*Discorsi*, 8–9).

The function of *diletto* or *piacere* is mentioned more frequently, particularly in relation to verisimilitude:

non attendono con quella espettazione e con quel diletto i successi delle cose, come farebbono se que' medesimi successi, o in tutto o in parte, veri stimassero (p. 5)

as well as the marvellous:

poco dilettevole è veramente quel poema che non ha seco quelle maraviglie che tanto movono non solo l'animo de gli ignoranti, ma de' giudiziosi ancora … prima d'ogn'altra cosa deve il poeta avvertire se nella materia, ch'egli prende a trattare, v'è avvenimento alcuno il quale, altrimenti essendo successo, avesse o più del verisimile e più del mirabile, o per qual si voglia altra cagione portasse maggior diletto (pp. 6, 17)

variety:

Né già io niego che la varietà non rechi piacere (p. 35)

and unity:

Quella [favola] in somma tanto meno dilettarà quanto sarà più confusa e meno intelligibile … Una dunque deve esser la favola e la forma (p. 36).

Pleasure is even posited as the actual end of poetry: 'essendo il fine della poesia il diletto'. This is underlined: 'Concedo io quel che vero stimo, e che molti negarebbono, cioè che 'l diletto sia il fine della poesia' (p. 34). Such emphasis is absent from the corresponding passage of the later *Discorsi*: 'Concedasi quel che si può negare, cioè che 'l diletto sia il fine della poesia' (p. 138).

The emphasis in these later *Discorsi*, where the functions are also treated more extensively, is on *giovamento*, which now replaces *diletto* as the ultimate *fine* of poetry: 'Non dee dunque il poeta preporsi per fine il piacere … ma 'l giovamento, perché la poesia … è una prima filosofia, la qual sin dalla tenera età ci ammaestra ne' costumi e nelle ragioni della vita.' Tasso is now of the opinion that 'l'ottimo fine è quello di giovare a gli uomini con l'essempio dell'azioni umane … La poesia è dunque imitazione dell'azioni umane, fatta per ammaestramento della vita' (pp. 66–9). He compares the functions, concluding, in open disagreement with Horace, that they cannot be of equal importance. *Diletto* must take second place to *giovamento*, as poetry is written 'affine di giovar dilettando' (p. 69).

Man as *uomo civile* now dominates man as *poeta*: 'ma in quanto è uomo civile e parte della città, o almeno in quanto la sua arte è sottordinata a quella ch'è regina delle altre, si propone il giovamento' and 'de' due fini dunque i quali si prepone il poeta, l'uno è proprio dell'arte sua, l'altro dell'arte superiore' (*Discorsi*, 68). The excellence of a poem is even made to depend on the excellence of the government under which the poet writes: 'l'eccellentissimo poema è proprio solamente della eccellentissima forma di governo'. The poet is therefore not regarded as completely in control of his creation. As a consequence, he is not responsible for writing imperfect poetry within an imperfect state, in which case 'il difetto non è dell'arte poetica, ma della politica, non del poeta, ma de' legislatori' (p. 98). The later *Discorsi* thus reveal a change of emphasis as regards the functions of the epic poet. In the early *Discorsi*, *giovamento* was considered an important aspect of poetic activity, insofar as the role of poet cannot be divorced from that of citizen. Despite this, the main concern of the epic poet was to inspire pleasure. The later *Discorsi* place more emphasis on the social responsibilities of the poet, and these now tend not only to eclipse the pleasurable end of poetic art, but also to diminish the autonomy of the art itself.

Neither of Tasso's positions is particularly unusual when compared with those of other Renaissance theorists, in that pleasure and instruction are each given varying emphasis. Mazzoni, writing as late as 1587, states in his *Della difesa della comedia di Dante* that pleasure is the end of poetry ('lo diletto, che è il suo fine') because poetics is a game that involves the cessation of political activity:

La facoltà civile si deve dividere in due principalissime parti, l'una delle quali considera la rettitudine dell'operationi, e fù nomata col nome generale Politica, cioè Civile. L'altra considera la rettitudine della cessatione o la rettitudine delle operationi de' giochi, e fù nomata Poetica (Weinberg 1961, 25 n. 48).

Similarly Malatesta comments in *Della nuova poesia, overo delle difese del Furioso* (1589) that the subject-matter of poetry is 'tutte le cose dilettabili' (Weinberg 1961, 663). Erizzo, on the other hand, while claiming in his *Espositione nelle tre canzoni di M. Francesco Petrarca* (1561) that the poet should treat any subject, at the same time automatically classifies under the moral sciences the subjects in which the poet should be especially well-versed. His priority is that the subject-matter should be suitable for the purpose of *giovamento*:

dovendo di qualunque cosa trattare … delle cagioni delle cose, de i vitii, de gli huomini, de i piaceri, del dolore, della morte, de gli affetti, e di tutte le perturbationi dell'animo, dell'onesto, del vero bene, di tutte le virtù, della vita, de i costumi, le quai cose tutte sotto la scientia morale si contengono (Weinberg 1961, 165 n. 14).

Correa, like Erizzo, specifies the useful in his *In librum de arte poetica Q. Horatii Flacci explanationes* (1587), together with the socially excellent, as fitting subject-matter for the high style predominantly used by the epic poet:

The highest style contains important personages and excellent actions ... to speak of God or describe heroes, kings, military leaders, governments ... Excellent matters are such things as wars for peace, deliberative councils, trials for selection, the virtues useful for the regulation of life, and great actions (Weinberg 1961, 217 n. 28).

These subjects recall not only the *Gerusalemme liberata* itself, but also the type of subject-matter stipulated by Tasso the theorist: 'quelle imprese che o per la dignità dell'Imperio o per essaltazione della fede di Cristo furo felicemente e gloriosamente operate' (*Discorsi*, 13). Tasso's ideas regarding the functions of the poet do not appear to differ particularly from those of his contemporaries. Of note, rather, is the change of emphasis in his own theory over time.

History vs. fiction

The issue of whether a poet should invent his material, or take it from history, is yet another area in Tasso's theory that reflects the kind of change in treatment already observed taking place from the early to the late *Discorsi*. The basic question of whether to use found or invented material can be traced back to classical rhetoric. Cicero, for example, says in his *De oratore*:

For purposes of proof, however, the material at the orator's disposal is twofold, one kind made up of the things which are not thought out by himself, but depend upon the circumstances ... the other kind is founded entirely on the orator's reasoned argument. And so, with the former sort, he need only consider the handling of his proofs, but with the latter, the discovery of them as well (II. xxvii. 116–17).

Delminio in his rhetorical treatise on the *materia* of the *eloquente* in 1540 also deals with this distinction, albeit rather more figuratively: 'disputaremo della materia sola, di quella dico che non è partorita dell'eloquente, ma viene a lui per chiedergli ancor quel beneficio che esso darle può con l'artificio suo' (Weinberg 1970–4, i. 323).

The distinction between found and invented material is already present in Aristotle's discussion of the narration in his *Rhetoric*: 'for it is necessary to go through the actions which form the subject of the speech. For speech is made up of one part that is inartificial (the speaker being in no way the author of the actions which he relates), and of another that does depend upon art' (1416^b III. xvi. 1). The distinction is also raised in Aristotle's *Poetics*, where it is treated parenthetically. It is the handling of the material that is given greater emphasis: 'The stories, whether they are traditional or whether you make them up yourself, should first be sketched in outline and then expanded by putting in episodes' and 'Now it is not right to break up the traditional stories, I mean, for instance, Clytaemnestra being killed by Orestes and Eriphyle by Alcmaeon, but the poet must show invention and make a skilful use of the tradition' (1455^b xvii. 5, 1453^b xiv. 10, trans. Hamilton Fyfe). Horace deals with the question rather more fully in his *Ars poetica*. First of all, he posits both possibilities: 'Either follow tradition or invent what is self-consistent' (119). He then opts for the former alternative, attributing greater difficulty to certain areas of the latter: 'It is hard to treat in your own way what is common' (128). Horace therefore advises that 'you are doing better in spinning into acts a song of Troy than if, for the first time, you were giving the world a theme unknown and unsung' (129–30). This does not rule out individual invention under certain conditions: 'In ground open to all you will win private rights, if you do not linger along the easy and open pathway, if you do not seek to render word for word as a slavish translator' (131–4).

Elements of the distinction between true/historical and false subject-matter, the actual point at issue in Tasso's poetics, can also be traced back to rhetoric. The *Rhetorica ad Herennium* makes a threefold division of the most literary of the quantitative parts of the speech, namely the narration or statement of facts: 'The kind of narrative based on the exposition of the facts presents three forms: legendary [*fabulam*], historical [*historiam*] and realistic [*argumentum*].' The clarification of this division would fit easily into poetic theory:

The legendary tale comprises events neither true nor probable, like those transmitted by tragedies. The historical narrative is an account of exploits actually performed, but removed in time from the recollection of our age.

Realistic narrative recounts imaginary events, which yet could have occurred, like the plots of comedies (I. viii. 13).

Aristotle's *Poetics* deals not with the distinction between the true/historical and the false, but, rather, with the distinction between the true and what appears to be true, in other words the probable or verisimilar. In relation to this, he distinguishes between history and poetry on the basis of the type of truth involved, namely that history deals in particular truths (the true as embodied in facts), while poetry is concerned with general truths (not necessarily the factual, but the probable):

> What we have said already makes it further clear that a poet's object is not to tell what actually happened, but what could and would happen either probably or inevitably. The difference between a historian and a poet is … that one tells what happened and the other what might happen … poetry tends to give general truths while history gives particular facts (1451^a ix. 1–3, trans. Hamilton Fyfe).

The formulation of the entire issue of found as opposed to invented *materia* in sixteenth-century poetics appears to have variously combined the classical rhetorical notions of found vs. invented, true/historical vs. false/legendary/improbable or false/realistic/probable, with the essential classical poetic notion, as discussed by Aristotle, of the true vs. the probable/verisimilar. His highly influential conception of verisimilitude can be seen to occupy a prime position in many Renaissance discussions of the alternative types of *materia* to be used, in whatever combination these are formulated.

Salviati, for example, states the case for false/invented/verisimilar as opposed to true/found/historical material, as follows in his *Risposta all'Apologia di Torquato Tasso* (also known as the *Primo Infarinato*) of 1585: 'la 'nvenzion del poeta … non è … di cose vere, anzi … è di cose false. Delle quali cose false quelle solamente, che *paion vere*, s'elegge per suo soggetto la poesia, e chiamale finzioni' (Weinberg 1961, 1017 n. 55). Frachetta, opting for true, historically based, rather than invented, material, says in the *Dialogo del furore poetico* (1581): 'essendo materia della tragedia le cose *avenevoli*, di gran vantaggio più convenevol materia saranno le cose già state, che le pensate o immaginate dal poeta … senza fallo molto meglio è se son vere, che se non sono … il poeta tragico, o l'epopeico pigliando un fatto avenuto' (Weinberg 1961, 594 nn. 52, 53). Pigna uses the distinction to differentiate between epic and romance in *I romanzi* (1554):

Evvi questa sola differenza; che il fondamento della costoro imitatione [of romances] non è con l'Epico un'istesso: percioche l'Epico sopra una cosa vera fonda una *verisimile*, & vera intendo io ò per historie, ò per favole: cio è ò in effetto vera, ò vera sopposta. Questi altri alla verità risguardo alcuno non hanno (Weinberg 1961, 445 n. 50).

Muzio also distinguishes between genres on the basis of true vs. invented material, allocating true material to the high style, and invented material to comedy in his *Dell'arte poetica* (1551): 'Finga 'l comico adunque, e intorno al vero / Vada il maggior poeta poetando' (Weinberg 1970–4, ii. 174). Other writers who believe that historical material is required as the basis for the epic are Lionardi, who says in his *Dialogi della inventione poetica* (1554): 'dico la favola principalmente trarsi dall'istoria' (Weinberg 1970–4, ii. 275); and Guastavini in his *Risposta all'Infarinato Academico della Crusca* (1588): 'l'inventione poetica in un certo modo è sempre di quella guisa di cose, che si trattano dalla istoria, cioè di cose vere, e reali, & non fantasmi' (Weinberg 1961, 1038 n. 98). Varchi, on the other hand, prefers the invented (*finto*) and the false (*favoloso*) as the subject-matter of poetry in his *Due lezzioni* (1549) (Weinberg 1961, 8). Robortello adopts a similar position in his *In librum Aristotelis de arte poetica explicationes* (1548): 'poetics, then, has as its subject-matter fictitious and fictional discourse' (Weinberg 1961, 391 n. 70). Tasso takes issue with him on this in his later *Discorsi*, while continuing to use the traditional expression of the issue in terms of true/historical material vs. the false/invented (*Discorsi*, 86).

In the early *Discorsi* he posits both possibilities: 'La materia, che argomento può ancora comodamente chiamarsi, o si finge, e allora par che il poeta abbia parte non solo nella scelta, ma nella invenzione ancora, o si toglie dall'istorie.' He goes on to state his preference for the latter: 'Ma molto meglio è, a mio giudicio, che dall'istoria si prenda.' He justifies his choice on the basis of the *verisimile*: 'perché, dovendo l'epico cercare in ogni parte il verisimile (presupongo questo come principio notissimo), non è verisimile ch'una azione illustre, quali sono quelle del poema eroico, non sia stata scritta e passata alla memoria de' posteri con l'aiuto d'alcuna istoria' (p. 4). After a short section clarifying the importance of the *verisimile* and of *novità* in producing *diletto* (*novità* taking place not in the choice of the material, but in its disposition), he concludes: 'Deve dunque l'argomento del poema epico esser tolto dall'istorie' (p. 6).

In the later *Discorsi* his statement of the two possibilities and of his own preference are almost identical, apart from the addition of one clause ('che non sarebbe se egli in tutto si fingesse') (*Discorsi*, 83). However, the explanation that follows is greatly expanded by the inclusion of further arguments in support of the true as opposed to the false, and also by open disagreement with other writers of his time. He introduces the argument that poets are imitators, that they must by definition imitate the true, for the false does not exist, and that any composition not obeying this law cannot be called poetry, nor its writer a poet:

> se i poeti sono imitatori, conviene che siano imitatori del vero, perché il falso non è; e quel che non è, non si può imitare; però quelli che scrivono cose in tutto false, se non sono imitatori, non sono poeti, e i suoi componimenti non sono poesie, ma finzioni più tosto; laonde non meritano il nome di poeta, o non tanto (*Discorsi*, 85).

Another argument added by Tasso in favour of choosing true material involves the classification of poetry. He believes that poetry should not be placed under sophistic, which is the art of the false and the non-existent, but under dialectic, in other words, under the art of the probable:

> la perfetta poesia, la qual ripone sotto la facoltà sofistica, di cui è soggetto il falso e quel che non è ... Però io non posso concedere né che la poesia si metta sotto l'arte de' sofisti, né che la perfettissima specie di poesia sia la fantastica ... Dico adunque che senza dubbio la poesia è collocata in ordine sotto la dialettica insieme con la retorica, la qual, come dice Aristotele, è l'altro rampollo de la dialettica facultà, a cui s'appertiene di considerare non il falso, ma il probabile (pp. 86–7).

Yet another line of reasoning is adduced, drawn from Thomas Aquinas and concerning the interchangeability of the good with the true:

> Con un'altra ragione possiam provare che 'l soggetto del poeta sia più tosto il vero che 'l falso; la quale è derivata da la dottrina di san Tomaso nella Somma e in altre opere sue. Dice egli ch'il bene e 'l vero e l'uno si convertono, e che 'l vero è bene de l'intelletto (p. 91).

As part of his extended treatment of this topic in these later *Discorsi*, Tasso also takes issue with other writers who are in favour of false material, such as Robortello ('Però molto s'inganna il Rubertello in assegnar al poema per materia il falso'), Piccolomini ('Dunque poco

meno errò monsignor Alessandro Piccolomini, volendo che il soggetto del poema sia più tosto il falso che il vero') and Mazzoni ('E in
questo medesimo errore, s'io non m'inganno, è il signor Iacomo
Mazzon') (p. 86).

His *Apologia* reveals a similarly expanded discussion of this area,
particularly in relation to the *Gerusalemme liberata*. Here, for
instance, Tasso counters the statement 'Il poeta non è poeta senza
l'invenzione. Però, scrivendo storia o sopra storia scritta da altri,
perde l'essere interamente' with the argument that the false does not
exist and cannot, therefore, be invented: '*Seg.* Ho sempre udito dire
per voi filosofi, che 'l falso è nulla. *For.* E quel che è nulla, non è;
dunque le cose false non sono: e l'invenzione non è delle false, ma
delle vere che sono, ma non sono ancor state ritrovate ... dunque la
poesia dee porlo [fondamento] sopra l'istoria.' He also replies to the
claim that invention is not merely a part, as he himself had stated in
his early *Discorsi*, but the foundation ('l'invenzione non è parte, ma
fondamento del tutto') with the argument that it cannot be the
foundation without being a part ('l'uno dice che l'invenzione è
parte del poeta ... l'altro risponde che non è parte, ma fondamento: quasi il fondamento non sia parte di quelle che fanno il tutto
intiero; ma io negherei che fosse il fondamento'). He then provides
further justification that invention cannot be the foundation: some
things are *trovate* and some *non trovate*, and invention, being of the
non trovate, which necessarily came afterwards, cannot be the foundation of the *trovate*, which already exist ('Delle cose alcune sono
trovate, alcune non trovate; ma l'invenzione è delle non trovate, le
quali sono dopo; dunque l'invenzione non è fondamento dell'altre')
(*Prose*, 428–9).

The discussion then focuses on criticism that the *Gerusalemme liberata* is 'murato sul vecchio', in that it does not contain sufficient
invented matter in comparison with Ariosto's *Orlando furioso*. Tasso's
response is that Ariosto is more guilty of this, because he merely continues the work of Boiardo: 'l'Ariosto, dunque, ha murato su 'l vecchio, avendo murato sovra quella parte così grande già cominciata dal
Boiardo; ma io, c'ho preso parte della materia da l'istoria solamente,
non ho murato su 'l vecchio, ma formato novo edificio.' The sphere
of the marvellous in Tasso's poem is then attacked on the same
grounds: 'Il Tasso non ha però trovato di proprio ingegno cose di
meraviglia' (*Prose*, 447). The poet defends his work by contradicting

this view outright and drawing attention to the inventions to be found there: 'tutte le cose le quali nel mio poema son governate da la providenza di Dio, sono degne di meraviglia ... e s'alcun dirà che non sia trovato da l'ingegno mio lo scudo della verità che ricoperse Raimondo, o tutte l'arme ...' (p. 449).

The criticism of the *Gerusalemme liberata* to which the poet responds in the *Apologia* signals one of the major reasons behind the changing treatment he gives to the various subjects discussed so far. He is no longer merely engaged in the formulation of an abstract poetic theory, as he was in the early *Discorsi*. On the contrary, he now defends his own poetic composition against criticism. This discussion took the form of a debate of comparison and contrast between the *Gerusalemme liberata* and the *Orlando furioso*, otherwise known as the Tasso–Ariosto polemic.

The Tasso–Ariosto polemic

As early as 1576, five years before the first publication of the *Gerusalemme liberata* and the onset of the polemic, Tasso had already appended an allegory to his poem by way of explanation. Letters asking for advice on particular cantos during the composition of the poem also testify to his early awareness of the opinions and judgements of others (see Ch. 3). The first stirrings of the polemic can be discerned in 1581 with Lombardelli's enthusiastic defence of Tasso expressed in a letter to Maurizio Cattaneo on 28 September 1581, and published by Tasso together with his *Apologia* in 1585. The *Orlando furioso* had long been a subject for argument in its own right, as testified by Fornari's *Apologia brieve sopra tutto l'Orlando Furioso* of 1549, and the Pigna–Giraldi Cinthio pamphlet of 1554 (Weinberg 1961, 954–83). The publication of the *Gerusalemme liberata* provided an opposite extreme to the *Orlando furioso*, and in this capacity it entered the existing assessment of Ariosto's poem.

The Tasso–Ariosto polemic flared up in a spate of treatises (usually in dialogue form), sparked off, in particular, by Pellegrino's *Il Carrafa, o vero della epica poesia* in 1584. Pellegrino responds in this work to pre-existing criticism of the *Gerusalemme liberata*, as he makes clear: 'in questa seconda parte del costume *notano alcuni* il Tasso, che pone in bocca d'un pastore sentenze non pur da uomo di città ma da filosofo ... *Dicono* ancora che non convenga ad Armida né a Tancredi innamorati dir ne' loro lamenti parole così colte et artificiose'

(Weinberg 1970–4, iii. 324). He also refers to the existence of a *commun parere* on Tasso and Ariosto: 'poiché contra il commun parere, nel paragone di questi due poeti' (p. 342).

There followed a series of treatises, beginning with Salviati's *Degli Accademici della Crusca Difesa dell'Orlando Furioso dell'Ariosto contra 'l Dialogo dell'epica poesia di Cammillo Pellegrino, Stacciata Prima* (1584), which constituted the first printed attack on Tasso's poem, and was known as the *Stacciata Prima*; Tasso's own *Apologia in difesa della Gerusalemme liberata* (1585); Salviati's *Dello Infarinato Accademico della Crusca Risposta all'Apologia di Torquato Tasso intorno all'Orlando Furioso e alla Gierusalèm liberata* (1585), known as the *Primo Infarinato*; Pellegrino's *Replica di Camillo Pellegrino alla Risposta degli Accademici della Crusca Fatta contra il Dialogo della Epica Poesia, in difesa, come e' dicono, dell'Orlando Furioso* (1585); Tasso's *Risposta al Discorso del Signor Orazio Lombardello intorno a' contrasti che si fanno sopra la Gerusalemme Liberata* (1586); Tasso's *Delle differenze poetiche* (1587); and Salviati's *Lo Infarinato Secondo Ovvero dello 'Nfarinato Accademico della Crusca, Risposta al Libro Intitolato Replica di Camillo Pellegrino* (1588), known as the *Infarinato Secondo*—to name but the most important works.

With the polemic, issues regarding *materia* became convoluted and complex, with much hair-splitting. The same passages, and the same lines of argument, originating predominantly in *Il Carrafa*, recur in each treatise, sometimes word for word, but not always in full, leading at times to a lack of clarity that does little to facilitate the understanding of an already intricate debate. As one treatise succeeded another, recognition of this difficulty becomes apparent in what seems to have been an attempt at a remedy in the presentation of an up-to-date, cumulative text including all previous discussions on each particular point. This was Salviati's treatise of 1588. The dialogue form employed by most of the treatises is perhaps partly responsible for the diffuse and difficult nature of the discussion. The matter was also complicated by the fact that the motivating force behind most of the polemic lay outside the realm of the poem itself. One instance of this is the dispute which resulted when the Accademia della Crusca took offence at Tasso's so-called anti-Florentine interpretation of some letters by Martelli in his dialogue *Il Gonzaga ovvero dell'Onesto Piacere* (1583).[14] Certain letters contributing to this dispute were published, significantly enough, together with Salviati's first treatise sup-

[14] See Brand 1965, 119; Brown 1970, 5 n. 6; Weinberg 1961, 1004.

porting Ariosto. Other external factors suggested are personal ani-
mosity against Tasso, or simply the polemical spirit of the age.
Another, more specific suggestion, is that Salviati's criticism of the
Gerusalemme liberata should be seen in the context of his desire,
expressed also in other of his writings, to promote a literary tradition
free from classical influences (thus aligning his position with that of
the Moderns in the Ancients vs. Moderns debate). Pellegrino's *Il
Carrafa* would have presented, in Salviati's eyes, a provocative antithesis to this principle (Brown 1970, 5).

The polemic itself appears somewhat unjustified in that Tasso's
intended revision of the poem had not yet taken place, as he points
out in his *Apologia*: 'né questa opera mia né l'altre sono mai state né
riviste né ricorrette né publicate da me: piaccia a Dio che mi sia con-
ceduto di farlo' (*Prose*, 462). He also draws attention to his poem as
'un poema che già dieci anni sono io non ho letto: nel quale molte
cose avrei mutate, non sol mutate parole, s'io gli avessi data l'ultima
perfezione' (p. 466). This even appears to have been accepted by
Salviati at one point in his *Stacciata Prima*:

> S'intende che il volume stampato ultimamente in Ferrara sia stato da lui
> riveduto? Io non so: ho bene inteso dire dal Padre Don Benedetto dell'Uva,
> che il Tasso prima che gli fusse sopravenuta questa disgratia, disse a lui, che
> egli non haveva intera sodisfattione in quest'opera. *Risposta.* Aveva buon
> giudicio. *Dial.* e che haveva in anima di mutar molti luoghi, parte de' quali
> veramente ha mutati, si come giudicar si può da diversi testi de' volumi
> stampati in diverse città d'Italia (Tasso, *Apologia*, 26–30).

Much of the criticism aimed at the *materia* of the *Gerusalemme liberata* during the course of the polemic centres on issues of poetic theory expounded upon in the early *Discorsi*, in other words, issues already
current in contemporary literary discussions. One important point of
contention concerned the relative merits of the true/historical vs. the
false/invented. Opposition to the *Gerusalemme liberata* was based on
support for the notion of complete invention by the epic poet, a
notion with which Tasso disagrees in his *Apologia*. A passage in the
Stacciata Prima, but not among those quoted by Tasso (despite the fact
that the *Stacciata* was printed alongside the *Apologia* in 1585) goes as
far as to say:

> e nella favola ecci l'Ariosto senza comparazione, dato, che quella della
> Gierusalem fosse favola, la quale è storia tolta di peso, com'ognun sa. Onde
> l'Autore in quell'opera non è poeta, ma riducitor d'altrui storia in versi,

laquale storia comparisce così bene con quelle pastoie, quanto farebbe la Metafisica ridotta in canzone à ballo (Tasso, *Apologia*, 14).

Tasso's poem is also compared by Salviati to a meagre 'casetta ... murata in su 'l vecchio' (*Prose*, 445). In his reply to the poet's *Apologia*, in the *Primo Infarinato* of the same year, Salviati reiterates his view on the matter:

la 'nvenzion del poeta ... non è ... di cose vere, anzi ... è di cose false. Delle quali cose false quelle solamente, che paion vere, s'elegge per suo soggetto la poesia, e chiamale finzioni (Weinberg 1961, 1017 n. 55).

It is therefore not surprising to find this topic undergoing a considerable change in treatment from the early *Discorsi* (where it already stood, significantly, at the beginning of the discussion on *materia*) to the later, extended work.

Having wrongly founded his poem on history, Tasso is further criticized for the inclusion of negative elements that distort and pervert historical truths:

se però poema dir si potesse l'imbrattar istoria pia con sozzure di vizi carnali, e omicidi in persone di cristiani ed amici, e sì fatti? E ad uomini celebri di santità di vita ed onorati di fama di martirio, attribuire affetti e peccati immondi, infino a lo innamorarsi di saracine, e per esse volersi uccidere, ed aver mutata religione? (*Prose*, 451)

Tasso vindicates these elements in his poem on the basis that they represent involuntary actions, are historically verifiable and, in any case, allegorically meaningful:

Niuna sceleraggine è nel mio Goffredo, o negli altri Cristiani; ma tutte incontinenze, o violenze d'incanti, le quali non sono scelerate, perché l'azioni non son volontarie semplicemente: e niuna io ne descrivo ne' cavalieri, della quale non si veda nell'istoria menzione, almeno in universale: niuna è senza costume, o senza allegoria (*Prose*, 452).

However, the lengthy, normative and highly detailed lists of subjects for exclusion and inclusion that make their appearance in the later *Discorsi* testify to the impact on the poet of this type of attack on the *Gerusalemme liberata*.

The element of love, already observed receiving greater emphasis and justification by Tasso after the early *Discorsi*, can also be found as the target of negative criticism of a moral and religious nature, voiced in expressions such as *vizi carnali* and *affetti immondi*. Tasso does not take issue with this at great length in the *Apologia*. However, as has already been suggested, the polemic by no means represents the first sign of the poet's preoccupation with the reception of his work by the arbiters of socio-religious norms. In his *Allegoria della Gerusalemme liberata*, the element of love (together with that of *ira*, which was also to receive censure) is already firmly situated by Tasso within an allegorical, and in other words normative, framework. Love is accredited with a symbolic role as one of the *intrinseci impedimenti* to the ultimate earthly good, namely *civile felicità*:

Ma venendo a gli intrinseci impedimenti, l'amor che fa vaneggiar Tancredi e gli altri cavalieri, e gli allontana da Goffredo, e lo sdegno che desvia Rinaldo da l'impresa, significano il contrasto che con la ragionevole fanno la concupiscibile e l'irascibile virtù, e la ribellion loro (*Prose*, 303).

The *ragionevole*, he argues, is the seat of political activity in man: 'l'operazion politica, che procede da l'intelletto' (p. 302). The *Allegoria* itself claims to show 'come il poeta serva al politico', and indeed emphasizes the political function of the *Gerusalemme liberata*, with frequent use of the term *civile* in expressions such as *vita civile* and *civile felicità* (it appears twelve times, on average once every twenty-three lines).

The historical justification for the inclusion of love elements in the poem also makes an appearance at an earlier date. In a letter to Orazio Capponi in July–August 1576, Tasso claims:

in Paulo Emilio e in Roberto Monaco si legge che ne gli ultimi anni de la guerra ne' cristiani s'era intiepidito il zelo de la religione, e che commisero molti peccati con le donne saracine: sì che da alcuni santi sacerdoti fu detto che l'avversità de' cristiani procedevano da i loro amori scelerati. Eccovi l'origine de la fama, eccovi l'occasione con la quale io introduco gli amori nel poema: non punto di cattivo esempio, poiché gl'introduco come instrumento del diavolo; né trovandosi ne le istorie alcun particolare de gli amori de' cristiani e de le loro concupiscenze carnali, ben poss'io particolarizzare questo universale a mia voglia, senza contradire a l'istoria (*Prose*, 799).

Another example can be found in a letter written on 30 March 1576 to a future cardinal, Silvio Antoniano (and beginning with an acknowledgement not only of the addressee's *giudicio*, but of his *dottrina*, *religione* and *pietà*): 'Né minor occasion mi viene offerta da gli istorici di vagar ne gli amori' (*Prose*, 777). He ends a lengthy explanation with a remark that brings the topic of love explicitly under the jurisdiction of the *politico*: 'Ma poiché io ho parlato a lungo de gli amori e de gli incanti, accioch'essi con minore difficultà siano accettati dal politico, non sarà forse fuor di proposito ch'io soggiunga alcune ragioni' (p. 779).

Both the format in which these issues are presented in the polemic and the issues themselves mirror contemporary preoccupations, namely the obsession with classification that characterizes the poetic theory of the period. As Pellegrino explains in his treatise *Il Carrafa, o vero della epica poesia* (1584), in order to decide: 'in che cosa il Tasso sia in bontà poetica superiore all'Ariosto, et in che cosa per avventura l'Ariosto in ciò avanzi il Tasso … Converrebbe che sottilmente si esaminassono tutte le parti, così principali come minuti, di poesia, non solo le formali e le materiali della epopea' (Weinberg 1970–4, iii. 320). He then examines the two poems primarily in their 'parti formali o di qualità' (*favola, costume, sentenza* and *locuzione*), for 'delle parti di quantità, o materiali, dell'epopea Aristotile non ragiona' (p. 342). Although two such material parts are recognized as having been posited ('Ma come alcuni vogliono, si può dir che non sieno più che due, legame e discioglimento'), Ariosto's poem is considered to contain too many of these to facilitate an analyis of this nature (p. 342). Consequently the final judgement is contained within the format of the qualitative parts: 'Voi avete conchiuso il Tasso avanzar l'Ariosto nella favola, nel costume e nella locuzione, e l'Ariosto avanzar il Tasso nella sentenza' (p. 341).

The *Apologia* represents Tasso's major contribution in treatise form to his own defence as part of the polemic. In this treatise the poet also makes use of notions of structure in response to criticism aimed at certain areas of the poem. In relation to *materia*, this involves the precise demarcation of zones in the overall structure of the subject-matter which the poet may alter, and those which he may not. In keeping with his belief that the poet should take his material from history, he advocates that the essence of this material should be preserved, and the circumstances altered: 'si debbono variar le circonstanze, non l'essenza dell'istoria'. The circumstances are then defined in detail under the headings of *chi* (the doer of the action), *che* (the action itself), *intorno a che* (the material of which the action forms a part), *in che* (the time and the place), *con che* (the instrument) and *in grazia di che* (the purpose of the action) (*Prose*, 457).

The criticism to which Tasso is replying, and which he quotes in part at this point, is the following: 'Quando non se gli attribuisca a fallo l'aver finto Rinaldo, tronco di casa d'Este, figliuolo di Bertoldo, aver militato nella guerra di Gerusalemme, ec.' This quotation is an excerpt taken from a longer passage in Salviati's *Stacciata Prima* which continues, by way of explanation, as follows: 'poi che si sa per l'historia, egli essere stato al tempo dello Imperator Federigo primo, che fu sessanta, o ottanta anni poi della guerra. Ma questo fallo ha per compagno Vergilio' (Tasso, *Apologia*, 24). To counter this, Tasso uses the elements of *in che* and *chi*:

Dunque, fra le circonstanze, è 'l tempo e la persona; e non importa se Rinaldo, il quale fu settanta o ottanta anni dopo l'impresa di Gerusalemme, sia numerato fra' principali che passarono a l'acquisto; perché l'alterazione non si fa nell'azione istessa, la quale altramente si potrebbe dir negozio, o nell'essenza sua, ma nelle circonstanze che sono attribuite al negozio o a la persona (*Prose*, 457–8).

This type of structural consideration concerning *materia* is already in evidence in the early *Discorsi*, where Tasso states that the beginning and the end should be left unchanged, together with a few well-known aspects, although the latter may be slightly modified: 'Lassi il nostro epico il fine e l'origine della impresa, e alcune cose più illustri, nella lor verità o nulla o poco alterata.' Other parts, such as the means and the circumstances, may be altered: 'muti poi, se così gli pare, i mezzi e le circonstanze, confonda i tempi e gli ordini dell'altre cose, e si dimostri in somma più tosto artificioso poeta che verace istorico' (*Discorsi*, 18). Relevant passages in the later *Discorsi* are almost identical. Similarly in a letter of 1576 he speaks of the possibility 'che si variino per maggior vaghezza alcune circostanze' (*Prose*, 777).

In his treatise on the revised version of the *Gerusalemme liberata*, the *Giudizio sovra la Gerusalemme conquistata* (1594), Tasso reiterates the early *Discorsi* on beginnings and endings, and posits episodes as the correct area for invention:

Io, in quel ch'appartiene a la mistione del vero co 'l falso, estimo che 'l vero debba aver la maggior parte; sì perchè vero dee esser il principio, il quale è il mezzo del tutto; sì per la verità del fine, al quale tutte le cose sono dirizzate: e dove è vero il principio ed il fine della narrazione, il falso può esser ascoso agevolmente nelle parti di mezzo, e fraposto, ed inserito con gli episodi (*Prose diverse*, 454).

Guastavini, in his quantitative division of the *Gerusalemme liberata* in 1592, likewise suggests that the prologue and epilogue (the beginning and end) should be based on history, while the central area, containing episodes, gives the poet scope for invention (Weinberg 1961, 1053).

The actual relationship of structure to *materia* is assessed by Tasso in terms of its presence or absence in *materia* as an entity preceding disposition: 'Ma questa che, prima che sia caduta sotto l'artificio dell'epico, materia si chiama.' This *materia nuda* or *materia prima* is judged to be without form: 'Ma avendo … assomigliata quella materia, che nuda vien detta da noi a quella che chiamano i naturali materia prima, giudico che, sì come nella materia prima, benché *priva d'ogni forma*' … (*Discorsi*, 14). In the later *Discorsi* Tasso also describes this *materia* as *informe* ('nella materia nuda o informe') (p. 100). *Materia* acquires form once it has passed through the stage of disposition, at which point it is no longer simply *materia*, but 'un composto di materia e di forma' (p. 14).

Before disposition, *materia* is merely in a state of receptivity in relation to form. It is, in effect, this aspect of *materia* which the poet must consider first of all when undertaking the composition of an epic poem: 'A tre cose deve aver riguardo ciascuno che di scriver poema eroico si prepone: a scegliar materia tale che sia *atta a ricever in sé* quella più eccellente forma che l'artificio del poeta cercarà d'introdurvi' (*Discorsi*, 31). This receptivity is primarily governed by another structural consideration, namely that of quantity: 'il poeta debba in questa nostra materia, inanzi ad ogni altra cosa, la quantità considerare' (p. 15). In particular, the chosen *materia* must not be too long, thereby leaving no room for the inventive faculty of the poet ('non lassando luogo alcuno all'invenzione e all'ingegno del poeta') who must have space to 'interserirvi molti episodii e adornare e illustrar le cose' (p. 14). In other words, 'deve la quantità della materia nuda esser tanta, e non più, che possa dall'artificio del poeta ricever molto accrescimento senza passare i termini della convenevole grandezza' (p. 16).

These structural notions pinpoint the difference between the first two faculties of composition. In particular, they throw into relief Tasso's conception of the first rhetorical faculty of *inventio*. He sees this in terms of selection, and not invention, of *materia*, a point of view which derives from his belief that *materia* should be historical and true. This view is reflected by Giraldi, who also saw *inventio* in terms of selection and receptivity, and who says in his *Discorso intorno al comporre de i romanzi, delle comedie, e delle tragedie* (1554): 'devesi porre grandissima cura nello *scegliere* tal materia ... che sia *capace* di ornamento e di splendore' (Giraldi, 49). It is, according to Tasso, at the second stage of the poetic process (*dispositio*), following the judicious selection of the subject-matter, that actual inventiveness comes into play: 'cominciando dal giudizio ch'egli deve mostrare nell'elezione della materia, passerò all'arte e all'invenzione che se gli richiede servare prima nel disporla e nel formarla' (*Discorsi*, 80). Tasso's ideas regarding this cardinal stage in poetic composition will be examined in the next chapter.

CHAPTER 2

Dispositio

Dispositio is the second and most important of the three classical rhetorical faculties still current in the Renaissance (*memoria* and *pronuntiatio* having lapsed during the Middle Ages).[1] According to Tasso and other Renaissance theorists, it is in *dispositio* that the inventiveness of the epic poet is to be exercised. The faculty of *dispositio* involves the various processes of adding to the basic selected material (*aggiungendo*), or removing elements from it (*scemando*), and generally changing it (*variando*) according to the dictates of poetic *ingegno*. It is consequently during this stage of composition, namely that of reordering the subject-matter, rather than that of *inventio*, or its selection, that the poet faces his greatest challenge.

Aristotle had declared in his *Poetics* not only that the poet 'must be a maker of plots', but that the plot 'is the first essential of tragedy, its life-blood'(1451^{b} X. 9, 1450^{a} VI. 19, trans. Dorsch).[2] Of all the six qualitative parts of tragedy (plot, character, diction, thought, spectacle and song), he concluded that 'the most important is the plot, the ordering of the incidents'(1450^{a} VI. 12). His explanation of the primary role of plot centres on the function of the tragic poet, which is to represent action, rather than men:

For tragedy is a representation, not of men, but of action and life, of happiness and unhappiness—and happiness and unhappiness are bound up with action. The purpose of living is an end which is a kind of activity, not a quality; it is their characters, indeed, that make men what they are, but it is by reason of their actions that they are happy or the reverse. Thus the incidents

---

[1] An earlier version of this chapter appeared as 'Tasso's *Materia–Favola* Distinction and the Formalist Notion of *Fabula* and *Sjužet*', *Romance Philology*, 37/2 (Nov. 1983), 151–64.

[2] Different translations of classical texts, such as Aristotle's *Poetics*, are used in this study depending on the greater clarity and transparency of the particular passage in question.

and the plot are the end aimed at in tragedy, and as always, the end is every-thing (1450ᵃ VI. 12–13, trans. Dorsch).

Epic poetry is similarly driven by action: 'Epic poetry agrees with tragedy to the extent that it is a representation, in dignified verse, of serious actions' (1449ᵇ V. 7). Aristotle opens chapter 23 on epic poetry with a discussion of plot and action:

As for the art of representation in the form of narrative verse, clearly its plots should be dramatically constructed, like those of tragedies: they should cen-tre upon a single action, whole and complete, and having a beginning, a middle, and an end, so that like a single complete organism the poem may produce its own special kind of pleasure (1459a XXIII. 1, trans. Dorsch).

The qualitative element of plot is the particular concern of *dispositio*. *Dispositio* is expressed in the following passage in terms of the effec-tive handling of traditional material or stories, the actual choice of which can be said to pertain to *inventio*:

Thus it will not do to tamper with the traditional stories, the murder of Clytemnestra by Orestes, for instance, and that of Eriphyle by Alcmaeon; on the other hand, the poet must use his imagination and handle the tradition-al material effectively (1453ᵇ XIV. 10–11, trans. Dorsch).

One sixteenth-century writer who placed more importance on *dis-positio* than on *inventio* was Guastavini. He noted in his *Risposta all'Infarinato Academico della Crusca* (1588) that: 'se ben non fosse sua l'invenzione della materia principale, sarebbe sua l'inventione della forma, e maniera poetica, & egli per quella sarebbe poeta, & l'opra poema' (Weinberg 1961, 1038 n. 97). Tasso himself writes in his early *Discorsi*: 'Scelta ch'avrà il poeta materia per se stessa capace d'ogni perfezione, li rimane l'altra assai più difficile fatica, che è di darle forma e disposizion poetica: intorno al quale officio, come intorno a proprio soggetto, quasi tutta la virtù dell'arte si manifesta', an evalua-tion that remains unchanged in the later *Discorsi* (*Discorsi*, 17). Like Aristotle's poet, Tasso's *poeta* is a maker of plots.

Tasso's discussion of *dispositio* in the *Discorsi dell'arte poetica* is of par-ticular interest because it displays a striking affinity with theories on literature put forward four centuries later by the Russian Formalists. This affinity manifests itself in Tasso's interpretation of general rhetor-ical and particular Aristotelian ideas on composition. His discussion of the poet's shaping and disposition of the subject-matter is of sig-nificance when viewed in connection with the emphasis given by the

Formalists to the ordering of material as the prime task of the poet. This notion finds specific expression in the distinction between *fabula* and *sjužet*, or story and plot, developed by the Formalists and first postulated in the 1920s in the writings of Viktor Šklovskij.[3] The distinction has been summarized as follows:

> The Russian Formalists distinguished between *fabula* and *sjužet* in discussing plot-construction. *Fabula* refers to the raw material of a story, the story stuff, the basic causal–temporal relationships. *sjužet* refers to the presentation and manipulation of this basic story stuff—what we would call plot (Matejka and Pomorska 1971, 226 n. 2).

Tasso proposes in the opening lines of his *Discorsi* that the poet begin by carefully selecting 'materia tale che sia atta a ricever in sé quella più eccelente forma che l'artificio del poeta cercarà d'introdurvi' (*Discorsi*, 3). The poet should then proceed to *disporla* and *formarla* with *arte* (skill) (p. 3). The elaboration of this proposition reveals a close correspondence between Tasso's notion of *materia* and the Formalist concept of *fabula*, while his use of *favola* appears analogous to the Formalist *sjužet*. In examining this correspondence, this chapter traces the development of the particular type of distinction represented by the *materia/fabula–favola/sjužet* differentiation, with the aim of providing the background against which its formulation by both Tasso and the Formalists can be set.

From *materia* to *favola*: aims and effects

At the outset it should be noted that the context of the Formalist notion of *fabula* and *sjužet* differs from that of Tasso's *materia–favola* distinction in that it does not form part of a practical, step-by-step treatise on composition. The Formalists are more interested in how literature works, and their approach is therefore more oriented towards theoretical speculation involving the analysis of literature that has already been composed. The Formalist distinction is the culmination of a line of enquiry beginning, as indeed had Aristotle, at the opposite starting point from that of Tasso, with an examination into the effect produced by a work of art. In his essay 'Art as Technique'

---

[3] Translations and developments of the distinction between *fabula* and *sjužet* have taken various forms, such as *histoire* and *récit* or *discours*, Chatman's *story* and *discourse*, and Ricoeur's *events* and *story* (Chatman 1979, Ricoeur 1983). Details of these developments are taken from Brooks 1995, 12–14, where Scholes 1974 is also recommended for further discussion of the relevant issues.

(1925), Šklovskij concentrates on the particular type of response induced by a work of art (Lemon and Reis 1965). This takes the form of a vivid, lifelike vision of the events represented, as opposed to the mechanical, unconscious process of automatic recognition. However, Tasso also deals with vividness (*energia*). For him, it is an important aspect of style:

Stando che lo stile sia un instrumento co 'l quale imita il poeta quelle cose che d'imitare si ha proposte, necessaria è in lui l'*energia*, la quale sì con parole pone inanzi a gli occhi la cosa che pare altrui non di udirla, ma di vederla (*Discorsi*, 47).

His term *energia* is equivalent to the Greek *enargeia*, which also appears in Quintilian's *Institutio oratoria*:

Consequently we must place among ornaments that *enargeia*, which I mentioned in the rules which I laid down for the statement of facts, because vivid illustration [*evidentia*], or, as some prefer to call it, representation [*repraesentatio*], is something more than mere clearness, since the latter merely lets itself be seen, whereas the former thrusts itself upon our notice (VIII. iii. 61).[4]

Tasso enlarges on *energia* in his later *Discorsi*:

quella che da' Latini è detta 'evidenzia', da' Greci 'energia'; da noi si direbbe 'chiarezza' o 'espressione' non men propriamente; ma è quella virtù che ci fa quasi veder le cose che si narrano, la quale nasce da una diligentissima narrazione, in cui niuna cosa sia tralasciata (*Discorsi*, 243).

He believes this quality to be particularly necessary in the epic poem, which has no actors or scenery to supplement the words, and offers specific directions on how it is to be achieved:

Nasce questa virtù da una accurata diligenza di descrivere la cosa minutamente, alla quale però è quasi inetta la nostra lingua . . . Nasce questa virtù

---

[4] Quintilian refers to Cicero's mention of the figure *sub oculos subiectio* (*De oratore* III. liii. 202) in another elaboration of *evidentia* where he draws attention to 'appeal to the eye rather than the ear' (*Inst. orat.* IX. ii. 40). Isidore of Seville also used the idea of *energia* in his *Origines*, explaining it as follows: 'energia est rerum gestarum aut quasi gestarum sub oculis inductio' (II. xxi. 33; Lausberg 1960, 400). My thanks to Leofranc Holford-Strevens for providing classical references, and for the observation that Isidore, as Tasso was to do, 'confused *enargeia*, "vividness", with *energeia*, "effectiveness", which amongst its many other meanings is also a rhetorical term (Quintilian VIII. iii. 89); in fact the two words are variants in the manuscripts of Aristotle's *Rhetoric* (III. x. 1410^{b}36, III. xi. 1411^{b}28–9), but there *energeia* is correct, in the sense of "being in action". I suppose Tasso got the notion that one seems to see rather than hear from Quintilian IX. ii. 40.'

quando, introdotto alcuno a parlare, gli si fa fare quei gesti che sono suoi propri ... È necessaria questa diligente narrazione nelle parti patetiche, peroché è principalissimo instrumento di mover l'affetto ... Nasce questa virtù ancora se, descrivendosi alcuno effetto, si descrive ancora quelle circonstanze che l'accompagnano come, descrivendo il corso della nave, si dirà che l'onda rotta le mormora intorno. Queste translazioni che mettono la cosa in atto portano seco questa espressione, massime quando è dalle animate alle inanimate ... Deriva molte volte l'energia da quelle parole che alla cosa che l'uom vuole esprimere sono naturali (*Discorsi*, 47–8).

The notion of vividness in the works of both Tasso and Šklovskij is particularly reminiscent of the Aristotelian concept of *enargeia*. In a passage of the *Poetics* delineating the effects of tragic representation, Aristotle indicates the importance of vividness:

Secondly, tragedy has all the elements of the epic—it can even use the hexameter—and in addition a considerable element of its own in the spectacle and the music, which make the pleasure all the more vivid; and this vividness can be felt whether it is read or acted (1462^a XXVI. 9–12, trans. Hamilton Fyfe).

Aristotle expands on *enargeia* in his *Rhetoric* in the context of diction, but with clear reference to action and to the 'actuality' of its verbal representation, saying that words should 'set things "before the eyes"; for we ought to see what is being done rather than what is going to be done. We ought therefore to aim at ... actuality' (1410^b III. x. 6). He elaborates further, adducing examples of vividness from an oration entitled *Philippus* by Isocrates, the Euripidean tragedy *Iphigenia*, and Homer's epic poems, the *Odyssey* and the *Iliad*:

We have said that smart sayings are derived from proportional metaphor and expressions which set things before the eyes. We must now explain the meaning of 'before the eyes', and what must be done to produce this. I mean that things are set before the eyes by words that signify actuality ... 'thee, like a sacred animal ranging at will' expresses actuality, and in 'Thereupon the Greeks shooting forward with their feet' the word 'shooting' contains both actuality and metaphor. And as Homer often, by making use of metaphor, speaks of inanimate things as if they were animate; and it is to creating actuality in all such cases that his popularity is due, as in the following examples: 'Again the ruthless stone rolled down to the plain' ... 'The spear-point sped eagerly through his breast' (1411^b III. xi. 1–3).

Another classical Greek text, known as the *De elocutione* by Demetrius, also deals with vividness as an effect in relation to diction.

For Demetrius, vividness is a quality of representation facilitated particularly by the plain style:

> As, however, the plain style will welcome vivid representation and persuasiveness in an especial degree, we must next speak of these two qualities. We shall treat first of vividness, which arises from an exact narration overlooking no detail and cutting out nothing (208–9).

The concern of Demetrius with vividness as 'exact narration' aligns his perspective, which is broadly speaking that of actuality and verisimilitude, with that of Aristotle, to whose *Rhetoric* he frequently refers. Aristotle also advises in the *Poetics* that, in order to achieve the effect of *enargeia*, the poet must 'keep the scene before his eyes' during the stages of plot-construction (*dispositio*) and diction (*elocutio*):

> In putting together his plots and working out the kind of speech to go with them, the poet should as far as possible keep the scene before his eyes. In this way, seeing everything very vividly, as though he were himself an eyewitness of the events, he will find what is appropriate, and will be least likely to overlook inconsistencies (1455ᵃ XVII. 1, trans. Dorsch).

As indicated by the final two clauses, Aristotle links vividness with notions of the fitting, or appropriate, and the verisimilar. Šklovskij, however, focuses his attention not on verisimilitude, but on the means used by the artist to de-automatize perception, in other words, to convey the object in the process of becoming, rather than already complete. He maintains that 'the technique of art is to make objects "unfamiliar", to make forms difficult, to increase the difficulty and length of perception because the process of perception is an aesthetic end in itself and must be prolonged' (Lemon and Reis 1965, 12).[5] From this attitude stems the Formalist conception of art as form, as arrangement (*sjužet*) of pre-existing material (*fabula*), rather than creation from zero.

In addition to *enargeia*, two other important effects were believed by Aristotle to be produced in the audience of a well-composed tragedy, namely the cathartic emotions of pity and fear. By contrast, the Formalist focus on 'making strange' the subject-matter in its

[5] Translations into English of some works by the Russian Formalists can be found in Lemon and Reis 1965 and Matejka and Pomorska 1971. Quotations from Italian translations are given for works not available in English. In the case of Tomaševskij's essay 'La costruzione dell'intreccio', the Italian translation is given in preference to the English.

reordering and representation as plot would have induced the opposite of the empathizing response inherent in catharsis. A contemporary of the Formalists, the dramatist and theorist Brecht, added a politicizing dimension to the process of 'making strange' the subject-matter for an audience, by means of what he called the *Verfremdungseffekt*, or *alienation-effect*. Willett notes that the term *Verfremdungseffekt*, coined as a translation of Šklovskij's phrase *priem ostrannenija* ('device for making strange'), first appears in Brecht's 'Verfremdungseffekte in der chinesischen Schauspielkunst'. Brecht wrote this essay after he had seen a performance of a Chinese play in Moscow in 1935 (while his earlier exploration of the notion of *Entfremdung* appears to precede any Formalist influence) (Brecht 1986, 99, translator's note). While Brecht's epic theatre represented action (*gestus*) rather than characters, as advocated by Aristotle in his *Poetics*, these two theorists part company in the area of effects. Brecht argued that the alienation-effect produced the opposite response of Aristotle's catharsis, whereby the audience expended its precious emotional and political energy by squandering it empathically and in a de-politicized manner. The alienation-effect, on the other hand, had the effect of awakening a critical response in the audience, who would then feel compelled to become politically active.

The basic point of interest in Aristotelian and Formalist thinking as far as coincidence with Tasso is concerned lies in the notion that the artistic process is located primarily in the arrangement and disposition of material. The ideas expressed on this subject by Èjxenbaum in his essay 'The Theory of the "Formal Method"' (1927):

the specific quality of art is shown in its particular use of the material (Lemon and Reis 1965, 113)

and Šklovskij in his essay 'Il legame tra i procedimenti di composizione dell'intreccio e i procedimenti generali dello stile' (1929):

libertà dell'autore, che costruisce l'opera, che prende un frammento e lo colloca vicino ad altri frammenti (Šklovskij 1976, 64)

seem to re-echo Tasso's notion of the poet primarily as arranger:

scelta ch'avrà il poeta materia per se stessa capace d'ogni perfezione, li rimane l'altra assai più difficile fatica, che è di darle forma e disposizione poetica; intorno al quale officio, come intorno a proprio soggetto, quasi tutta la virtù dell'arte si manifesta (*Discorsi*, 17).

This artistic process of disposition is encapsulated in Šklovskij's *fabula* *–sjužet* distinction and Tasso's analogous *materia–favola* formulation.

For Tasso, material (or, more precisely, raw material: 'materia nuda è detta quella che non ha ancor ricevuta qualità alcuna dall'artificio dell'oratore e del poeta'; *Discorsi*, 3) undergoes the essential poetic process of organization to become *favola*:

> ma questa che, prima che sia caduta sotto l'artificio dell'epico, materia si chiama, doppo ch'è stata dal poeta disposta e trattata, e che favola è divenuta, non è più materia (*Discorsi*, 14).

This description of the transition from *materia* to *favola* does not, however, appear in Aristotle's *Poetics*. Aristotle himself is only mentioned by Tasso with reference to the central importance of plot: 'Ma è forma e anima del poema; e tale è da Aristotele giudicata.' The particular sentence in the *Poetics* that Tasso refers to here is the following: 'The plot, then, is the first essential of tragedy, its life-blood, so to speak' (1450ª VI. 19, trans. Dorsch).[6] Tasso's concluding remark in this section of the *Discorsi* shows his own particular concern to define *favola* in terms of its relationship with *materia*, in other words, with the stage preceding its formation: 'e se non forma semplice, almeno un composto di materia e di forma il giudicaremo'.

Similarly for Šklovskij, in his essay 'Sterne's *Tristram Shandy*: Stylistic Commentary' (1925), *fabula* or *story* is formed by the writer into *sjužet* (translated here by *plot*):

> the description of events ... what I propose provisionally to call the story. The story is, in fact, only material for plot formulation (Lemon and Reis 1965, 57).

Tomaševskij discussed this particular distinction in his essay 'La costruzione dell'intreccio' (1928). According to him, the *avvenimenti* of the *fabula* are distributed (the importance of this act being indicated by his italicizing of the appropriate word) in such a way as to become transformed into a sequence (the *intreccio*) that qualifies as art:

> bisogna dar loro una *distribuzione*, ordinarli in una costruzione determinata, esporli in modo che le componenti della *fabula* si trasformino in una composizione letteraria. La distribuzione in costruzione estetica degli avvenimenti nell'opera ne è chiamato l'intreccio (Todorov 1968, 314).

---

[6] The relevant passage, found at *Poetics*, 1450ª VI. xix. 38–9, is translated by Robortello in his *In librum Aristotelis de arte poetica explicationes* (1548) as follows: 'Est igitur principium, ac velut anima Tragoediae, fabula' (p. 63).

He offers a further definition of the structure both of the *fabula* and the *intreccio*, expressed in terms of the causal–temporal relationship between narrative units which he calls *motivi* (a *motivo* being 'il tema di una particella indivisibile'):

la fabula è costituita dall'insieme dei motivi nei loro rapporti logici causali–temporali, mentre l'intreccio è l'insieme degli stessi motivi, in quella successione e in quei rapporti in cui essi sono dati nell'opera (p. 315).

Tomaševskij suggests that one way in which the organization of the *intreccio* could differ from the order of the *fabula* is by means of *trasposizioni temporali*. Tasso's discussion of the freedom of the epic poet to alter the nature and the circumstances of the *avvenimenti* of his *materia* in transforming them into *favola* also includes the device of temporal transposition, thereby showing a similar view of narrative material in terms of a certain order that undergoes rearrangement:

Lassi il nostro epico il fine e l'origine della impresa, e alcune cose più illustri, nella lor verità o nulla o poco alterata; muti poi, se così gli pare, i mezzi e le circonstanze, confonda i tempi e gli ordini dell'altre cose, e si dimostri in somma più tosto artificioso poeta che verace istorico (*Discorsi*, 18).

Tomaševskij's interpretation of the *intreccio* as the sequence or interrelationship of *motivi* that is found in the final product ('l'intreccio è l'insieme degli stessi motivi, in quella successione e in quei rapporti in cui essi sono dati nell'opera') also finds a parallel in Tasso's definition of the *favola* as that particular combination of *avvenimenti* of which the poem itself is composed: 'favola chiamo la forma del poema che definir si può testura o composizione degli avvenimenti' (*Discorsi*, 19). He takes this definition directly from the *Poetics*, in which Aristotle says: 'By "plot" I mean here the arrangement of the incidents' (1450ᵃ VI. 8, trans. Hamilton Fyfe).[7] Tasso's concept of *favola*, the 'artificiosa testura de' nodi', can clearly be equated with the notion of *sjužet*, and parallels a similar correspondence between his concept of *materia* and the Formalist use of *fabula* (*Discorsi*, 22). The ordering process of art that leads to the transition from *fabula* (story) to *sjužet* (plot) is expressed by the Formalists in terms of structure, or construction:

The line between the idea of plot as structure and the idea of the story as material was drawn (Lemon and Reis 1965, 122),

---

[7] Robortello's translation of *Poetics*, 1450ᵃ, VI. viii. 4–5, is as follows: 'fabulam vero rerum ipsum compositionem appello' (p. 56).

organization:

un risultato dell'organizzazione del materiale in un intreccio (Todorov 1968, 340)

and formation:

The story is, in fact, only material for plot formation (Lemon and Reis 1965, 57),

and by Tasso in terms of disposition ('darle [materia] forma e disposizion poetica'), texture and formation ('formare la testura della favola') (*Discorsi*, 17, 14). Robortello, in his influential commentary of 1548, *In librum Aristotelis de arte poetica explicationes*, has in mind a concept similar to that of Tasso, which he describes as *fabulas contexere* (p. 164).

Tasso's *materia–favola* distinction can be set against analogous sixteenth-century discussions, and these will be outlined later. However, it can also be illuminated by direct reference to his interpretation of Aristotle. The fundamental nature of this interpretation does not lie predominantly in any significant development or alteration of Aristotelian ideas as such, although some amplification does take place. It is, rather, the actual organization of these notions in the *Discorsi* that culminates in the particular *materia–favola* polarization absent from the *Poetics*. For Aristotle the notion of material is secondary to that of plot, and as such it is treated under considerations of the latter. Tasso, on the other hand, deals with *materia* in its own right as the first of three stages of composition outlined in his opening paragraph, and linked, as a separate entity, by the *artificio* of the poet to the second stage, epitomized by *favola*.

The *materia–favola* distinction that emerges from this reformulation of Aristotle's ideas clearly has a strong rhetorical flavour. It forms the first two parts of Tasso's tripartite division of the process of composition outlined at the beginning of the *Discorsi*, which, as mentioned above, is equivalent to the three surviving faculties of rhetorical composition, namely *inventio*, *dispositio* and *elocutio*. It is Tasso's superimposition of these rhetorical categories onto Aristotle's *Poetics* (the six constituent parts of tragedy listed therein constituting no analogous division) that helps to give rise to the *materia–favola* distinction itself. The fact of formulating a distinction of this nature, and of classifying such stages of composition in the context of poetry, betokens the continuing influence of rhetoric on poetics.[8] This influence can be seen to extend from the broad categor-

---

[8] For further discussion of the influence of rhetoric over poetics, see Clark 1922, Norden 1909 and Weinberg 1961.

ization of the faculties of rhetorical composition to discussions on specific details concerning each individual faculty.

A history of dual order in rhetoric and poetics

The arguments particularly relevant here concern the act of ordering
which, by definition, entails the rearrangement of one order into a
second, different sequence. A brief explanation of the development
of the notion of such a dual-order system in rhetoric will help to
place in perspective Tasso's expression of the reordering transition
from *materia* to *favola*, while at the same time indicating the type of
rhetorical background to which the Formalist distinction would seem
to be related. This notion of a dual order or, more precisely, the possibility of more than one type of order, has its roots in various areas
of classical rhetoric. It appears, first, under the faculty of ordering
itself, namely *dispositio*; second, in the context of that part of the oration which is also its most literary component, namely the *narratio*;
and third, in the section dealing with word-order, which lies in the
grammatical zone of *compositio* to be found under the faculty of *elocutio*.

Rhetoric itself, as Aristotle pointed out in his *Rhetoric*, can be seen
to derive directly from dialectic, with which it has a notable affinity:

Thus it appears that Rhetoric is as it were an offshoot of Dialectic ...
Rhetoric is a sort of division or likeness of Dialectic, since neither of them
is a science that deals with the nature of any definite subject, but they are
merely faculties of furnishing arguments (1356ᵃ I. ii. 7).

In this passage Aristotle underlines the fact that both rhetoric and
dialectic are *forms* of reasoning. They are linked in this respect, he
argues, by the use made in rhetoric of the enthymeme. The
enthymeme is a particular formula in reasoning that is 'a kind of syllogism', and the syllogism is also to be found in dialectic (1355ᵃ I. i. 11).

The origins of the notion of a dual order, such as that expressed by
the Formalist distinction, can thus be seen to lie ultimately in logic,
a domain concerned predominantly with forms of reasoning; dealing,
in other words, with relationships and links rather than with pure
meaning, and with arguments rather than with subject-matter. There
is an obvious correlation here with the essence of Formalist and
Structuralist thought in general, characterized by its emphasis on
arrangement and sequence, and on the pre-eminence of the formal

rather than the content level.

A brief glance at the discussion of dual order in classical rhetoric will help to orient its treatment during the Renaissance, and by Tasso in particular. Under the faculty of *dispositio*, the rules of rhetoric in themselves are seen to present a duplex order, one for the whole speech and one for the parts of each argument used within it, as stated in the *Rhetorica ad Herennium*:

This Arrangement [*dispositio*], then, is twofold [*duplex*]—one for the whole speech, and the other for the individual arguments—and is based upon the principles of rhetoric (III. ix. 17).

In its commonest form the notion appears in the *Rhetorica ad Herennium* as the difference between the rules of the art of rhetoric as opposed to their modification according to the requirements of particular circumstances:

The kinds of Arrangement [*dispositionum*] are two [*duo*]: one arising from the principles of rhetoric, the other accommodated to particular circumstances (III. ix. 16).

This particularly concerns the sequence followed by the standard oration, namely *exordium, narratio, confirmatio* and *peroratio*, which could appear in a reordered format, as well as not always necessarily including all of these parts.[9] In this case, there is a departure from the *ordine artificioso*, in other words, 'the order imposed by the rules of the art' (III. ix. 17).

Significantly, it is in the realm of the *narratio*, that part of the oration which relates most closely to literary writing, that the concept of two types of order recurs, and in a manner more directly relevant to the modern *fabula–sjužet* distinction. It is interesting to note in this connection that Aristotle in his *Rhetoric* deals with a dual order in narration. He does so in the section on the statement of facts in epideictic speeches, epideictic oratory being traditionally considered the branch of oratory, as opposed to the forensic and the deliberative, that was most akin to literature:

In the epideiktic style the narrative should not be consecutive, but disjointed ... it is sometimes right not to narrate all the facts consecutively, because a demonstration of this kind is difficult to remember. From some facts a man may be shown to be courageous, from others wise or just. Besides, a speech

---

[9] See also Quintilian VII. x. 11–13.

of this kind is simpler, whereas the other is intricate and not plain. It is only necessary to recall famous actions; wherefore most people have no need of narrative—for instance, if you wish to praise Achilles; for everybody knows what he did, and it is only necessary to make use of it (1416^b III. xvi. 1–4).

Aristotle makes mention of two different orders of narration, the 'consecutive', or 'continuous', and the 'disjointed', or 'broken up'.[10] Emphasis is on the use of facts, which should not necessarily all appear in detail or keep their order. This implies a standard type of order of facts that are presented consecutively. In the second type of order, the facts should be arranged (in this case grouped together to illustrate bravery, wisdom or justice) according to the aim of the par- ticular speech ('sometimes'). An actual as opposed to a false or unreal order of events, or chronological vs. achronological order, is not overtly mentioned by Aristotle here, but some form of dual order is certainly implied. This particular Aristotelian passage was to be cited in the sixteenth century in the context of the dual order of *ordine naturale* vs. *ordine artificiale* in Lionardi's *Dialogi della inventione poetica* (1554):

Vero è che ci sono due *ordini*, l'uno *naturale* e l'altro *artificiale* … In questo poi si raccontano solamente i fatti et accidenti più importanti o più notabili … secondo quello che dice Aristotile nella *Retorica* ove parla della narrazione dimostrativa (Weinberg 1970–4, ii. 252).

Quintilian further polarizes Aristotle's 'continuous' and 'broken up' forms of narrative into two distinct possibilities of order in his dis- cussion of the orator's ability to decide which type of order to use in the statement of facts: 'when we should make our statement of facts continuous [*continue*], and when we should subdivide it [*partita*]' (VII. x. 11). Indeed by Roman times treatment of order in the *narratio* included a particular stress on this specific type of dual order. Dual order was to reappear during the Renaissance in the *materia–favola* ordering process, with the normal order of events being modified according to the requirements of the plot.

In classical rhetoric it is the use of the chronological order itself, however, that is normally advocated. This is specifically in the inter- ests of a clear *narratio* (clarity having been considered essential by Aristotle). The *Rhetorica ad Herennium* also proposed that:

[10] The terms 'continuous' and 'broken up' are used by Jebb in his translation of Aristotle's *Rhetoric*.

Our Statement of Facts will be clear if we set forth the facts in the precise order in which they occurred, observing their actual or probable sequence and chronology (I. ix. 15).

In his *De inventione*, Cicero said:

It will be possible to make the narrative clear if the events are presented one after another as they occurred, and the order of events in time is preserved so that the story is told as it will prove to have happened or will seem possible to have happened (I. xx. 29).

There may be exceptions when an achronological order should be adopted, as Quintilian's *Institutio oratoria* points out:

Neither do I agree with those who assert that the order of our *statement of facts* should always follow the actual order of events, but have a preference for adopting the order which I consider most suitable (IV. ii. 83).

However, this is the exception rather than the rule, and inappropriate use of such reordering may have negative effects:

On the other hand this is no reason for not following the order of events as a general rule. Indeed inversion of the order has at times a most unhappy effect, as for example if you should mention first that a woman has brought forth and then that she has conceived, or that a will has been read and then that it has been signed (IV. ii. 87).

Fifth-century discussions on how to produce a clear *narratio* similarly mention the alteration of the chronological order in negative terms. For instance, Victorinus says: 'Hic erit considerandum, ne quid perturbate, ne quid contorte dicatur' (Halm 1863, 206).[11]

The notion of a dual order is also present in classical rhetoric in the grammatical area of word-order. Demetrius refers in his *De elocutione* to a 'natural order' and a 'reverse order', once again in the context of clarity:

In general, the natural order of the words should be followed, as in the sentence 'Epidamnus is a town on your right hand as you sail into the Ionian gulf'. First of all is mentioned the subject, which is then defined to be a town, and next come the other words in due succession. Of course the order might be reversed, as in the words 'There is a town Ephyra'. We do not absolutely approve the one order nor condemn the other, when simply setting forth the natural method of arranging the words ... These are a few remarks, where much could be said, on the subject of clearness (199–200, 203).

---

[11] See also Albinus, *De arte rhet. dial.*, 22, 10 (Halm 1863, 536).

The same terminology is used by Quintilian in his *Institutio oratoria*:

there is also another species of order which may be entitled natural, as for example when we speak of 'men and women', 'day and night', 'rising and setting', in preference to the reverse order (IX. iv. 23).

Classical rhetoric thus already contained the basic elements inherent in the notion of two possible types of order in discourse, a notion that in itself was clearly related to wider, philosophical discussions on nature as opposed to art, as well as to theorization on the psychological effects, and thence requirements, of various aspects of communication. Classical poetics, which did not constitute a comparable corpus in terms of size or, in its day, importance (being, for one reason, an offshoot of rhetoric rather than an independently developed body of precepts), contained no such explicit schematizations of dual order. However, two passages from the one major work on poetics, Horace's *Ars poetica*, which dominated and indeed represented this field until the late fifteenth-century rediscovery of Aristotle's *Poetics*, provided a basis for rhetorical-style schematization into two distinct types of order:

The virtue and attraction of order, I think I am right in saying, is that the poet will at any moment be saying exactly what his poem at that moment requires; he will be keeping back points for the time being or leaving them out altogether, and showing what he thinks admirable and what beneath notice (42–5);

and:

This poet … does not trace Diomede's return right back to the death of Meleager, or the Trojan War to the twin eggs of Leda. All the time he is hurrying on to the crisis, and he plunges his hearer into the middle of the story [*in medias res*] as if it were already familiar to him; and what he cannot hope to embellish by his treatment he leaves out. Moreover, so inventive is he, and so skilfully does he blend fact and fiction, that the middle is not inconsistent with the beginning, nor the end with the middle (146–52).

Like Horace's *Ars poetica*, Aristotle's *Poetics* contained no overt, comprehensive treatment of a dual order. Castelvetro was to comment on the Greek philosopher's lack of explicitness in this context in his *Poetica d'Aristotele vulgarizzata, et sposta* (1570), when he applied the distinction *ordine della natura* vs. *ordine artificiale* to Aristotle's work: 'la qual cosa a me non pare dire Aristotele' (p. 211). However, certain passages in the *Poetics*, in particular the following section concerning historical as opposed to poetical writing, were to lend themselves readily to such an interpretation and amplification:

The difference between a historian and a poet is not that one writes in prose and the other in verse ... The real difference is this, that one tells what happened and the other what might happen ... poetry tends to give general truths while history gives particular facts. By a 'general truth' I mean the sort of thing that a certain type of man will do or say either probably or necessarily ... A 'particular fact' is what Alcibiades did or what was done to him (1451^a IX. 2–1451^b 4, trans. Hamilton Fyfe).

While Aristotle does not overtly discuss a dual order in the *Poetics*, he does, however, mention order itself:

The representation of the action is the plot of the tragedy; for the *ordered* arrangement of the incidents is what I mean by plot (1450^a VI. 8, trans. Dorsch);

and:

a plot giving an *ordered* combination of incidents (1450^a VI. 16).

In relation to the arrangement of the incidents in the context of the representation of an action that is complete, Aristotle also explains the beginning, the middle and the end in terms of the sequential relationship each has with the other two:

I have already laid down that tragedy is the representation of an action that is complete and whole ... Now a whole is that which has a beginning, a middle, and an end. A beginning is that which does not necessarily come after something else, although something else exists or comes about after it. An end, on the contrary, is that which naturally follows something else either as a necessary or as a usual consequence, and is not itself followed by anything. A middle is that which follows something else, and is itself followed by something. Thus well-constructed plots must neither begin nor end in a haphazard way, but must conform to the pattern I have been describing (1450^b VII. 2–7, trans. Dorsch).

A dual order of sorts is hinted at later when he uses the notion of logic to delineate one way in which events might possibly unfold, while another, alternative, order is that of things happening 'unexpectedly' (albeit still within the realms of verisimilitude):

However, tragedy is the representation not only of a complete action, but also of incidents that awaken fear and pity, and effects of this kind are heightened when things happen *unexpectedly as well as logically*, for then they will be more remarkable than if they seem merely mechanical or accidental (1452ª IX. 11).

Aristotle's elaboration of simple as opposed to complex plots deals more obviously with a dual order. His discussion at this point in the *Poetics* is reminiscent of his treatment in the *Rhetoric* of the *narratio* in an oration. There he speaks of dual order in terms of the 'continuous' or the 'broken up', while in the *Poetics* he defines a simple plot as 'one which is single and continuous ... and in which the change of fortune comes about without a reversal or a discovery' (1452ª X. 2, trans. Dorsch). The complex plot, on the other hand, 'is one in which the change is accompanied by a discovery or a reversal, or both' (1452ª X. 3).

A predominant feature of rhetorical schematization was the standardized terminology that in time became the conventional expression of the concept of dual order, namely *ordo naturalis* vs. *ordo artificialis*. This was accompanied, after the recovery of Aristotle's *Poetics*, by the more specialized literary (as opposed to philosophical) formulation of historical as opposed to poetic order. Use of the terms *ordo naturalis* and *ordo artificialis* as a pair seems not to have been a common feature of the classical rhetorical period itself. Although the second component of the pair does appear in the section on *dispositio* in the *Rhetorica ad Herennium* as *ab ordine artificioso*, referring to the rules of the art of rhetoric, it is not coupled with any mention of *ordo naturalis*.[12]

[12] It is not until the 5th c. AD that these two terms appear together with any regularity. When they do occur prior to this period, *ordo naturalis* serves to refer to the order stemming from the rules of the art of rhetoric, for which *ordo artificiosus* is used, for example in the *Rhetorica ad Herennium* (trans. Caplan; see p. 184 n. b). In the 5th c. these terms are found in discussions of *dispositio* by rhetoricians such as Sulpitius Victor (*ordo naturalis* and *ordo artificiosus*) (Halm 1863, 320). Fortunatianus uses *ordo naturalis* and *ordo artificialis* (ibid. 120–1); and Martianus Capella says: '*naturalis est ordo, aut oratoris artificio comparatur*' (ibid. 472). Furthermore, the *narratio* itself is classified under the *artificiosus ordo* of *dispositio* by Sulpitius Victor, in cases when it is 'subdivided' and 'interrupted' ('*artificiosus ordo* est ... aliquando subdividenda et interrumpenda narratio') (ibid. 320). By at least the 9th or 10th c., this essentially rhetorical pair of terms was applied to poetics, as can be seen in the following excerpt from the *Scholia vindobonensia ad Horatii artem poeticam*, a commentary on Horace's *Ars poetica*: '*omnis ordo naturalis aut artificialis est. Naturalis ordo est si quis narret rem ordine quo gesta est; artificialis ordo est si quis non incipit a principio rei gestae, sed a medio*' (Faral 1962, 56).

The application of these terms in treatises on poetics continued throughout the Middle Ages. Another example occurs at the beginning of the 13th c. in Geoffroi de

The Renaissance was therefore to inherit a concept of dual order originating in *dispositio*, *narratio* and *compositio* (*elocutio*), all discussed in the context of classical rhetoric, and recurring in the Middle Ages in, for instance, arts of poetry, *artes grammaticae* and *artes dictandi*. By the ninth or tenth century, the terms *ordo naturalis* and *ordo artificialis*, first used with any regularity, it will be recalled, by rhetoricians of the fifth century AD, had become adopted as a conventional, standardized expression of the distinction. A major development in the sixteenth century was the addition of Aristotle's *Poetics* (following Giorgio Valla's Latin translation of 1498) to the body of classical texts open to commentary and interpretation. Here it joined Horace's *Ars poetica* in the field of poetics, a work that was similarly to undergo the super-imposition of rhetorical schematization in terms of a dual order.[13]

One illustration of the type of distinction that crystallized during this period can be found in Castelvetro's commentary on Aristotle's *Poetics*, the *Poetica d'Aristotele vulgarizzata, et sposta* (1570). In this work Castelvetro uses the expressions *ordine della natura* and *uno [ordine] artificiale* to interpret and amplify Aristotle's statement on the

Vinsauf's *Poetria nova*: 'Ordo bifurcat iter: tum limite *nititur artis*, / Tum *sequitur stratam naturae*' (ibid. 200). The distinction recurs in the discussion on how to begin a poem in Vinsauf's *Documentum de modo et arte dictandi et versificandi*: 'Circum principium ita distinguitur: *principium aliud naturale, aliud artificiale. Principium naturale est quando sermo inde incipit unde res geri incipit ... Principium artificiale est quando sermo aliunde incipit ... Sumitur enim tum a medio, tum a fine*' (Faral 1962, 265). By the 11th c., the *artes grammaticae* had also adopted the concepts of *ordo naturalis* and *ordo artificialis* in their treatment of word-order (Scaglione 1972, 106 ff). *Artes dictandi* were to use these terms in the early 13th c., where they appear, for example, in the *Summa dictaminis* by Guido Faba (or Fava) of Bologna (*c.*1200–50): 'in constructione duplex est *ordo*, scilicet *naturalis* et *artificialis. Naturalis* est ille qui pertinet ad expositionem, quando nominativus cum determinatione sua precedit et verbum sequitur cum sua, ut EGO AMO TE. *Artificialis* ordo est illa compositio que pertinet ad dictationem, quando partes pulcrius disponuntur' (Scaglione 1972, 117).

[13] For a detailed study of the 16th-c. position regarding reinterpretation of the *Ars poetica* in the light of Valla's 1498 translation of Aristotle's *Poetics*, discernible in the merger of Horatian and Aristotelian ideas that characterized 16th-c. literary theory, see Herrick 1946.

difference between history and poetry (quoted above), while at the same time incorporating the ever-influential Horatian idea on where to begin a poem:

che l'ordine della narrazione poetica sia molto differente dall'ordine della narrazione istorica; percioché in questa si conserva l'*ordine della natura* e si comincia narrando dal principio delle cose che prima sono state fatte e poi, passando per lo mezzo, si segue infino al fine; e in quella non si conserva simile *ordine di natura*, ma se ne tiene *uno artificiale*, che è di cominciare dal mezzo o dal fine, e poi, per alcune opportunità o digressioni, di raccontare le cose prima avenute, o poi, o in mezzo (p. 210).

Other terms used by Castelvetro for the artificial order of poetry are *ordine tramutato, ordine turbato, ordine transmutato* and *ordine trasportato*. In the same way, some Renaissance commentators on the Horatian precept on where to begin the poem used *ordo naturalis* and *ordo artificialis*, thereby continuing the ninth- or tenth-century tradition, while at the same time incorporating Aristotle's comparison between history and poetry.[14]

The distinction is also formulated by Daniello in his *Della poetica* of 1536 in terms, interestingly, of *dispositio*. He uses the notions of *disposizione naturale* and *disposizione artificiale* in differentiating between the two types of order that are observed in historical and poetic writing respectively. In the process, he emphasizes the chronological element found in *disposizione naturale*, thereby recalling the treatment of the *narratio* in classical rhetoric:

La *disposizione* in due guise fare si può: *naturale* et *artificiale*. *Naturale disposizione* è quando 'l poeta dal principio della cosa ch'egli vuol trattare incomincia ad ordire il suo poema e segue ordinatamente dal principio sino al fine, quella istessa narrando e così isponendola come stata è, l'ordine tuttavia de' tempi ne' quali esse cose che si narrano avenute sono, servando. *Artificiale* è poi quella, quando egli non dal principio, ma nel mezzo della cosa suol incominciar a narrare, e poscia con bel modo introdurre una terza persona che tutta quella tralasciata parte ripigliando, racconti. Ma la *naturale* è molto più propria dello istorico (al quale si convien seguire l'ordine delle cose fatte, dal principio sino al fine) che non è del poeta (Weinberg 1970–4, i. 255).

Renaissance discussions on rhetoric in fact show the continuing presence of the notion of a dual order. Lionardi in his *Dialogi della inven-*

---

[14] Relevant passages from Parrhasius and Willichius, two such commentators, are adduced by Herrick 1946, 17 n. 42.

tione poetica (1554) mentions 'due *ordini*, l'uno *naturale* e l'altro *artifi-ciale*, nell'orazione così dimostrativa come giudiciale' (Weinberg 1970–4, ii. 252). Denores, in his *Breve trattato dell'oratore* of 1574, speaks in terms of the 'manner' of the disposition: 'segue a ragionar brevemente della *disposizione* ... Di questa, l'una *maniera è naturale* ... l'altra è *artificiosa*' (Weinberg 1970–4, iii. 126). He also echoes classi-cal rhetorical advice on the need to observe chronological order in the *narratio* for the purpose of clarity:

averà la chiarezza se la sarà piana, facile, distinta, se commincerà dalle cose non molto lontane, se averà riguardo all'ordine de' tempi e delle cose occorse (Weinberg 1970–4, iii. 126).

The concept of reordering as part of poetic rather than rhetorical composition is again expressed in terms of chronology by Lionardi in his *Dialogi*. He implies that poetry, in order to delight, does not fol-low the chronological order of history:

sì come è proprio del poeta dilettare e giovare, e dell'istorico narrare la ver-ità delle cose seguendo l'ordine de' tempi e dell'azioni (Weinberg 1970–4, ii. 253).

Indeed, he goes so far as to assert that no true poet can leave this his-torical order unchanged:

non troverete mai che colui si possa chiamare veramente poeta il quale narri per ordine tutte le cose da lui scritte, come fa l'istorico (p. 258).

By implication, Lionardi also sees the reordering process of poetry in terms of causal links, a formulation that points to the ultimate roots of the distinction in logic, which ultimately governs the cause-and-effect sequence of the *ordine di natura* of history:

l'ordine di questa [istoria] ... che è una regolata norma di ciò che si scrive o parla, o a persone o a fatti ha riguardo. E nel trattare d'amendue bisogna seguitar l'*ordine di natura*, la quale va *dalle cause agli effetti* nell'operare (p. 222).

He goes on to add:

bisogna che lo scrivere istorie séguiti l'ordine dell'azioni. E come gli effetti sono causati dalle cose precedenti, così possono diventar cause delle cose a loro sussequenti (p. 225).

One narrative device recommended in the sixteenth century for use as part of the reordering process in poetic composition is the introduction of a third person, whose function is to narrate the part

of the story that has been left out (presumably so that the new structure will have its own inner, logical coherence). This device is illustrated in the following quotation from Lionardi:

et il trasportar delle cose appresso de' poeti non è altro che incominciar a
narrare nel mezzo e presso al fine dell'istoria, e poscia prendere occasione di
dire o *fare altrui riferire ciò che dal principio è stato lasciato*, e poi cercar di venire
al fine dell'introdotta e narrata azione (Weinberg 1970–4, ii. 274).

Lionardi's *altrui* is equivalent to Daniello's *terza persona* in the latter's
Della poetica, written eighteen years before Lionardi's *Dialogi*. The
terza persona is introduced by the poet into narrative that follows a *dispositio artificiale* beginning *in medias res*, a persona who recounts action
that has been omitted:

e poscia con bel modo introdurre una *terza persona* che tutta quella tralasciata
parte ripigliando, racconti (Weinberg 1970–4, i. 255).

It would seem, then, that Renaissance treatises express an interest in
the dual possibility of order in discourse. This interest specifies
chronology and causality as systems of links to be considered in the
reordering process of poetic composition, as well as indicating the
type of narrative device through which such reordering may be
effected.[15] Twentieth-century movements in literary theory are clearly foreshadowed here. One modern formulation that springs to mind
in this connection is Tomaševskij's reference in 'La costruzione del-
l'intreccio' (1928) to the *rapporti logici causali–temporali* of the *fabula*.
This example dates from the early stage in Structuralist development,
epitomized by Formalism, that has since led to the logic-oriented
schools of New Rhetoric and Narratology. (Interestingly, the term
struttura already appears in a definition of plot in Capriano's *Della vera
poetica* of 1555: 'Fabula cosa altra non è che una … composizione, o
struttura che ci piaccia di chiamarla' (Weinberg 1970–4, ii. 301).)

New Rhetoric and Narratology continue the emphasis on the particular effect produced in the addressee (audience or reader) as a result
of the ordering process of narrative composition. In this context, too,
the roots of contemporary narrative theory, as of poetics in general,
are discernible in classical rhetoric. With its rules of selection of

---

[15] For a discussion of natural as opposed to artificial order in the Renaissance, see
Herrick 1946, 16–20. There is also a useful historical survey of relevant terminology
and notions, including references to the art of logic in the 16th c., in Herrick 1950,
89–129. See Scaglione 1972 for treatment of 18th-c. discussions of natural as opposed
to artificial order.

subject-matter, arrangement, expression and delivery, classical rhetoric was geared specifically to producing a range of desired effects in an audience in order to persuade its members of a particular viewpoint. Brooks, writing recently on the *fabula* and *sjužet* distinction, maintains this focus on the effect generated on the reader by the ordering of material. He draws attention to the illusory and, one might infer, illogical, nature of the (presumably causal and temporal) priority that *fabula* is assumed to possess over *sjužet*, when assessed from the point of view of the reader:

We must, however, recognize that the apparent priority of *fabula* to *sjužet* is in the nature of a mimetic illusion, in that the *fabula*—'what really happened'—is in fact a mental construction that the reader derives from the *sjužet*, which is all that he ever directly knows (Brooks 1995, 13).

On the one hand, when compared with the theories of both Aristotle and Tasso, this modern reader-response perspective appears to betoken a shift of emphasis away from classical rhetorical models of composition grounded in the rhetorical faculties. According to Aristotle's discussion of 'consecutive' and 'disjointed' order in *narratio* in his *Rhetoric*, elements of a well-known story should only be selectively used in the reordering of the subject-matter, rather than narrated in full to an audience for whom the story was common knowledge (1416^b III. xvi. 1–4, quoted above). In other words, for Aristotle, Brooks's reader *would* know more than what (s)he derives from the *sjužet*. Interestingly, however, the faculty of *dispositio is* implicated in Brooks's view of plot as an 'interpretative activity', an 'active' or 'dynamic shaping force':

'Plot' in fact seems to me to cut across the *fabula/sjužet* distinction in that to speak of plot is to consider both story elements and their ordering. Plot could be thought of as the interpretive activity elicited by the distinction between *sjužet* and *fabula*, the way we *use* the one against the other. To keep our terms straight without sacrificing the advantages of the semantic range of 'plot', let us say that we can generally understand plot to be an aspect of *sjužet* in that it belongs to the narrative discourse, as its active shaping force, but that it makes sense (as indeed *sjužet* itself principally makes sense) as it is used to reflect on *fabula*, as our understanding of story. Plot is thus the dynamic shaping force of the narrative discourse (Brooks 1995, 13, author's italics).

For Tasso, on the other hand, the rhetorical faculties, and especially *dispositio*, were not merely implicit in considerations of poetic
composition, but still provided the schema within which theories of
composition were to be elaborated upon. An assessment of the nature
of Tasso's contribution to the debate on ordering subject-matter in
his *Discorsi dell'arte poetica*, when seen in relation to the development
of the Renaissance background outlined above, reveals, first of all, an
absence of the conventional expression of the distinction in terms of
natural as opposed to artificial order. This receives its nearest approx-
imation in the reference to the poet who 'confonda i tempi e gli ordini dell'altre cose, e si dimostri insomma più tosto artificioso poeta che
verace istorico' (*Discorsi*, 18). The conventional formulation is present, however, in the second version of the *Discorsi*, the *Discorsi del
poema eroico* of 1594. In this later work it appears in addition to the
previous quotation as a supplement to the *materia–favola* distinction:

> oltre a ciò, l'ordine osservato da Lucano non è l'ordine proprio de' poeti,
> ma l'*ordine dritto e naturale* in cui si narran le cose prima avvenute; e questo
> è commune all'istorico. Ma nell'*ordine artificioso*, che perturbato chiama il
> Castelvetro, alcune delle prime deono esser dette primieramente, altre
> posposte, altre nel tempo presente deono esser tralasciate e riserbate a
> miglior occasione, come insegna Orazio (*Discorsi*, 121).

In the second sentence quoted here from the later *Discorsi*, Tasso
refers to Castelvetro, whose 1570 commentary on Aristotle he had
not seen before writing the first *Discorsi* (composed, it will be
remembered, in 1561–2, and published in 1587). In a letter to Curzio
Ardizio dated 25 February 1585, he actually says:

> Ed io scrissi già ne la mia fanciullezza alcuni discorsi in questo subietto,
> molto prima che fossero stampate e ch'io vedessi i commenti del Castelvetro
> … sovra la *Poetica* (*Prose*, 913).

However, he would obviously have been aware of the basic concept
itself, as well as being well-versed in the rhetorical tradition of which
it forms a part.

This state of affairs, together with Tasso's comment in his letter to
Ardizio on the period of his life during which the *Discorsi dell'arte
poetica* were composed ('ne la mia fanciullezza'), makes it tempting to
surmise that his initial, rather uncommon expression of the distinction in terms of the reordering transition from *materia* to *favola* stems,
at least in part, from the enthusiasm of a young poet imbued with a

knowledge of rhetoric and eager to theorize on the art of poetic composition itself. This may help to account for the contrast between Tasso's particular form of expression of the *materia–favola* progression, and the usual reiteration of the conventional formulation by theorists not motivated by any such poetic impulse.

Whether or not this is actually the case, the correspondence between Tasso's views on literature and those of the Formalists, as indicated by their respective *materia/fabula–favola/sjužet* distinctions, remains thought-provoking. The common rhetorical background that nurtured both distinctions clearly contributes to an explanation for this affinity. Another consideration might be that both Tasso and the Formalists have succeeded in expressing notions on art that actually reflect the intrinsic nature of its processes. This explanation finds some support, as far as an appraisal of Tasso is concerned, in Weinberg's fundamental work on the period. Weinberg repeatedly describes Tasso's early *Discorsi* as 'remarkable' (a label he uses four times in this context). Commenting on Tasso's preoccupation with the intrinsic nature of art, he says: 'Tasso's work is also remarkable for its defence of Aristotle not as an authority on poetry, but as one who represents the eternal and invariable conditions of the art' (Weinberg 1961, 647). He concludes:

In its totality, Tasso's conception of poetry is quite remarkable. One of its most remarkable qualities is, in a sense, its totality. For Tasso constructs a complete and self-consistent theory, which maintains its integrity between certain rhetorical conventions and a basic Aristotelianism (Weinberg 1961, 652).

Of the three rhetorical faculties brought into play by the Renaissance poet, it is the transition from the first to the second, as encapsulated by the *materia–favola* transformation, that takes centre stage for Tasso, both as theorist and practitioner of epic poetry. The final matter for consideration in this first section on epic theory is Tasso's attitude to the third, and last, faculty, namely *elocutio*. This forms the subject of the following chapter.

CHAPTER 3

Elocutio

Elocutio, the third of the classical rhetorical faculties engaged in composition, was very much the poor sister in relation to *inventio* and *dispositio*. For Tasso, as argued in the previous chapter, the most interesting stage in poetic writing was the arrangement of selected subject-matter into *favola*. Writing to Scipio Gonzaga on 11 February 1576, eleven months after beginning work on the *dispositio* of the *Gerusalemme liberata*, Tasso reveals a lack of enthusiasm, and even a degree of impatience, regarding the choice of words, and language in general, with which to clothe his plot:

ma io per ancora non ho avuto alcun diligente riguardo a le voci ed a la lingua, riserbandomi sempre di far ciò in ultimo ed in fretta (*Lettere*, i. 129).

This somewhat disparaging attitude to *elocutio* was not unique to Tasso. He would have found justification for it in Aristotle's *Poetics*, in conjunction with an elevation of *dispositio* as the primary concern of the poet. 'The poet must be a maker of plots rather than of verses', Aristotle had said (1451^b IX. 9, trans. Dorsch). The classical philosopher further dismissed *elocutio* because it presented the poet with less of a challenge than the devising of plot:

beginners can achieve accuracy in diction ... before they can construct a plot out of the incidents, and this could be said of almost all the earliest dramatic poets (1450^a VI. 18, trans. Dorsch).

Tasso's use of *sempre* in the above letter to Gonzaga suggests that his negative attitude towards *elocutio* had long been a feature of his writing. Almost twenty years later in the *Discorsi del poema epico* he was to put forward quite a different view, defining the poet in terms of his skill with words: 'Anzi il poeta dal finger dei nomi prende il suo nome' (*Discorsi*, 180). He even gives equal weight to word-invention and plot-construction in this context: 'Laonde così dal finger i nomi come dal far la favola è denominato' (*Discorsi*, 180). Of particular significance in his letter of 11 February 1576 is the adjective *diligente*, which describes the attention he considers he should have accorded to *elocutio*. Interestingly, however, other letters dating back to the period when he was working on the *favola* of the *Gerusalemme liberata* show that he was in fact already concerned with diction, and particularly with the choice of individual words. Eleven months earlier, in another letter to Gonzaga dated 13 April 1575, the poet had expressed doubts that certain verses in the first four stanzas were not sufficiently polished, referring to them as *duretti* and *troppo inculcati*. Concerning the lexicon, he fears that he has been too free in his use of Latinisms ('Dubito ancora di non essere alquanto licenzioso ne le voci latine'), intending to remove them only if this does not reduce the *maestà* of his verses. Indeed, in the same letter in which he says he has begun work on the *favola* of the poem (20 May 1575), Tasso is already deliberating on the use of prepositions (although not with the requisite degree of diligence, if his letter of 11 February 1576 is to be believed).

The area of *elocutio* was to prove among the most laborious for Tasso in terms of complying with rules that all forms of composition were expected to observe. The *lettere poetiche* show Tasso sending out freshly written cantos or verses of his major poem to benefactors and censors, not merely for their comment and criticism, but even, on occasions, for them to edit and rewrite. As a consequence, the concept of the solitary, inspired poetic genius as the sole, or even primary force behind poetic creation, is called into question. More importantly for any study of the *Gerusalemme liberata*, the issue of single or multiple authorship is raised. Not only is the 'standard' 1581 edition of the poem known not to have received Tasso's approval; a further doubt now emerges concerning the precise nature of the authorship of the poem. It is possible that Tasso's dissatisfaction with the 1581 edition arose from a sense of hostility towards words and phrases that were not his own, as well as fear of the censors regarding certain elements of the *favola*. A study of the poem therefore has to acknowledge this basic reservation, however inconsequential it may be considered to be in the last resort.

The role of inspiration in the composition of the *Gerusalemme liberata* would seem to take second place in the overshadowing context of norms and precepts. Rules are omnipresent in Tasso's ideas on style, as in his notions on other aspects of the epic poem. As indicat-

ed earlier, this originates in the authoritarian climate of post-
Tridentine Italy, which made itself felt, in its most benign form,
through ecclesiastical censorship of literary production in the spheres
of both composition and printing. Censorship necessitated the con-
stant justification by writers of their art, which often took the form
of argued recourse to the approved authority of the ancients. Rules
taken from ancient rhetoric were rigorously applied to poetic composition in all its areas. The authority of classical writers in matters of
art was also accepted on philosophical grounds. Art was seen as per-
fect and therefore not open to change. As a consequence, rules for art
established by the ancient world would always be applicable and, it
was assumed, never need changing, except for minor modifications.

In practice, however, these rules and norms were often manipulated in order to justify a desired end. In other words, they were not
really seen to contain any inherent, irrefutable truth, but could be discussed and expanded, and their emphasis shifted according to the
requirements of a particular argument. At the same time, their fundamental authority over matters of poetic theory was seldom formal-
ly questioned, and literary debates in this era of treatises about
treatises were always contained within their normative framework.
Tasso's comments on style, written in close connection with the composition of his major poem, record his particular views on an accepted set of norms, with the aim of explaining, vindicating, or
apologizing for, stylistic aspects of his poem. It is significant that none
of his prose works is devoted exclusively to a discussion of *elocutio*.
There is, however, a proportional increase in space allotted to this faculty in the later *Discorsi* (1594), of which three-sevenths (Books IV, V
and VI) deals with matters relating to diction and language, in comparison with three-tenths (Book III) of the early *Discorsi*. This is perhaps largely in response to the criticism directed at his style in the
Gerusalemme liberata during the course of the Tasso–Ariosto polemic,
which followed on the heels of the publication of the poem in 1581
(see Ch. 1).

For Tasso and his contemporaries, *elocutio* constituted not only the
third rhetorical faculty, but also the fourth component of the product
of the faculties. The accepted Aristotelian formula, noted in the
Poetics, enumerated the *parti formali* of tragedy and epic as *favola*,
costume, *sentenza* and *elocuzione*. The last of the three classical faculties
to be retained in the Renaissance, *elocutio* was eventually to remain

the sole surviving element of ancient rhetoric and was the precursor of the modern concept of style. The notion of poetry purely as a source of pleasure and beauty, which would have accorded to style (as it was to do in later centuries) a more predominant position, made little headway during the sixteenth century. This period was still very much oriented towards classical rhetoric, and consequently remained in sympathy with the main functions of rhetoric and, by extension, poetry, as established by the ancients. The Ciceronian *docere* (to educate politically and ethically) and *delectare* (to delight the literary and artistic sensibilities) were both taken into consideration in writing as well as criticizing poetry. Emphasis was given equally to the choice and arrangement of subject-matter, and to its formal presentation. The severely ascetic censorship imposed during the era of the Counter-Reformation meant that greater importance came to be placed on the utility of poetry, and so on its subject-matter, than on any pleasure it might produce through stylistic beauty. Tasso himself saw pleasure closely linked with the didactic function of poetry: 'il diletto è fine ordinato al giovamento' and spoke of the need to *dilettare giovando* (see Ch. 1).

As well as the term *elocuzione*, that of *stile* itself appears in his works. *Stile* is used to indicate the Ciceronian concept of the three styles, high, middle and low: *stile magnifico*, *stile mediocre* and *stile umile*. Each of these *stili* requires the use of a particular set of rhetorical devices classified according to the rules of *elocutio*. A different tone of composition is produced by each style, for which some figures of speech are considered appropriate, while others are not. Some overlap in the use of these figures does, however, occur on occasion, especially between the high and the middle styles. Epic poetry, a genre requiring the high style, may use certain figures assigned to lyric poetry, which belongs to the middle style.

In addition to the use of *stile* specifically to indicate one of the three Ciceronian tones of composition, the term is also employed in a sense much more akin to its modern meaning, that is, with reference to style as the idiosyncratic characteristics observed in a particular author. These are seen to result from the individual application of poetic rules. In Tasso's day this would include stylistic features judged negatively according to the criterion of rules that were misapplied in attempting, say, the *stile magnifico*, a style regarded as inevitably bearing the danger of a lapse into the *stile gonfio*. The three

Ciceronian styles were therefore not, as may appear at first glance, the only styles to be recognized. They constitute three positive peaks, each regarded as suitable for a particular genre of composition, but between which lie unfavourably regarded styles not fit for any genre. These latter represented stylistic pitfalls into which an author who missed his aim at one of the three accepted styles might blunder.

Tasso offers some definitions of the terminology he uses. Such procedure is in keeping with the tenor of poetic treatises of the period, characterized as they were by the search for new, original interpretations and reworkings of an accepted set of rhetorical precepts. The setting down and illustration in detail by Tasso of the eight parts of *elocutio* according to Aristotle (*Discorsi del poema eroico*, Book IV), for instance, is not, therefore, intended to communicate new information, for the ideas of Aristotle were well known. Tasso's purpose in doing so was, rather, to establish his own position in relation to the Aristotelian plumb line, with a reiteration of Aristotle's definition of *elocutio* as an indication of assent. The detail with which this acceptance is expressed serves to illustrate his specific application of the Aristotelian concept to his own case.

This chapter offers a comparison between the earlier *Discorsi dell'arte poetica* and the later *Discorsi del poema eroico*, in the general realm of style. It also gives an account of Tasso's specific response to stylistic criticism of the *Gerusalemme liberata*, which he formulated as the *Apologia in difesa della Gerusalemme liberata* in 1585. A survey of some of the *lettere poetiche* sheds further light on his experience of writing the poem.

General theory of style

In Tasso's threefold treatment of the composition of the epic poem in the early *Discorsi*, Books I and II deal with *inventio* and *dispositio*, and Book III deals with *elocutio*. However, matters of diction and language appear not only in the third book. Likewise, discussion of stylistic matters in Book III often includes what can be categorized as subject-matter rearranged into elements of the plot, in the form of concepts (*concetti*).

In Book II, for example, consideration of the properties of different languages enters the discussion of the romance in Tasso's account of the suitability of the Italian language (*lingua* or *idioma*) for this genre: 'Ogni lingua ha dalla natura alcune condizioni proprie e naturali di lei, ch'a gli altri idiomi per nissun modo convengono' (*Discorsi*, 25). *Elocutio* is further linked to matters of *materia* and *favola* in his disagreement with the view that languages have different effects on the unity of action to be portrayed. The languages Tasso concerns himself with are the vernacular, Latin and Greek: 'Concludendo adunque dico che, se ben è vero ch'ogni lingua abbia le sue proprietà, è detto nondimeno senza ragione alcuna che la moltitudine delle azioni sia propria de' vulgari poemi, e l'unità de' latini e de' Greci' (*Discorsi*, 30). He also differentiates between Latin and Greek in other ways, characterizing the Greek language as 'molto atta alla espressione d'ogni minuta cosa', unlike Latin, which is 'molto più capace di grandezza e di maestà' (p. 29).[1] This is perhaps one reason why Tasso favours Latinisms, since *grandezza* and *maestà* were regarded as desirable attributes of the epic poem. This aspect of his style in the *Gerusalemme liberata* was to attract severe criticism from one school of theorists. Regarding the vernacular, he singles out its sweet sounds, created by vowels and harmonious rhymes, that make it especially suitable for love scenes:

> la nostra lingua toscana, se bene con egual suono nella descrizione delle guerre non ci riempie gli orecchi, con maggior dolcezza nondimeno nel trattare le passioni amorose ce le lusinga ... per le vocali della toscana, e per l'armonia delle rime, più convenevole alla piacevolezza de gli affetti amorosi (*Discorsi*, 29, 30).

A modern-sounding observation on the intrinsically social nature of words also appears in this second book. These are seen to depend for their meaning and aesthetic quality not on any inherent natural properties, but, as man-made creations, on usage:

> le parole non siano opere dalla natura composte, né più in lor natura una cosa che un'altra significhino (ché se tali fossero, da l'uso non dependerebbono), ma che siano fattura de gli uomini, nulla per se stesse dinotanti, onde, come a lor piace, può or questo or quel concetto esser da esse significato; e non avendo bruttezza o bellezza alcuna che sia lor propria e naturale, belle e brutte paiono secondo l'uso le giudica; il quale mutabilissimo essendo, necessario è che mutabili siano tutte le cose che da lui dependono (*Discorsi*, 31).

The notion of *concetti* is explained in similar terms in Book III on style. Like words, concepts have no real existence in themselves in the

---

[1] Tasso learnt the rudiments of Greek at the age of 8 in a Jesuit school in Naples (Hasell 1882).

real, natural world, but are human perceptions of reality: 'Concetti non sono altro che imagini delle cose, le quali imagini non hanno soda e reale consistenza in se stesse come le cose, ma nell'animo nostro hanno un certo loro essere imperfetto, e quivi dall'imaginazione sono formate e figurate' (*Discorsi*, 43). *Parole* are later linked to *concetti*: 'le parole sono imagini ed imitatrici dei concetti … adunque le parole devono seguitare la natura de' concetti' (p. 49). The series *cose–concetti–voci* is usefully embraced by the following passage:

Cose sono quelle che sono fuori degli animi nostri, e che in se medesime consistono. I concetti sono imagini delle cose che nell'animo nostro ci formiamo variamente, secondo che varia è l'imaginazione degli uomini. Le voci, ultimamente, sono imagini delle imagini: cioè che siano quelle che per via dell'udito rappresentino all'animo nostro i concetti che sono ritratti dalle cose (*Discorsi*, 50).

At the same time, *elocutio* is equated with *stile*, which is defined as a combination of *concetti* and *voci*:

Avendosi a trattare dell'elocuzione, si tratterà per conseguenza dello stile: perché non essendo quella altro che accoppiamento di parole, e non essend'altro le parole che imagini ed imitatrici de' concetti, che seguono la natura loro, si viene per forza a trattare dello stile, non essendo quello altro che quel composto che risulta da' concetti e da le voci (*Discorsi*, 40).

In relating these definitions to the Aristotelian formula, the parts *favola*, *costume* and *sentenza* are presumably all to be seen as consisting of *concetti* which are then clothed by means of the fourth part, *elocuzione*. The distinction, if any, between Tasso's *voci* and *parole* is not clear, unless *voci* become *parole* when they are brought into a specific, in this case, poetic, context: in other words, when they no longer exist as abstract counters of vocabulary, but are extracted from this collective stock to be fused with particular *concetti* as concrete, contextual *parole*. The linking together of these *parole* ('accoppiamento di parole') is the domain of *elocuzione*, and the whole procedure is labelled *stile*. This is perhaps the most explicit statement on style made by Tasso in his writings.

Tasso also explores *stile* in the early *Discorsi* in terms of the three Ciceronian styles, namely the high, middle and low: 'Tre sono le forme de' stili: magnifica o sublime, mediocre ed umile' (*Discorsi*, 40). In accordance with the elevated nature of the selected subject-matter which it befits the epic poem to relate (the task of *inventio*), the manner or tone of its diction (that of *elocutio*) must also be elevated and magnificent. The first of the three styles is therefore appropriate: 'la prima è convenevole al poema eroico ... perché le cose altissime, che si piglia a trattare l'epico, devono con altissimo stile essere trattate' (p. 40). The choice of subject-matter therefore precedes and indeed dictates stylistic choices. In addition, the purpose of the epic poem (the marvellous) must be taken into account when selecting a particular style, since style forms an integral part of the poem: 'lo stile è parte del poema epico; adunque lo stile opera a quel fine che opera il poema epico, il quale ... ha per fine la meraviglia, la quale nasce solo dalle cose sublimi e magnifiche' (p. 40).

Reference is also made to the stylistic pitfalls that lie between the three acceptable Ciceronian peaks: 'ogni forma di stile ha prossimo il vizioso, nel quale spesso incorre chi bene non avvertisce. Ha il magnifico, il gonfio ...' (p. 41). Some overlapping of styles, however, is admissible. In any case, each genre of poem has its own definition of *magnifico*, *mediocre* (or *temperato*) and *umile*: 'Il magnifico, il temperato e l'umile dell'eroico non è il medesimo co 'l magnifico, temperato e umile de gli altri poemi; anzi, sì come gli altri poemi sono di spezie differenti da questo, così ancora gli stili sono di spezie differenti da gli altri' (p. 41). Even within one genre, some intermingling of styles is inevitable: 'Non è disconvenevole nondimeno al poeta epico ch'uscendo da' termini di quella sua illustre magnificenza, talora pieghi lo stile verso la semplicità del tragico, il che fa più sovente, talora verso le lascivie del lirico, il che fa più di rado' (p. 42).

The subject-matter narrated by the epic poem, although basically of one type, may also vary at certain points, and so require a variation of style. However, just as there must not be any distracting digressions from the *favola*, the high style of the epic must not be departed from too much either:

l'epico vedrà che, trattando materie patetiche o morali, si deve accostare alla proprietà e semplicità tragica; ma, parlando in persona propria o trattando materie oziose, s'avvicini alla vaghezza lirica; ma né questo né quello sì che abbandoni a fatto la grandezza e magnificenza sua propria. Questa varietà di stili deve essere usata, ma non sì che si muti lo stile non mutandosi le materie; ché saria imperfezione grandissima (*Discorsi*, 42).

What actually constitutes a digression from the *favola* and a departure from *magnificenza* are of course debatable points. These were in fact to become two major bones of contention around which polemics raged, with Tasso, according to some, winning on the first count, and Ariosto on the second.

The ingredients that make up the *stile magnifico* include concepts as well as words: 'Può nascere la magnificenza da' concetti, dalle parole e dalle composizioni delle parole; e da queste tre parti risulta lo stile' (p. 43). The art of *elocuzione* caters for all three areas, with rules on figures of speech, individual words and sentence structure, respectively. In the first place, once magnificent *concetti* have been elected, a particular set of rhetorical figures must be used to represent their *grandezza* successfully. Secondly, as well as figures, individual words are also of importance in *elocuzione*, especially if they are unusual: 'Sarà sublime l'elocuzione se le parole saranno non comuni, ma peregrine e dall'uso popolare lontane' (p. 43).

Tasso divides *parole* into four groups: the *semplici* or *composte*, and the *proprie* or *non proprie*. All categories of the *non proprie* (foreign borrowings or words used in an unusual way) produce laudable effects, but also carry certain risks, notably that of *oscurità*:

Nasce il sublime e 'l peregrino nell'elocuzione dalle parole straniere, dalle traslate e da tutte quelle che proprie non seranno. Ma da questi stessi fonti ancora nasce l'*oscurità*, la quale tanto è da schivare quanto nell'eroico si ricerca, oltra la magnificenza, la chiarezza ancora (p. 44).

Oscurità was a stylistic fault of which Tasso was to be accused in the *Gerusalemme liberata* (Brand 1962). Here he instructs on how to avoid this by means of a very careful choice and juxtaposition of words:

Però fa di mestieri di giudicio in accoppiare queste straniere con le proprie, sì che ne risulti un composto tutto chiaro, tutto sublime, niente *oscuro*, niente umile. Dovrà dunque sceglier quelle traslate che avranno più vicinanza con la propria; così le straniere, l'antiche e l'altre simili, e porle fra mezzo a proprie tali che niente del plebeio abbiano (p. 44).

On the use of certain types of words in figures such as the metaphor, Tasso suggests that, while too much daring is inadvisable, a certain degree is laudable. He himself was accused of being excessively *artificioso*.

The combining of words and figures into sentences is dealt with as the last, syntactic constituent of style. Tasso prefers long clauses and sentences, arguing that this produces a magnificent style: 'La composizione, che è la terza parte dello stile, avrà del magnifico se saranno

lunghi i periodi e lunghi i membri de' quali il periodo è composto'
(p. 45). As well as the length of sentences and their component parts,
other syntactic features contributing to *magnificenza* by means of
asprezza are mentioned:

S'accresce la magnificenza con l'asprezza, la quale nasce da concorso di
vocali, da rompimenti di versi, da pienezza di consonanti nelle rime, dallo
accrescere il numero nel fine del verso, o con parole sensibili per vigore d'ac-
centi o per pienezza di consonanti. Accresce medesimamente la frequenza
delle copule che, come nervi, corrobori l'orazione. Il trasportare alcuna volta
i verbi contro l'uso comune, benché di rado, porta nobiltà all'orazione
(p. 45).

Certain syntactic features, on the other hand, are to be avoided if a
stile gonfio is not to be the result:

Per non incorrere nel vizio del gonfio, schivi il magnifico dicitore certe
minute diligenze, come di fare che membro a membro corrisponda, verbo a
verbo, nome a nome; e non solo in quanto al numero, ma in quanto al senso
(p. 45).

Similarly, figures that contain syntactic mirroring, such as antithesis,
are to be avoided as mediocre and affected. Tasso was, however, to
make frequent use of antithesis in the *Gerusalemme liberata*, as will be
illustrated in Chapter 4.

 Gonfiezza, characterized as 'vizio sì prossimo alla magnificenza',
results from misapplication of the rules established for the creation of
the magnificent style. Tasso's examples of such misuse include the categories of *concetti*, *parole*, *figure di sentenze* and *composizione delle parole*.
Basically, the magnificent style must portray magnificent *concetti* if it is
not to appear inflated and pompous: 'Per che lo stile, magnifico in
materie grandi, tratto alle picciole, non più magnifico, ma gonfio sarà
detto' (p. 46). Indeed, since each *stile* is composed of two elements
(*concetti* and *parole* or *elocuzione*), these two parts must match in order
to produce a *stile convenevole*:

da due cose nasce ogni carattere di dire, cioè da' concetti e dall'elocuzione
(per lasciare ora fuori il numero); e non è dubbio che maggiore non sia la
virtù de' concetti, come di quelli da cui nasce la forma del dire, che dell'e-
locuzione. È ben vero che quando d'altra qualità sono i concetti, d'altra le
parole o l'elocuzione, ne nasce quella disconvenevolezza che si vederebbe in
uomo di contado vestito di toga lunga da senatore (p. 49).

 Throughout these early *Discorsi*, Tasso emphasizes his belief that *concetti*, and not *parole*, are the starting point for *stile*. He is totally opposed to the idea that 'lo stile non nasca dal concetto, ma dalle voci' (p. 49). The predominance he accords to concepts (part of the *dispositio* of *materia*) over words (*elocutio*, the clothing of the *concetti*) is also evident in his account of the difference between epic and lyric styles. While some consider this to be rooted in *elocutio*, Tasso is adamant that these differences in style occur because the concepts they deal with are different (even though the *concetti* may well stem from the same *cose* or *materia*):

La materia del lirico non è determinata, perché … il lirico … tratta ogni materia che occorra a lui … con alcuni concetti che sono suoi propri, non comuni al tragico e all'epico: e da questa varietà de' concetti deriva la varietà dello stile che è fra l'epico e 'l lirico (p. 50).

Whether a style is high, medium or low will therefore depend not on *cose* (subject-matter), but primarily on *concetti*, and only secondarily on *elocuzione*:

trattando l'epico e 'l lirico le medesime cose, usino diversi concetti; dalla quale diversità de' concetti ne nasce poi la diversità dello stile che fra loro si vede … Appare dunque che la diversità dello stile nasce dalla diversità de' concetti, i quali sono diversi nel lirico e nell'epico, e diversamente spiegati (pp. 50, 54).

In case the reader is left in any doubt, Tasso concludes, using Virgil as a justification:

Si ha adunque che lo stile nasce da' concetti, e da' concetti parimente le qualità del verso: cioè che siano o gravi o umili ec. Il che si può anco cavare da Virgilio che umile, mediocre e magnifico fece il medesimo verso con la varietà de' concetti. Ché se da la qualità del verso si determinassero i concetti, avria trattato con l'esametro, nato per sua natura a la gravità, le cose pastorali con magnificenza (p. 54).

The *Discorsi del poema eroico* are an extended version of the earlier *Discorsi dell'arte poetica*, with the last three of the six books devoted to *elocuzione*. Opening Book IV, Tasso refers to *elocuzione* as 'questa ultima parte di qualità', namely the last of the Aristotelian parts of the tragedy or epic, and links it with what he calls the *forme del parlare*:

Dovendo io trattare dell'elocuzione, si tratterà per conseguente delle forme del parlare, perché, essendo egli pieghevole a guisa di cera, prende molte forme e quasi molti caratteri, ciascuno de' quali è diverso da gli altri e ha la sua propria eccellenza e la sua propria laude (*Discorsi*, 172).

The element of divine inspiration, absent from the earlier *Discorsi*, is introduced at this point: 'Ora consideriamo quel ch'appartiene all'e-locuzione, nella quale si dimanda l'aiuto divino per favellare alta-mente, non meno che per la memoria delle cose già sepolte nell'oblivione' (p. 177).

There follows a definition of *elocuzione* that echoes part of the def-inition of style given at the beginning of Book III of the earlier *Discorsi*: 'Io dico che l'elocuzione altro non è che uno accoppiamen-to di parole' (p. 177). However, no mention of *stile* is made here. Tasso goes on to elaborate on *elocuzione* in terms of speech compo-nents, beginning with the smallest parts (letter, syllable, conjunction, noun, verb, article, case, oration). *Elocuzione*, he says:

> si risolve ne' nomi e ne' verbi e nell'altre parti dalle quali è composta; e queste nelle sillabe; e le sillabe nelle lettere, che sono chiamate elementi … Ora darò la definizione delle parti dell'elocuzione, le quali sono: l'ele-mento, la sillaba, la congiunzione, il nome, il verbo, l'articolo, il caso, l'ora-zione (p. 178).

The element of content, treated under *concetti* in the earlier *Discorsi*, soon surfaces in the guise of the signifying properties, or otherwise, of the various parts of *elocuzione*. The syllable, conjunction and arti-cle are believed to contain no meaning, while the verb communicates the element of time: 'Verbo è una voce composta, la qual significa insieme co 'l tempo, e di cui niuna parte separata significa per sé, come abbiamo detto de' nomi' (p. 179). For *nome* there is a definition inserted by Gherardini, the first modern editor of the *Discorsi*, due to a gap in the text noted but not rectified by Tasso. This definition is taken from Aristotle to match the remainder of the section: 'Nome è voce composta significativa, ma senza tempo, del quale non è parte alcuna che per se stessa significhi, conciossiaché ne' nomi doppi s'osservi ancora che le parti da per loro non vi significhino nulla' (*Prose*, 633 n. 3). These seven parts are grouped together to form a whole, the oration, whose signifying properties receive particular attention:

> l'orazione è una voce, o vero un parlar composto, il qual significa; e le sue parti significano ancora per sé qualche cosa. Ma l'orazione si dice una in due modi: o quella che significa una sola cosa, come la definizione dell'uomo 'l'uomo è animal ragionevole', o quella la qual, congiungendo molte cose insieme, ne fa una di molte, come l'*Iliade* (*Discorsi*, 179).

This section reveals the concept of presence or absence of semantic content as a guiding principle in defining elements of speech. Most *voci* are classified as either conveying meaning ('quelle che hanno significazione') or not. As indicated above, the *sillaba, congiunzione* and *articolo* are in themselves without meaning (they are described respectively as 'una voce che non significa cosa alcuna', 'una voce che non significa alcuna cosa' and 'una cosa che non significa'). *Nome* and *verbo*, on the other hand, are meaningful, while *orazione* conveys meaning both as a whole, and in each of its parts. As far as the *elemento*, or letter, is concerned, no use is made as such of *significazione* or derivative terms in describing it, perhaps because the non-significative nature of this part of *elocuzione* was considered obvious. However, Tasso's discussion of the *elemento* hints at the communication of a type of meaning. Letters, he says, as well as being distinguishable from each other due to the varying movements of the mouth that produce them, also differ according to the *acume* and *gravità* they convey. This links up with discussions later on in these *Discorsi* on the qualities of some letters of the alphabet, and consequently which of the *elementi* are to be used or avoided, and in what combination they should appear.

The category of *nomi* is enlarged upon, as in the earlier *Discorsi*, where the term used was *parole*. To give an idea of the kind of detailed alteration that took place from the earlier to the later works, the following quotation indicates in square brackets the words used in the earlier version:

Ma le specie de' nomi [parole] son la semplice e la doppia [composta], che si può dir composta; ed ogni nome è o proprio, o straniero o trasportato [traslate], o usato per ornamento [d'ornamento], o fatto [finte], o allungato, o accorciato [scorciate], o mutato [alterate] (*Discorsi*, 43, 179).

Definitions follow of *proprio, straniero, fatto o finto, allungato, accorciato* and *mutato*, which vary slightly in wording from those in the first *Discorsi*, while details on *traslazione* help to clarify those given more tersely earlier. There is an additional definition of the *nome usato per ornamento*, or adjective. It is in the context of the vividness to be produced by *nomi* such as adjectives, that Tasso, as mentioned at the beginning of this chapter, appears temporarily to shift his earlier emphasis on *dispositio* as the defining faculty of the poet, to *elocutio*, or *elocutio* in conjunction with *dispositio*:

Fatto o finto è quel nome che, non essendo mai stato usato da alcuno, il
poeta il fa di nuovo ... ma particolarmente son lodati quelli che son più atti
all'imitazione e al por le cose avanti gli occhi ... Anzi il poeta dal finger de'
nomi prende il suo nome ... Laonde così dal finger i nomi come dal far la
favola è denominato. Il nome usato per ornamento è l'epiteto, o 'l nome
aggiunto che vogliam dirlo (p. 180).

Linked with vividness, the effects of *oscurità*, *grandezza* and *chiarezza*
are then discussed in connection with *nomi propri* and *non propri*, as
they were in the *Discorsi dell'arte poetica*, but with a slight change in
emphasis. The earlier *Discorsi* stress the avoidance of *oscurità* (the concomitant stylistic pitfall of the high style) and mention the need for
chiarezza, but without *umiltà* (p. 44). Here clarity, the characteristic
quality of the low style, is deemed inappropriate to the requirements
of the high style. However, while it is to be shunned, clarity is at the
same time regarded as a virtue in *elocuzione*: 'Ma la virtù della
elocuzione, se crediamo ad Aristotele, è che sia chiara, non umile,
quasi nell'umiltà non possa essere alcuna virtù' (p. 181). In both earlier and later *Discorsi* the epic poet is recommended to follow a middle path between the two opposite poles of *oscurità* and *chiarezza*, to
be achieved by means of careful juxtaposition of *nomi propri* with *non
propri*.

As in the earlier *Discorsi*, the discussion on *nomi* and their effects is
extended to the metaphor. The later *Discorsi* now elaborate on the
metaphor, relating it to allegory. Properties that were ascribed to *stile*
in the earlier work are now applied solely to the metaphor, which by
implication now plays a major role. A discussion of metaphor is followed by one on *figure del parlare*, first of all in relation to *elocuzione*.
Tasso opts for the opinion that 'l'elocuzione sia il tutto, e le figure
sieno alcune parti in lei tessute in molti e diversi modi' (p. 188). His
definitions of *figura* echo those of *inventio* and *dispositio*: 'non debbiam diffinir la figura forma fatta di nuovo con qualche artificio, ma
una parte artificiosamente rinovata e mutata e diversa dall'altre' (pp.
188–9).

Attention is thereafter focused on the *forme del parlare* whose mention opens this fourth book. These *forme* refer to the styles established
by Cicero, whose tripartite division is preferred by Tasso to other suggestions: 'Più breve e più spedita mi par la divisione di Cicerone nel
suo *Oratore*, che tre siano i generi del parlare: l'alto, il mediocre e l'u-
mile' (p. 190). He notes that such division of speech into modes was

unknown to Aristotle: 'Ma questa divisione fu fatta dopo Aristotele, il quale non distinse le forme del parlare in quel modo che dopo lui furono distinte da Demetrio' (p. 190). Alternatives mentioned for the term *forme*, which predominates in these *Discorsi*, are *idee*, *caratteri* and *generi* (while *stile*, *forma* and *forma de' stili* were used in the earlier work). The characteristics of each *forma* are given, using the term *genere* for each of the three Ciceronian modes, with *spezie* and *forma* to denote the attributes of each:

Chiamandosi generi, pare che le spezie quasi più minute sotto a lui sian contenute. Laonde se le forme sono spezie, conviene che sian soggette al genere. E se ciò è vero, il sublime e l'alto genere avrà, come sue spezie, la grande, la bella, la splendida, la grave forma e quella ch'è piena di dignità, e l'aspra, l'affettuosa e la veemente; il mediocre: la graziosa, la soave, la dolce, la piacevole, l'ornata e la fiorita; l'umile: la chiara o ver la facile, la semplice, l'acuta, la sottile, la motteggevole o ver quella che move a riso, e altre simiglianti (pp. 191–2).

Three components go to make up a Ciceronian *stile* or *forma del parlare*: 'Tre condizioni dunque concorrono in queste che noi dimandiamo forme del parlare: le parole (quasi materia che dee ricever la forma), il numero, e 'l concetto, o sentenza che vogliam dirla' (p. 193). This contrasts with the earlier *Discorsi* where, as cited above, only two elements were mentioned: 'da due cose nasce ogni carattero di dire, cioè da' concetti e dall'elocuzione (per lasciare ora fuori il numero)' (p. 49). *Numero* receives no further mention in the later *Discorsi*, but the remaining two elements, Tasso advocates here as in the *Discorsi dell'arte poetica*, should be compatible. In the *Discorsi dell'arte poetica* he says: 'È ben vero che quando d'altra qualità sono i concetti, d'altra le parole o l'elocuzione, ne nasce quella disconvenevolezza che si vederebbe in uomo di contado vestito di toga lunga da senatore' (p. 49).

In the *Discorsi del poema epico*, the concept of *disconvenevolezza* is replaced by that of humour: 'le cose ampie si deono dire ampiamente, e tutte l'altre deono esporsi con parole acconcie e proprie del concetto; e facendosi altrimenti par che si scherzi' (p. 186). As in the earlier work, particular reference is made to the magnificent style in this context. In the early *Discorsi* Tasso writes: 'Perché lo stile, magnifico in materie grandi, tratto alle picciole, non più magnifico, ma gonfio sarà detto', and in the later version: 'Laonde nelle materie gravi non è lecito che le parole discordino dalle cose, benché alcuni

stimassero che sia gran segno d'eloquenza il dir le cose picciole alta-
mente' (pp. 46, 196). The subject-matter and the words used to
express it should therefore correspond.

The three Ciceronian *forme* are also linked to different genres of
poetry. At the same time, some intermingling of styles is permissible,
and even inevitable, as has been noted. In *La Cavalletta overo de la poesia toscana* (1584), Tasso says: 'ciascuna maniera di parlare è mescolata
... in quelle che sono stimate gravissime c'è qualche mistione di
piacevolezza' (Tasso 1958, 629). Absence of intermingling may even
lead to a decline in pleasure and readability, so that verses 'ne' quali
non è qualche mescolanza sì fatta assai meno sogliono piacer de gli
altri, né possono lungamente esser ascoltati senza fastidio' (p. 630).
The poet must not, however, wander from the high style into the
realms of another that is inappropriate, such as the low style of comedy. In the later *Discorsi*, Tasso states: 'e se fosse pur lecito al poeta usar
lo stil dimesso nell'epopeia, non dee però inchinarsi a quella bassezza
ch'è propria de' comici' (*Discorsi*, 196–7).

The epic poet may at times borrow from other poetic genres that
belong to the same high style (such as the tragic genre) or to the
neighbouring middle style (such as the lyric). However, when borrowing from the lyric genre, care must be taken not to stoop to 'la
mediocrità lirica senza decoro'. In the early *Discorsi* Tasso says:

Lo stile eroico è in mezzo quasi fra la semplice gravità del tragico e la fiorita vaghezza del lirico, ed avanza l'una e l'altra nello splendore d'una
meravigliosa maestà; ma la maestà sua di questa è meno ornata, di quella men
propria. Non è disconvenevole nondimeno al poeta epico ch'uscendo da'
termini di quella sua illustre magnificenza, talora pieghi lo stile verso la semplicità del tragico, il che fa più sovente, talora verso le lascivie del lirico, il
che fa più di rado (*Discorsi*, 41–2).

These early *Discorsi* also contain a summary of how, and on which
occasions, such borrowing must take place, emphasizing that the high
style of the epic must not be departed from too much:

l'epico vedrà che, trattando materie patetiche o morali, si deve accostare alla
proprietà e semplicità tragica; ma, parlando in persona propria o trattando
materie oziose, s'avvicini alla vaghezza lirica; ma né questo né quello sì che
abbandoni a fatto la grandezza e magnificenza sua propria. Questa varietà di
stili deve essere usata, ma non sì che si muti lo stile non mutandosi le
materie; che saria imperfezione grandissima (p. 42).

The tragic and the lyric genres are described in relation to the epic.

The use of the term *stile* in this section does not have the Ciceronian connotation of high, middle or low style, but refers, rather, to the characteristics of the genre in question (bearing in mind that each genre belongs to one of the three styles). According to Tasso, the *stile del tragico* is 'meno sublime e più semplice dell'eroico', despite the fact that it describes 'avvenimenti illustri e persone reali' (*Discorsi*, 198). There are two reasons for this:

l'una, perché suol trattar materie più affettuose; e l'affetto richiede purità e semplicità, perch'in tal guisa è verisimile che ragioni uno che sia pieno d'affanno o di timore o di misericordia o d'altra simile perturbazione. L'altra cagione è che nella tragedia non parla mai il poeta, ma sempre coloro che sono introdotti agenti ed operanti; a' quali si dee attribuire una maniera di parlare men disusata e men dissimile dall'ordinaria (p. 198).

The *stile tragico* is similarly dealt with in the early *Discorsi*, but there are extra comments on *elocuzione*, *stile* and the *verisimile* that are omitted in the later version. This is the corresponding passage in the *Discorsi dell'arte poetica*, with the extra comments italicized:

Lo stile della tragedia, se ben contiene anch'ella avvenimenti illustri e persone reali, per due cagioni deve essere e più proprio e meno magnifico che quello dell'epopeia non è; l'una, perché tratta materie assai più affettuose che quelle dell'epopeia non sono; e l'affetto richiede purità e semplicità *di concetti, e proprietà d'elocuzioni*, perché in tal guisa è verisimile che ragioni uno che è pieno d'affanno o di timore o di misericordia o d'altra simile perturbazione; *e oltra che i soverchi lumi e ornamenti di stile non solo adombrano, ma impediscono e ammorzano l'affetto*. L'altra cagione è che nella tragedia non parla mai il poeta, ma sempre coloro che sono introdotti agenti e operanti; e a questi tali si deve attribuire una maniera di parlare ch'assomigli alla favola ordinaria, acciò che l'imitazione riesca più verisimile (p. 42).

On this occasion, then, the later *Discorsi* do not represent an amplification of the early version. The *stile lirico* is also related to that of the epic in the *Discorsi del poema epico*. Both earlier and later *Discorsi* state that the lyric style is not as magnificent as the epic, belonging to the middle style by virtue of its greater ornamentation.

Book V introduces an equation of *elocuzione* with *parlare* ('il parlare, ch'altramente si dice elocuzione'), and relates eloquence to the former ('l'eloquenza, che prende il nome da l'elocuzione') (pp. 200, 201). For Tasso, *elocuzione* pertains to the orator as *eloquente*, and not, as a histrionic aid, to the actor. He thereby places it once again firmly in the realm of *parlare* and *parole*: 'Grande è stato adunque l'errore

di coloro ch'estimarono che l'elocuzione non fosse propria dell'oratore e dell'eloquente, ma parte che si concede all'istrione' (p. 201).
He remarks on the ability of words to persuade, the implication being
that this applies to all words, however they are used. Consequently
parlare, or *elocuzione* (in turn equated with *stile*), is in itself a persuasive act, while rhetoric is regarded as the art of persuasion that estab-
lishes an appropriate set of rules for *elocuzione*.

Tasso associates poetry with persuasion (and thence with logic)
because, by imitating, it offers proof by means of example and sheer
plausibility: 'nel parlar poetico, il quale non è senza imitazione, è una
tacita prova e molte volte efficacissima; perché non si può imitare
senza similitudine e senza essempio, ma ne l'essempio e in ogni cosa
che paia verisimile è la prova' (*Discorsi*, 201). *Stile*, in the sense of the
poet's choice, positioning and general manipulation of words, was
referred to in the earlier *Discorsi* as a tool to be used by the poet in
such a way as to imitate with great vividness (p. 47). Vividness now
finds its rational justification in this rhetorical, logical function of persuasion through proof. *Stile* is therefore not merely an ornament (as
Tasso suggests in the earlier *Discorsi* when he refers to the relationship
of *stile* or *elocuzione* to *materia* in terms of clothing and adornment),
but an essential, vital factor contributing to the persuasive qualities
characteristic of poetry as a branch of rhetoric.

This preamble situating poetry alongside rhetoric and logic serves
almost as an explanation and justification of the relevance of
elocuzione. It also functions as an introduction to a highly detailed
account of all the elements of *elocuzione* to be used in the magnificent
style. The account opens with no mention of which categories of
elocuzione are to be dealt with, such as individual *parole*, *composizione
delle parole*, or *figure di sentenze*. In the earlier *Discorsi*, on the other
hand, a breakdown of the high style was given: 'Può nascere la magnificenza da' concetti, dalle parole e dalle composizioni delle parole;
e da queste tre parti risulta lo stile' (p. 43). Moreover, in the earlier
work the section of *elocuzione* directly expressing *concetti* was clarified
as that of *figure di sentenze*: 'La magnificenza de' concetti sarà se si trat-
tarà di cose grandi … Per isprimere questa grandezza accommodate
saranno quelle figure di sentenze' (p. 43). The later *Discorsi* offer no
such clarification.

Tasso discusses thirty-four elements of *elocuzione* in the later
Discorsi. Only a minority of these elements are categorized, perhaps

because their classification was common knowledge in cultured circles. They are drawn either from the syntactic section called *composizione delle parole*, or from the figurative section of *figure di sentenze*. The third section, that of individual *parole*, is not drawn upon here (with the exception of *trasportazione de le parole*), presumably because *parole*, or *nomi*, were considered in detail in the previous book as one of the eight Aristotelian parts of *elocuzione* (*elemento, sillaba, congiunzione, nome, verbo, articolo, caso, orazione*) (p. 178). With reference to the wider context of all the constituents that strictly speaking go to make up the Ciceronian *stile* ('parole … numero, e 'l concetto, o sentenza che vogliam dirla'), *numero* is the only section to be omitted (*concetti* or *sentenza* being expressed via *figure di sentenze*) (p. 193). *Numero* is not classified under *elocuzione* and is certainly not part of *concetti*, but is always treated as a separate section. In the early *Discorsi*, it appears as follows: 'da due cose nasce ogni carattere di dire, cioè da' concetti e dall'elocuzione (per lasciare ora fuori il numero)' (p. 49). In the later version it is again mentioned as a separate entity on its own: 'in ciascuna forma, oltre il numero, sono considerate l'elocuzioni e i concetti' (p. 223). In effect, *numero* receives relatively little attention, as the words 'per lasciare ora fuori' and 'oltre' indicate.

Of the thirty-four elements of *elocuzione* presented by Tasso as appropriate to the magnificent style, the first eleven appear to belong under *composizione delle parole*. These are as follows: *lunghezza de' membri e de'periodi, senso largamente sospeso, asprezza della composizione, concorso delle vocali, versi spezzati, consonanti doppie, ordinare i nomi, congiunzioni raddoppiate, dissoluzione, antipallage,* and *duplicare le parole*. The remaining twenty-three can be categorized mostly as *figure di sentenze*, the group to which Tasso then tacitly turns: *allegoria, reticenza, epifonema, prosopopea, definizione invece del nome, gradatio, metafora, similitudini, comparazioni, conversione, esclamazione, pervertimento dell'ordine, sineddoche, parentesi o interposizione, endiadys, zeugma, trasportazione de le parole, perturbar l'ordine naturale, hiperbaton, pleonasmo, verbo s'accorda co 'l nome più vicino, sillepsi,* and *apposizione*.

Allegory, the first of these figures, is of special interest as an indispensible part of the epic poem:

Ha del grande ancora l'allegoria … fu detto che l'allegoria fosse simile alla notte e alle tenebre; laonde ella dee esser usata ne' misteri, e per conseguente ne' misteriosi poemi, come è il poema eroico (*Discorsi*, 210–11).

Tasso notes that Aristotle spoke not of allegory but of enigma, Demetrius Phalereus being among the first to rename the concept. The poet mentions allegory earlier in the *Discorsi del poema epico*, describing it as an extended metaphor (p. 183). He also provided the *Gerusalemme liberata* with an allegory, although this had not been his original intention. In a letter to Gonzaga written on 15 June 1576, he speaks of the difficulties of including allegorical content in a poem due to the subjectivity of allegorical interpretation (*Prose*, no. 15, p. 791). The final sentence in his history and advocacy of allegory indicates that both allegory and enigma are in fact *figure di parlare*: 'Ma non era questo luogo di trattar de l'enigma o de l'allegoria, se non considerandoli come figure di parlare' (*Discorsi*, 213). It is difficult to know whether Tasso would actually bother to distinguish this category of *figure* from that of *figure di sentenza*; his views on the categorization of *figure* are by no means transparent. This seems also to be the case of the classical theorists. The *Rhetorica ad Herennium*, for instance, appears to divide figures into those of diction and those of thought:

> The divisions under Distinction are Figures of Diction and the Figures of Thought. It is a figure of diction if the adornment is comprised in the fine polish of the language itself. A figure of thought derives a certain distinction from the idea, not from the words (IV. xii. 18).

However, as Caplan observes of the ancient rhetoricians: 'The line of demarcation between tropes and figures, and that between figures of thought and figures of diction were often vague' (p. 275 n. c).

Tasso includes a discussion of the figures belonging to the *stile mediocre*, from which the *stile magnifico* may borrow. He argues that, although both epic and lyric poets at times deal with the same topics (*cose*), their manner of formulating them as *concetti* may differ. It is from the latter area of poetic composition, he believes, that any difference in style arises. Each *stile* and each genre therefore has its own repertoire of *concetti*. Speaking of the lyric genre, he says: 'usa alcuni concetti suoi propri, che non sono così convenienti al tragico e all'epico' (*Discorsi*, 223). In the earlier *Discorsi* he had similarly said: 'il lirico … tratta ogni materia che occorra a lui; ma ne tratta con alcuni concetti che sono suoi propri, non comuni al tragico e all'epico: e da questa varietà de' concetti deriva la varietà dello stile che è fra l'epico e 'l lirico' (p. 50). Just as a particular *forma del parlare* does not derive from *cose*, similarly it does not derive directly from *elocuzione* (a

Dantesque view that Tasso criticizes in the earlier *Discorsi*). According to Tasso, it springs from the area of poetic composition between the two, namely that of *concetti*, the qualities of which filter into *elocuzione*.

When both epic and lyric poet use the same *concetti*, similarity between high and middle styles occurs: 'E quinci si può raccogliere che, se l'epico e 'l lirico trattasse le medesime cose co' medesimi concetti, adoprerebbe per poco il medesimo stile' (p. 227). Interestingly, this possibility was not mentioned in the earlier *Discorsi* when the same point was discussed. Tasso provides an account of the figures of diction to be used when writing in the lyric *parlar grazioso* in the epic poem. Although Tasso uses the term *figure*, some of the points he mentions seem to belong to *composizione delle parole*. The thirteen 'figures' he mentions are as follows: *repetizione, traslazione o metafora, parole basse e volgari, proverbi, comparazione, alcuna cosa soverchia, scherzi, opposizione, render a ciascuna cosa il suo proprio, aggiunti, distribuzione o componimento, membri e parole c'hanno il medesimo fine*. After a minutely detailed discussion of rhyme, including specific types of rhyme words, their vowel–consonant ratio, and the use or avoidance of particular letters in alliteration, he passes on to an analyis of *gravità*.

Tasso usually associates *gravità* with tragedy, while *magnificenza* is linked with the epic and *vaghezza* with the lyric. Both *gravità*, along with *magnificenza*, belong to the high style. Tragic and epic genres share the same style, although the epic, according to Tasso, surpasses tragedy 'nello splendore d'una meravigliosa maestà'. The 'illustre magnificenza' of the epic, on the other hand, differs from the 'semplice gravità del tragico' (p. 196). The components leading to *gravità* are divided into three parts, as in the case with the high and middle styles: 'nella grave ancora, nella quale tre cose parimente si considerano: le sentenze, le parole e la composizione' (p. 237). In the earlier *Discorsi*, the term *concetti* was used instead of *sentenze*: 'Può nascere la magnificenza da' concetti, dalle parole e dalle composizioni delle parole' (p. 43). To bring *concetti* from the realm of *inventio* into that of *elocutio, figure di sentenze* were to be employed to express them.

Tasso begins by dealing with *sentenze* (using the term *cose*), often in such a way as actually to involve elements of *elocuzione*, before mentioning a series of figures of thought apt to produce *gravità*. His first point concerning *sentenze* in this context refers to the need for choosing suitable words to express them. Thus he says: 'ma non basta che le cose sian gravi, s'elle non son dette con gravità'. His second point relates automatically to diction, and particularly to brevity in *composizione delle parole*: 'La brevità in questa forma si richiede più ch'in tutte l'altre, perciò che il molto nel poco si mostra molto più grave' (p. 237). Thirdly, he advocates the use of symbols and allegory, which he presumably classes with figures of thought: 'I simboli ancor sono gravi, e l'allegoria' (p. 238). His fourth point again concerns *composizione delle parole* to some degree: 'Ma niuna cosa par più grave che 'l por nel fine quello ch'oltre tutte l'altre cose è gravissimo' (p. 238). The fifth point of interest under *gravità* sees a return to what was regarded in the earlier *Discorsi* as a vice into which the inept creator of the high style may lapse, except that here it is a virtue (see above, p. 77). On *oscurità* Tasso now says: 'l'oscurità suole ancora in molti luoghi esser cagione della gravità, perciò che tutto quello ch'è piano e aperto suole esser sprezzato' (p. 239). This change of heart in the later *Discorsi* may have been due to the fact that the criticism of *oscurità* was levelled at the *Gerusalemme liberata*. Certain figures are listed by Tasso as producing *gravità*, the most important one, in his view, being the first of the following: *prosopopeia, reticenza e omissione, ironia, raddoppiar le parole, epanaphora, dissoluzione, interrogazione, moderarsi e correggersi, affermar certamente, fermarsi molto in una cosa, dire le cose odiose come piacevoli.*

Tasso gives a cursory account of the *umil forma di parlare*. The low style is presumably too remote from the high style, which consequently does not borrow any special figures from it (although of course some figures are held in common by all three styles). Finally Tasso turns his attention to external factors relating to the reading or performance of the epic poem, a matter that affects the manner in which *elocuzione*, the expression of chosen *concetti*, is created. He believes that the diction of the epic poem is made to be read: 'l'elocuzione dell'epopeia è fatta per esser letta' (*Discorsi*, 257). There is consequently a difference between 'quella elocuzione che doveva essere scritta, e quella che ricercava l'aiuto dell'azione' (with *azione* referring to tragedy) (p. 257). Such action is not necessary to the epic poem: 'non è in modo alcuno necessaria al poema eroico, il quale ha la sua chiarezza per se stesso' (p. 258). *Chiarezza* is therefore an important product of the diction of the epic poem, which relies totally on the written word to convey its *concetti*.

As well as being read, the epic poem may be sung to appropriate music. While music remains an extrinsic element, the vernacular language itself provides a kind of natural harmony in its rhyme:

> se perfezione è la musica, è perfezione estrinseca; può nondimeno esser rice-
> vuta dal poeta eroico ... anzi possono i poemi eroici esser cantati con quel-
> la sorte di musica ch'è perfettissima ... e nella nostra lingua particolarmente
> il poema eroico ha la rima, la quale è una propria e naturale armonia
> (*Discorsi*, 257–8).

The type of music suitable for the epic poem is the majestic: 'la musi-
ca, la qual conservi il decoro de' costumi e la maestà' (p. 254).
However, music is not mentioned as an *aiuto*, in the way that *azione*
is for the tragedy, and is presumably to be regarded as an optional
accompaniment highlighting the essential characteristics of magnifi-
cence and majesty already present in the poem.

The style of the *Gerusalemme liberata*

The later *Discorsi* were published in 1594, thirteen years after the first
publication of the *Gerusalemme liberata*. In an earlier work, the dialogue entitled *Apologia in difesa della Gerusalemme liberata* of 1585,
Tasso undertook a detailed defence of his poem as it came under
attack in the Tasso–Ariosto polemic. Objections to the *Gerusalemme
liberata* were mostly, but not exclusively, located in the area of *elocutio*,
the third rhetorical/poetic faculty that shaped the *elocuzione*, or diction, of his composition. It seems that his father's poem, the *Amadigi*,
had undergone similar criticism. In the *Apologia* for his own poem,
Tasso defends the *Amadigi*, emphasizing, among other aspects, its
superiority to Pulci's *Morgante* and Boiardo's *Orlando innamorato* in
matters relating to the fourth Aristotelian epic constituent, *elocuzione*:

> qual più ricco, non solo dell'invenzioni, ma dell'elocuzioni e delle figure e
> degli ornamenti poetici ... eguali di bellezza e di numero ... con quelle
> parole ch'esprimono la sentenza (*Prose*, 419).

Sentenza is seen here to be in the same relationship to *parole* as *concetti*, and it is this stage of poetic composition, that of manipulating
words, phrases and figures to suit the ideas to be expressed, that is, as
in the *Discorsi*, represented by *elocuzione*.

Tasso defends himself against an unnamed opponent throughout
the *Apologia*. He turns to usage in order to defend his choice of words
in the *Gerusalemme liberata*, and indeed in determining how language
should be used. His diction is regarded not only as less poetic than

that of Ariosto, but also as 'oltre ogni natural modo di favellare'. Accused of using words, sounds (*suoni*), lines (*versi*) and expressions (*modi*) that are *bassi*, Tasso retorts that usage, both spoken and written, supports his choice of the particular words in question, namely *qualch'una* and *avventurieri*:

Né a me parevano basse; ma perché l'una, quantunque sia nova, è più in bocca de' cavalieri che del volgo; e l'altra, ch'è pure usata da popolari, non fu rifiutata dal Petrarca, che l'usò tre volte (*Prose*, 442).

Where he cannot call upon written usage, Tasso justifies such words by referring to their good qualities, which he finds praised in other writers.

Criticism was aimed at various aspects of Tasso's diction. These fall roughly into the following areas: individual words, linking of words, figures, and final effect. On the choice of individual *parole*, Tasso was accused of using too many Latin words ('voci latine … pedantesche … tante ne sono in quella opera') (*Prose*, 471). Other non-Tuscan words are also too numerous. To this Tasso responds that a number of great poets before him used most of the same words. Objections are also raised regarding words used in what is felt to be an inappropriate context. The word *fabbro* is taken as an example: 'voce che, per proprietà di lingua, non si lascia cavar del proprio per traslatarsi ad altro significato' (p. 478). At this point Tasso's understanding of the language is even thrown into doubt: 'Taccionsi quelli epiteti che da lui s'usano impropriamente … che non sono errori del Tasso, ma del suo non intender la lingua' (p. 478).

The basic tenet of the poet's opponent is that a metaphor cannot be derived from a *nome proprio*. Tasso argues that, if only the *nome non proprio* may be used, this does not allow for the essential feature of the metaphor, which is to transpose *to* the level of the *non proprio* (p. 482). He cites other writers, such as Petrarch, who have similarly used some of the adjectives on the list of forbidden words. Next, Tasso's adjectives are considered to be *oziosi*. To this he replies that if they work, they cannot be ineffective: 'ch'epiteto non ozioso sia quello che fa alcuno effetto'. This is re-echoed in the later *Discorsi* when he praises Homer's use of words: 'non s'astenne di alcuna, sol che gli paresse aver in sé qualche piacevolezza o qualche veemenza' (*Discorsi*, 245). Still in the sphere of individual words, Tasso has to answer an accusation of *cacofonia*, which he does by drawing attention to the effect of *vaghezza* it produces. Certain sounds are also found to produce an unwanted comic effect: 'spesso ci muove a riso, come alcuni di questi suoni che si sentono ne' suoi versi' (*Prose*, 460). This effect was also produced, it was believed, by inappropriate choice of words that were considered: 'di niuno o di lontanissimo sentimento da quel che s'aspettava da la continuazion del concetto: sì che spesso ci muove a riso' (p. 460).

Tasso's *composizione delle parole* is harshly criticized: 'e con legatura tanto distorta, aspra, sforzata e spiacevole ec. Tra l'altre cose, buona parte delle parole paiono appiastricciate insieme, e due e tre di loro ci sembrano spesso una sola.' The poet's answer to the criticism that his diction is *laconica* is that he is following Aristotle: 'aggiungendosi oltre la necessità o levandosi parte di quelle congiunzioni che son necessarie, s'accrescesse per diverse cagioni grandezza al parlare' (*Prose*, 463). Associated with the linking of words is the consideration of verse structure. On this aspect of Tasso's diction, his opponent declares: 'Di questi versi aspri, saltellanti … n'è pieno il libro del Tasso.' The poet, as on other occasions, refuses to comment at any length, deciding that: 'non adducendo né la ragione né l'autorità, non debbo rispondere' (p. 471).

On the matter of Tasso's *figure*, which are praised by his supporter Pellegrino on account of their vividness ('quanto al vivo delle figure'), his opponent states: 'Il concetto era bello, ma il Tasso nella scurezza l'ha affogato nel modo del favellare.' To this, Tasso replies succinctly: 'S'è vivo, non è affogato' (*Prose*, 482–3). In other words, if the opponent recognizes the beauty of the *concetto* through the words, this must mean that the words used to express it were aptly chosen. The use of a particular figure, the *scherzo*, is criticized:

Questi scherzi usati a suo luogo, e con parcità, stanno bene; ma il Tasso se n'empie tanto la bocca, e tanto gli adopera senza decoro e senza distinzione, che pare una fanciullaggine il fatto suo. Non son questi i propri ornamenti e le proprie figure dell'epopea (*Prose*, 466).

In the answer to this, an interesting point emerges concerning the classification of figures. In both the earlier and later *Discorsi*, no overt distinction is made between *figure di sentenze* and *figure del parlare*. In the *Apologia*, however, Tasso himself asks for clarification: 'vorrei sapere se l'oppositore chiama gli scherzi le figure delle sentenze o delle parole'. The reply is that 'scherzi sono le figure delle parole' (*Prose*, 467). Regarding the particular example quoted by his opponent, Tasso claims that:

non c'è scherzo alcuno, quantunque ci sia la figura detta da' Latini repetizione: la quale non è propriissima dell'epico, perch'è usata da gli altri; nondimeno gli è convenevolissima' (*Prose*, 469).

Negative effects believed to be produced by Tasso's diction are those of *oscurità*, rather than *chiarezza*, and *durezza* rather than *dolcezza*. Tasso justifies lack of clarity by outlining the dangers of *facilità*: 'ma quel della soverchia facilità, quando ella è volgare anzi che no, suol generar disprezzo' (*Prose*, 465). Lack of clarity is seen to arise from the poet's excessive use of *nomi e verbi propri*, whereas it is *nomi non propri* that are ultimately suited to producing *meraviglia*:

perché i nomi e i verbi propri fanno il parlare assai chiaro, ma l'ornamento l'è dato da gli altri. Laonde gli uomini non sono mossi altrimente da le parole che da' peregrini: perché quel solo è venerando e degno di riverenza: e peregrino dev'esser il parlar se dee mover maraviglia (p. 465).

In the earlier *Discorsi*, Tasso had in fact stated: 'Però fa di mestieri di giudicio in accoppiare queste straniere con le proprie, sì che ne risulti un composto tutto chiaro, tutto sublime, niente oscuro, niente umile' (*Discorsi*, 44). In the later *Discorsi*, he was similarly to advocate mingling the *propri* with the *non propri* to avoid *oscurità*:

Ma perché da una medesima cagione suol nascere l'oscurità e la grandezza, e derivar quasi da un medesimo fonte e dall'altro la umiltà e la chiarezza, fa di mestieri di gran giudizio e di grand'arte in accoppiare le voci proprie con le straniere e con le trasportate e con l'altre in guisa che ne risulti un parlare tutto splendido e tutto sublime (p. 181).

The criticism continues: 'il Tasso, ricercando troppo l'arte, anzi duretto che no a le volte par che divegna … molti luoghi, i quali ora a' leggenti mozzi ed oscuri s'offeriscono' (*Prose*, 465). Tasso at this point draws attention to the important matter of authorship: 'né questa opera mia né l'altre sono mai state né riviste né ricorrette né publicate da me' (*Prose*, 466). In effect, none of the editions of the poem, including that of Bonnà in 1581, was ever approved by Tasso (Brand 1965, 24–5).

The negative effects of *durezza* and *oscurità* are claimed to result from the diction expressing Tasso's *concetti*:

Vedete i concetti dell'Ariosto facili, e vestiti per lo più di voci *chiarissime* e *dolci*; e quelli del Tasso per lo più di traslati e vaghi di sensi esquisiti. Vedete nel medesimo luogo la *durezza* e l'*oscurità* del Tasso (*Prose*, 469).

According to Tasso, however, there can be no *oscurità* because the *concetto* is taken from a *luogo illustre*: 'Confesso di non conoscer l'oscurità, perché il concetto è tolto da luogo illustre' (*Prose*, 469). This links up with his discussions in both the earlier and the later *Discorsi* on the reasons for differences between the high and middle styles, which he concludes are located in the *concetti* and not in either *elocuzione* or *cose*. Similarly, areas of his poem that are found to be *duretti* are attributed by him to the type of *concetto* being expressed. He says:

E se peraventura son duretti, rammentisi che l'Ariosto descrive il giardino d'Alcina nell'India, in parte dove la natura poteva produr quegli effetti: ed io fingo questo d'Armida sovra un'asprissima montagna cinta di neve, dov'ella non ha parte alcuna, ma tutta la bellezza nasce da l'arte (*Prose*, 469).

Tasso's opponent proposes that: 'La bontà e la virtù della locuzione consiste principalmente nella chiarezza, e nella brevità, e nell'efficacia' (*Prose*, 475). Tasso quotes Aristotle in pointing out that the concomitant danger of *chiarezza* is in fact *umiltà*: 'La virtù dell'elocuzione è ch'ella sia chiara, non umile' (p. 475). On the type of words to use in this context (*proprie* or *non proprie*), he continues: 'e i nomi chiari [propri] e i verbi rendono chiara l'orazione, ma umile; e gli altri nomi [non propri], de' quai si ragiona nella *Poetica*, ornata' (p. 475). Tasso stresses the need for *ornamento* (as opposed to *parole proprie*), again with reference to Aristotle, 'da le quali parole mi par che si raccolga chiaramente che l'altezza e l'ornamento sian proprii del parlar poetico' (p. 475). The poet's use of the term *chiaramente* may be meant as a jibe against the opponent, who stresses the importance of clarity and yet is blind to the obvious meaning behind Aristotle's words. Tasso is criticized for believing that *gravità* leads to *dolcezza* in the poem: 'non sa che la gravità è nemica della dolcezza'. The poet contradicts this with: 'A me pare la gravità nimica dell'acume e della leggierezza' (p. 483). To the comment that a *dolcissima cosa*, such as *baci*, should be expressed using suitably sweet diction, Tasso retorts with the reminder that the epic form requires its own treatment: 'ch'in poema eroico io non voglia parlar di baci sì dolcemente, come in altro componimento si farebbe' (p. 483).

In addition to extensive and minutely detailed criticism of the diction in the *Gerusalemme liberata*, the poet's use of allegory also comes under attack. Allegory as used by the Greeks (and, it is implied, by Tasso himself) is problematized as a means of concealing impiety: 'Questa maschera dell'allegoria ... ritrovarono i Greci per ricoprir l'empietà delle lor sceleratissime finzioni' (*Prose*, 485). Tasso, as at other times, finds a suitable precedent in order to vindicate himself. In this case he turns to Dante's use of allegory. To clarify his own position, he reiterates the essential religious conformism of the allegory he provided to explain the poem:

E perché alcuni di loro dicono che Gerusalemme, secondo vari sensi, ora è nome di città, ora figura dell'anima fedele, ora della Chiesa militante, ora della trionfante, non sarà stimata vana l'allegoria ch'io ne feci, a la quale posso aggiungere il senso che leva in alto: perché nella visione di Goffredo ed in altri luoghi della celeste Gerusalemme significo la Chiesa trionfante (*Prose*, 485).

In conjunction with the severity of the religious context, a prescriptive academic aura particularly marks the *Apologia* and the later *Discorsi*.

In addition to these theoretical works in prose and dialogue form, Tasso also penned over 1,500 letters. The special interest of these letters is best expressed by Tasso himself. He compares his letter of 13 April 1575 to Scipio Gonzaga with the *Discorsi dell'arte poetica*, written just over a decade earlier. Of the *Discorsi* he says: 'quelli parlano in universale', whereas the letter 'avrà particolar riguardo al mio proprio poema'. The letters give a fascinating insight into precisely how Tasso composed and intended to revise his poem. They also reveal the cardinal role played both by his benefactors and censors, together with his reactions to criticisms and suggestions affecting all spheres of poetic composition. As some of the following sample letters also indicate, Tasso at times agreed to certain changes which did not always find their way into the *Gerusalemme liberata*.

Of the 1,565 letters published in chronological order in the standard edition of Tasso's correspondence by Guasti, forty-six are labelled *lettere poetiche*. This name was assigned to a group of letters published together with the earlier *Discorsi* in 1587, under the full title *Discorsi del signor Torquato Tasso dell'arte poetica et in particolare del poema eroico et insieme il primo libro delle lettere scritte a diversi suoi amici, le quali, oltra la famigliarità, sono ripiene di molti concetti et avertimenti poetici a dichiarazione d'alcuni luoghi della sua Gierusaleme liberata, gli uni e l'altre scritte nel tempo ch'egli compose detto suo poema*. It is the *famigliarità* of these letters that is their main attraction.

The *lettere poetiche* date from 31 March 1575 to 9 December 1587. This chapter concludes with a survey of twenty-nine selected letters of particular interest. The letters are presented in order of date (there-

by departing from Guasti's method), so as to match the progression of
Tasso's experience of writing the poem and his reaction to criticisms
of it. The second number refers to the letter as one of the *lettere poetiche* numbered by Guasti in his notes. The third number is that allotted by Guasti to the letter as part of Tasso's entire correspondence,
and it is under this number that the letter can be located in Guasti's
edition. Unless otherwise stated, the letters are addressed to Scipio
Gonzaga.

1 2 (22) 31 March 1575
Tasso shows concern for the precise use of vocabulary. Concerning a
line about Argante in battle ('ma raddoppiando / Va tagli e punte',
VII, 91), he deliberates on the use of *percosse* instead of *tagli*, if the latter term does not suitably convey the meaning of 'colpo tirato di
taglio' (*tagli* appears in the final version of the poem). Here he is
searching for an exact correspondence between the *concetto* he has in
mind (in this case, a particular type of sword-thrust), and the element
of *elocuzione* with which to express it. He mentions *purpurei tiranni*
(VII, 52) among phrases as his *capricci*, but notes that these were also
used by Horace and Dante.

2 1 (49) after March 1575
According to Guasti, this was classified as the first of the *lettere poetiche* because it deals with the first stanza of the *Gerusalemme liberata*. It
belongs to the period of the second revision of the poem. In this letter Tasso asks whether stanzas 3 and 4 should be removed.

3 3 (24) 13 April 1575
The poet writes of his doubts that certain lines in the first four stanzas are not sufficiently polished, referring to them as *duretti* and *troppo
inculcati*. Concerning the lexicon, he fears that he has been rather free
in his use of Latinisms. However, he intends to remove them only if
this does not reduce the *maestà* of the poem. From this letter it tran-
spires that Tasso sent out several versions of one line of poetry that
contained *de' luoghi dubbi* or were *detti in più modi*, presumably so that
Gonzaga could give advice.

4 4 (25) 15 April 1575
Tasso expresses concern that many passages will be criticized for conveying an excess of charm: 'Credo che in molti luoghi troveranno forse
alquanto di vaghezza soverchia, ed in particolare ne l'arti di Armida,
che sono nel quarto.' This again shows the poet's apparent dependence

on the assent of parties *in molti luoghi*. He also declares himself dissatis-
fied with the link between Canto VII and Canto VIII, as well as with
the transition between episodes in Canto V. Rhythm, an element not
much developed in the *Discorsi*, receives a mention in terms of *dolcezza*:
'ho avuto solamente riguardo d'addolcire il numero'.

5 5 (26) 27 April 1575
Tasso declares his willingness to rephrase certain cases of syncope
(*furno* and *rifondarno*) if required. Fearing that the poetry is tedious, he
asks for advice on the last stanzas of Canto X, which show Goffredo
gathering the princes so that Rinaldo can be recalled: 'saria forse bene
il dire più minutamente le cose dette da lui, e le risposte da l'altra
parte: dubito di tedio'.

6 6 (27) 3 May 1575
There is evidence in this letter that Scipio Gonzaga has contributed
some words or phrases to the poem by completing work begun by
Tasso on a section of Canto V: 'Vostra Signoria me l'ha rimosso,
facendo perfette, e quasi colorando quelle cose che nel mio disegno
erano rozze e abozzate; onde gliene resto con molto obligo.' This
brings to mind the way that figurative artists in the Renaissance
would sketch out the main design of a piece of work, leaving its completion to their assistants. Words that give pleasure to the reader are
mentioned, together with their rhetorical capacity of persuasion: 'mi
dà il cuore di far parlare Eustazio in modo che le sue parole saranno
lette con diletto, e che potranno trarre il consiglio nel suo parere'.

7 7 (28) 3 May 1575
Tasso stresses the need to impress the reader, a factor that influences
his *dispositio* of the *materia*. On this basis he decides to include every-
thing concerning the *Califfo* in Canto XVII: 'perché quello mi pare
luogo opportuno ... ed unisco insieme molte cose che dette sparsa-
mente, oltre che mi romperiano il filo de l'altre, non fariano a mio
giudizio tanta impressione ne' lettori'. He discusses whether he or
Tancredi should narrate the latter's imprisonment: 'Nel principio del
settimo potrà parere ch'io vaghi troppo; e che sarebbe meglio far poi,
che Tancredi stesso narrasse la sua prigionia.' The use of the third-
person narrator, also raised in the following two letters, came under
discussion in contemporary treatises in relation to the *dispositio* of the
subject-matter (see Ch. 2). Precision in the use of vocabulary is
stressed, in this case to convey geographical exactitude. When

Argante speaks to Alete about Gaza, he is therefore made to say *verso* instead of *in* Egypt, when Tasso discovered that Gaza was not in Egypt (II, 94).

8 8 (29) 14 May 1575

The question of whether the poet or the character should be made to convey information in certain instances is again raised. It is decided that the person of the poet, being neutral, should be used to convey factual information, a character like Argante, for instance, being too biased to impart such information with accuracy: 'a me pare che lo stato de la città si debba considerare da le parole del poeta e non da le parole d'Argante, il quale è di sua natura impazientissimo, e vuol persuadere il combattere; però non si disconviene ch'egli faccia la cosa maggior del vero'. An interesting link is made between real time (*lunghezza di tempo*) and the narrative space it occupies (*stanza*): 'Non confesserò dunque che siano ne l'arti di Armida tante stanze, che da esse si possa argomentare lunghezza di tempo.'

9 9 (30) 20 May 1575

Tasso's method of composition is revealed by his comment: 'Ho cominciato a distendere l'argomento de la favola e de gli episodi inseritivi, così in prosa'. He presumably began with a small plan of the plot in prose, which he then extended and converted into verse. The art of suspense is considered: 'Il lasciar l'auditor sospeso, procedendo dal confuso al distinto, da l'universale a' particolari, è arte perpetua di Virgilio.' Tasso attempts such suspense with Erminia: 'Siale ora per esempio Erminia, de la quale e de gli amori de la quale s'ha nel terzo canto alcuna ombra di confusa notizia: più distinta cognizione se n'ha nel sesto; particolarissima se n'avrà per sue parole nel penultimo canto.' Similarly with Armida and Rinaldo: 'Nel decimo non s'ha intiera cognizione de l'arti di Armida e del caso de l'armi di Rinaldo: s'avrà poi; e però questo sia per avviso.' Raising once again the issue of whether the poet or a character should impart information, Tasso comments that when the poet himself narrates, he may do so amply, whereas a character conveying information may not: 'c'a queste tali narrazioni si conviene minor larghezza, c'a quelle fatte dal poeta immediate'.

10 10 (31) 24 May 1575 (to Luca Scalabrino)

A consideration belonging originally to *costume*, but directly affecting *elocuzione* in dictating the use of 'parole smoderate ed iperboliche', is that of the language used by a character. This should be adapted to reflect state of mind:

Il poeta deve esprimere ed imitare in Eustazio il costume ed il parlare de' giovani e amanti o proni a l'amore; a' quali apparendo nova bellezza e maravigliosa, sono rapiti da l'affetto a dir cose sovra la lor credenza; a chi chiamare il luogo dove loro appare la donna paradiso, e lei dea: non già perché così veramente credano; ma perché la grandezza de l'affetto e l'uso e l'adulazione amorosa ricercano parole smoderate ed iperboliche.

In this way Tasso justifies his use of the word *angioletta* as *iperbole amorosa*. By glossing the word to mean that 'Eustazio la crede un angiolo', he counters criticism of *angioletta* as a heretical reference to an angel that is female, rather than male. However, he omits the word in the final version of the poem. The poet also replies to criticism of the Sofronia episode in Canto II as 'troppo vago, troppo tosto introdotto', and the resolution as happening *per machina*. The episode was nonetheless to remain in this early position in the poem. Importance is given here to the overall positioning of narrative sections, as well as to the tone and the credibility of the outcome. Concern is once again shown for the proper linking of episodes, as well as for the exclusion of nuances belonging properly to romance: 'la narrazione di Cato … né solo quell'episodio mi pare male attaccato, ma la ventura de la spada dubito che senta del romanzo'.

II 11 (32) 2 June 1575 (to Luca Scalabrino)
Tasso maintains that the poet is under no obligation to prove hyperbolic praise of a character by making that character perform certain actions:

Il poeta non è obligato a corrispondere a le comparazioni ed a l'iperbole poetica co' fatti … il poeta, fingendo un cavaliero, deve servar in lui un perpetuo tenor d'azioni e corrispondere a' fatti co' fatti; ma non è necessario che co' fatti corrisponda a le parole dette per aggrandimento poetico. Ed a me pare che Argante ne le sue operazioni sia sempre il medesimo, né mi pare d'esser obbligato a più.

12 12 (35) 11 June 1575
Tasso expresses the fear that he has repeated some words too often in Canto XI, a situation he will remedy later: 'alcune voci troppo spesso replicate nel undecimo, che spero di variar poi a più bell'agio'. Here the emphasis is on variety, whereas in the later *Discorsi* repetition will be listed as the eleventh element in the discussion of ele-

ments of *elocuzione* leading to the high style. Precise use of vocabulary is emphasized, and achieved by research into practical matters. A fascinating insight is given here into Renaissance machinery and the poet's acquaintance with this aspect of warfare: 'Fu tempo ch'io mi credetti che si potesse fare una torre, o altra machina tale da oppugnare le mura, stabile e di legno: ho poi imparato che stabile e di legno ne l'arti de la guerra sono termini incompatibili, perché le stabili si fanno di terra o di pietra, e le mobili di legno.' This fact has far-reaching effects on other parts of the poem: 'Sì che volendo fare questa torre di legno, per farla più facilmente sottoposta a l'incendio, mi è bisognato mutare molte cose ne l'undecimo, e in conseguenza, alcuna, ma di poca importanza, nel duodecimo.'

13 21 (43) 2 September 1575
Tasso's desire to use Tuscanisms is outweighed by his concern that the words should not sound harsh, and should also accord with other words: '*Scorgeano* e *scorgono*, credo toscanamente si dica; ma se 'l fare *scorgiense* par duro, o che non s'accorda, mutarò.'

14 22 (46) 17 September 1575
Tasso believes that a poet should be examined only on the literal, and not allegorical, level of his poetry. The allegorical level, as he was to declare in his letter of 15 June 1576, is open to various interpretations: 'crederei che potesse bastare l'esaminare il senso litterale, che l'allegoria non è sottoposta a censura; né fu mai biasmata in poeta l'allegoria, né può esser biasmata cosa che può esser intesa in molti modi'. (See also *lettera poetica* no. 16).

15 23 (47) 1 October 1575
In this letter Tasso expresses detailed doubts about his *stile* in the syntactic realm of *composizione delle parole*, an aspect of his poem that was to attract criticism later countered in his *Apologia*. The following extract is notable for its self-recriminations, evidence of earlier criticism, the characteristic prioritizing of meaning (*sensi*) over word-order, and qualification of the use made of classical authority, here in the form of Virgil:

Non so se Vostra Signoria abbia notato un'imperfezione del mio stile. L'imperfezione è questa: ch'io troppo spesso uso il parlar disgiunto; cioè, quello che si lega più tosto per l'unione e dependenza de' sensi, che per copula o altra congiunzione di parole. L'imperfezione v'è senza dubbio; pur ha molte volte sembianza di virtù, ed è talora virtù apportatrice di grandezza:

ma l'errore consiste ne la frequenza. Questo difetto ho io appreso de la continua lezion di Virgilio, nel quale (parlo de l'Eneide) è più ch'in alcun altro; onde fu chiamato da Caligula, arena senza calce. Pur se bene con l'autorità si può scusare e difendere, sarebbe meglio rimediarvi talora. Io mi ci son provato, e mi ci rimproverò.

Tasso's second stylistic worry is with *dolcezza del numero*, and with Gonzaga's apparent lack of concern for this area of his style, on which the poet appears to have been expecting advice: 'Secondariamente vorrei c'avvertisse a la dolcezza del numero ... anzi mi pare ch'ella non si curi punto ... del concorso de le consonanti e de le vocali d'una stessa natura come in quello, "Drudo di donna".'

16 24 (48) 4 October 1575
While maintaining his reservations about allegory, Tasso believes that it has its uses under certain circumstances. In particular, it can serve the purpose of rendering the *maraviglioso* more palatable to his censors, whom he calls *i severi*:

giudicai c'allora il maraviglioso sarebbe tenuto più comportabile, che fosse giudicato c'ascondesse sotto alcuna buona e santa allegoria. E per questo, ancora ch'io non giudichi l'allegoria necessaria nel poema, come quella di cui mai Aristotele in questo senso non fa motto; e ben ch'io stimi che 'l far professione che vi sia, non si convenga al poeta; nondimeno volsi durar fatica per introdurvela ... Se dunque i miracoli miei del bosco e di Rinaldo convengono a la poesia per sé, com'io credo, ma forse sono soverchi per la qualità de' tempi in questa istoria; può in alcun modo questa soprabondanza di miracoli esser da' severi comportata più facilmente, se sarà creduto che vi sia allegoria.

17 27 (51) 24 January 1576
Tasso is having difficulty with Canto XIV: 'Io mi affatico intorno al quarto-decimo; e veramente posso chiamar questa fatica, poich'è senza diletto. La musa non mi spira i soliti spiriti; sì che credo ch'in queste nuove stanze non vi sarà eccesso d'ornamento o d'arguzia. Spero nondimeno che ne' versi sarà chiarezza e facilità senza viltà.'

18 29 (52) 11 February 1576
Real time is considered in the light of verisimilitude: 'La navigazione non credo che sia possibile che resti tutta, poiché fra l'andare e 'l ritorno vi correrebbe un mese di tempo; e questo mi pare pur troppo lungo spazio.'

19 30 (8) 5 March 1576

Tasso responds to negative comments on the Sofronia episode, revealing that he is more worried by criticism of content than of individual lines: 'Se 'l dubbio si stenderà solamente ad alcun verso, com'a quello "Che vi portano i creduli devoti", ciò non mi dà noia'. In the event, he did not remove the line from the poem (II, 5). He continues: 'mi rincrescerebbe bene infinitamente che 'l dubbio fosse diretto contra la sostanza de l'episodio'. This comment shows yet again that *favola* was of more importance to him than *elocuzione*. In his reworking of Canto XIV, Tasso has also consolidated the allegory to which, almost to his own surprise, he has now come to attach greater importance. The reason may lie in an acute awareness of the need to provide a defensible allegory, as suggested by his determination to pre-empt any possible attack by eliminating material 'che non possa stare a martello': 'ma ancora migliorate molte cose che riguardavano l'allegoria, de la quale son fatto, non so come, maggior prezzatore ch'io non era; sì che non lascio passar cosa che non possa stare a martello'. He therefore removes the *mostro* from Canto XV, 'perch'in somma quel mostro era affatto ozioso ne l'allegoria'. Instead of this, he will introduce 'la fonte del riso', from which runs a stream that later forms a lake: 'ma questa fonte e questo lago mi servono mirabilmente a l'allegoria'.

20 33 (61) 3 April 1576

Tasso has decided to leave out the Sofronia episode, partly for stylistic reasons, and partly as the result of criticism: 'Io ho già condennato con irrevocabil sentenza a la morte l'episodio di Sofronia, e perch'in vero era troppo lirico, e perc'al signor Barga ed a gli altri pareva poco connesso e troppo presto.' Nonetheless, as indicated above, the episode remained in the *Gerusalemme liberata* (but was excluded from the *Gerusalemme conquistata*). This letter also deals with choice of character for the narration of a particular story. For instance Erminia, and not Goffredo, is chosen to tell of the fall of Antioch: 'non so da chi meglio possa esser fatto che da Erminia; perché narrando Goffredo, o alcun de' vincitori, la narrazione non potrebbe riuscire patetica, e la presa d'Antiochia, narrata senza l'affetto doloroso, avrebbe de l'insipido'. The general theory in this context is that victories should be magnified, but not by the victors themselves. Mishaps, on the other hand, should be narrated by their perpetrators: 'Qui metto in considerazione, che Ulisse ed Enea non narrano le vittorie loro, ma le sciagure, e più tosto quel c'han patito che quel c'han fatto.'

21 34 (63) 14 April 1576

Religious sanctions determine not only change of vocabulary, but also the removal of entire episodes. In relation to the former, Tasso agrees to replace *mago* with *saggio*. As a result, entry gained magically by using a *verga* was to be substituted by entry through a cave. However, *mago* was retained (XIV, 49), as was the *verga* (XIV, 33), which the *mago* gives Carlo and Ubaldo to use against Armida's magic. While Tasso agrees to remove episodes such as 'il miracolo del sepolto' and 'la conversione de' cavalieri in pesci' from Cantos XIV and XV, many magical elements are kept.

22 17 (64) 3–24 April 1576 (to Luca Scalabrino)

Tasso is worried by the possible lack of *diletto* in Canto II, which may turn out *nuda e stretta*:

Ma tre dubbi restano a me in questo racconto di Goffredo al patriarca: l'uno, che tutto questo canto secondo si leggerà con poco diletto; che le vittorie non possono esser magnificate, né ricever alcun ornamento da la bocca del vincitore; … dubito che la narrazione non sia per riuscire alquanto nuda e stretta; ma di questa giudicarsi nel fatto.

23 36 (63) 14 June 1576

The relationship between real time and narrative space comes under discussion, with compression considered a feat of poetic ingenuity: 'Lo scudier parte: e si dice in una sola stanza, come è raccolto da le guardie e introdotto a Tancredi, c'ascolta lietamente l'ambasciata; e come, lasciando lui pien di mille dubbi, se ne torna con felice risposta.' In a passage on rhyme in Italian poetry, he emphasizes his practical as well as theoretical interest: 'Tutto questo ho detto non solo come teorico, ma come pratico ancora: pur Vostra Signoria vedrà nel canto ch'io le manderò, sin a quanto giudico che si debba stendere questa moderazione d'ornamento, la quale in alcune cose in ogni modo è necessaria.'

24 13 (79) 15 June 1576

Tasso speaks of allegory. This aspect of his poem was to undergo criticism on religious grounds, as his *Apologia in difesa della Gerusalemme liberata* was to show. In this letter he claims that he had no allegorical intention when he began writing the *Gerusalemme liberata*, due to the subjective nature of allegorical interpretation:

Io, per confessare a Vostra Signoria illustrissima ingenuamente il vero, quando cominciai il mio poema non ebbi pensiero alcuno d'allegoria, parendomi soverchia e vana fatica; e perché ciascuno de gli interpreti suole dar l'allegoria a suo capriccio, né mancò mai a i buoni poeti chi desse a i lor poemi varie allegorie.

He maintains, moreover, that not every particle of a poem need necessarily have allegorical significance, claiming that this would be impossible. In this context he defends the lack of allegorical significance in the characters Carlo and Ubaldo, two warriors sent to bring Rinaldo back to fight the Christian cause.

25 37 (80) 23 June 1576
As in his letter of 24 January 1576, the poet is having difficulties with a particular canto. In this case it is Canto XVII: 'Ora m'affatico intorno al decimo-settimo canto, ove ho da fare molte faticose e noiose mutazioni; e dubito più di questo solo che di tutto il rimanente, perché omai mi par d'aver superati gli altri luoghi più difficili.' He shows how he can make allegory work in his favour by using it in order to excuse the presence of certain miracles. Some of these he intends to remove, but not those whose allegorical meaning is clear: 'ma fra questi miracoli non numero l'abitazion sua sotteranea, per'oltra che chiara è l'allegoria, c'altro non è abitar sotto terra che il contemplare le cose che ivi si generano; qual miracolo è questo così grande?'

26 19 (83) 27 July 1576
Tasso intends to moderate the content of certain passages for reasons that are only implied (*per altre cagioni*), but can be presumed to be religious in nature:

son risoluto di moderarlo in alcune parti; e tanto più mi confermo in questa deliberazione, quanto che per lo più l'eccesso de l'ornamento è ne le materie lascive, le quali per altre cagioni ancora bisogna moderare.

27 26 (88) 20 October 1576 (to Luca Scalabrino)
Meticulous concern is shown in the choice of the correct word. The word *nero* in Canto XX is changed because the terrain about which Tasso writes is white rather than black. Black is taken as a sign of humidity and fertility, characteristics that are inappropriate at this point. Thus 'E i duo che manda il nero adusto suolo' becomes 'E i due che manda il piú fervente suolo' (XX, 23).

28 41 (211) 10 July 1582 (to Orazio Lombardelli)
In this letter Tasso defends the title of his poem: 'i poemi, ne' quali sono scritte le guerre che sono state fatte in alcun luogo, non pren-

dono il nome dal capitano, ma dal luogo stesso'.

29 43 (216) 28 September 1582 (to Orazio Lombardelli)
Tasso again defends the title of the poem, this time against criticism
that it is sluggish: 'E perché la guerra fatta sotto Gerusalemme non fu
condotta al fine in pochi giorni ma in molti mesi, e fu piena di vari
impedimenti, i quali son accresciuti da me poeticamente; non le
poteva esser dato da me alcun titolo più convenevol di quello che è
fatto de' nomi, come voi dite, tardi e non ispediti.'

From the title of the poem to individual vowel and consonant,
from syntax to allegory, it seems that little of the poem escaped scrutiny and criticism, whether from scholarly or religious sources, or
indeed from the self-critical eye of Tasso himself. However, as has
been seen, not all the changes discussed in the letters were ultimately implemented, a factor which indicates the complexity of the interplay between the poet and the Counter-Reformation.[2] This first
section has concentrated on Tasso's epic theory in the context of
sixteenth-century rhetoric, poetics and religion, and on the implications of this context for the composition of the *Gerusalemme liberata*.
The second section carries out an analysis of the *Gerusalemme liberata*
from the perspective of modern theory and methodology. This analysis is not intended simply as a twentieth-century update of what may
strike the modern mind as pedantic and ultimately destructive sixteenth-century criticism. On the contrary, it is hoped that the contemporary methods of analysis employed will allow for an
illumination of the richness and complexity of Tasso's text.

---

[2] My thanks to Peter Brand for focusing my attention on this important point.

PART II

Poesia

Rhetorical Practice in the *Gerusalemme liberata*

CHAPTER 4

Negation

Negative constructions occur frequently in the *Gerusalemme liberata*. Even excluding negative words formed by affixes, and taking into account only constructions involving *non*, *né*, *nulla*, *nessun* and the verb *negare* itself, there are about 2,000 (once approximately every seven and a half lines). Of particular interest are those cases in which a negative is used to convey a positive by means of denial or contradiction of its opposite. It has been argued that all negation necessarily implies prior affirmation, and that negative thought as such does not exist.[1] In a similar vein, the negative is considered, in its function as a transformational marker, to occur in conjunction with statements of what *is* (like, for instance, the passive and the interrogative). The negative therefore behaves as a logical operator that acts on the proposition, rather than as an actual argument of the proposition (Chomsky 1969, 44, 61–84). While accepting as a premise that all negation somehow involves its contrary, namely affirmation, this chapter does not attempt to deal with all instances of the negative in the poem, but with some constructions in which actual denial of the opposite appears to be particularly evident. This includes various forms of litotes, the figure of intensification by understatement. Examples of this figure are antenantiosis, which expresses an affirmative by negation of the contrary, and the *non* + *ma* construction, a form of antithesis.

Turning to the consideration of historical context, the normative tendency characterizing the background of the Counter-Reformation against which Tasso composed his poem can itself be seen as based on negation. Prescription and censorship are inscribed in the drive towards narrative closure, as well as in the policing of the stylistic sphere, as seen in the previous chapter. On a psychoanalytical

---

[1] See Frege 1918–19 and Perelman and Olbrechts-Tyteca 1966, 163.

level this period of extreme socialization of the creative impulse can be seen as a kind of parallel to, or even extension of, the socialization processes undergone by the *id* during the mirror phase. Particular areas of the poem show a certain affinity with this phase, which has been theorized in terms of a stage in the development of the infant.[2]

Moreover, it is perhaps no coincidence that this delimiting phase, when the difference between self and non-self begins to be perceived, is also the period when the negative symbol (together with certain syntactical relations) is acquired. In other words, this is the stage of recognition, on the part of the symbolizing subject, of a particular relationship with what lies outside it. The effect of this newly distinguished *Umwelt* on the *Innenwelt* is to socialize the *id*, and to repress what is socially unacceptable. Freud argued in his essay entitled 'Negation' (1925) that negation provides a vehicle for the surfacing of the ideational content of these repressed elements, although the repression itself is not lifted (Freud *SE* xix. 235). It follows, then, that what is negated belongs to, or is, the *id*, in other words, the narcissistic part of the mirror phase that precedes the delimitation and repression of self-oriented desire and action.

This examination of the ideational content of negation in the poem aims at pinpointing and unmasking areas where the 'repressed' does indeed 'return'. In conjunction with this, attention is also paid to the mechanism of ideological reinforcement discernible at times in the negative construction. Dominant ideological patterns forming part of the repressive Symbolic order are imposed on the subject, which is forcibly inserted into a fixed, Other-dominated hierarchy. This is constantly reiterated and reimposed on the subject by structures of reinforcement which, when laid bare, can be seen to reveal the processes of repression. The negative construction provides a useful vehicle for this repression. A diachronic overview shows that ancient rhetorical treatises, such as the *Rhetorica ad Herennium*, included negation as part of antithesis (*contentio*) in which 'opposing thoughts ought to meet in a comparison' (IV. xlv. 58). Negation was one of four types of comparison: contrast, negation, detailed parallel, and abridged comparison. Each of these had its own purpose: 'to embellish or prove or clarify or vivify' (IV. xlv. 59). The function of negation was therefore one of logic, of proving the argument, thereby linking it closely with forensic oratory and establishing its

[2] See Lacan 1966 and below, Ch. 5.

connection with the original context of rhetoric in matters of law.

The appropriation and reduction of rhetoric by the Middle Ages and the Renaissance to the area of poetics, and particularly to considerations of style, led to an emphasis on the use of the negative to create certain stylistic effects. Novelty and variety, for instance, were achieved by means of negation, as Muzio stated in his *Dell'arte poetica* of 1551: 'Non sia del dir una sola sembianza, ma nova e varia; or dritto e or obliquo vuole esser il parlar. Dubitar vuolsi, *negar*, interrogar, chiamar altrui ecc.' (Weinberg 1970–4, ii. 202). Tasso himself makes little mention of negation in his *Discorsi*. In the revised version, carried out after the publication of the poem, a discussion of 'gli aggiunti i quali implicano contrarietà e contradizione', which are considered *bellissimi*, includes a reference to instances showing *la negazione espressa*. The examples cited are of negative affixes, such as '*in*sepulta sepultura' (*Discorsi*, 234). Again in the later *Discorsi*, in a section on the *forma graziosa* which may be 'agevolmente ... ricevuta dal poema eroico', Tasso says: 'particolarmente mi paion belli i contraposti come son quelli di Bembo'. These include the negative *non* as part of the antithetical *non* + *ma* construction: 'or *non* pur ardo, secco già e fral, *ma* incenerisco e pero' (*Discorsi*, 233).

Contraposti, *contrarietà* and *contradizione* can be seen to provide the context for these allusions to negation, and it is in terms of conflict and paradox that the resonance and tension characterizing the poem itself have traditionally been expressed. In the following chapter it is postulated that the true source of conflict lies in the process of the socialization of an individual, Rinaldo. His socialization is indispensable for the outcome of the overt conflict posited as the actual nexus of the poem, in other words, that of Christians vs. pagans. The elements repressed during this conflictual socialization process are among those that can be seen to surface on the stylistic level too, in certain uses of the negative construction.

The use of negation in epic poetry, a form of poetry dominated by action in terms of movement and change, may relate to what has been posited as 'the specific function of the negative, which is to signal a change of meaning, since it is used when an explicit or implicit assertion is being denied' (Greene 1970, 17). Another specifically rhetorical purpose of negation when used to convey a positive meaning is that of emphasis. This function of the negative in the *Gerusalemme liberata* can be explained in part by the fact that the epic is a genre characterized by the emphatic and the superlative. The negative occurs frequently in epic poems such as the *Aeneid* (about once every twelve lines), in Ariosto's *Orlando furioso* (about once every nine lines, based on the average of Cantos 1–6) and, as has been indicated above, in Tasso's *Gerusalemme liberata* (once every seven and a half lines). Interest in Tasso's use of negation lies, therefore, as much in its frequency as in the manner of its use. Clearly much deliberate, conscious use is made by Tasso of negation. As well as illustrating the various forms this takes, this chapter also examines particular examples in which negation appears to have a rather more involuntary, unconscious motivation and significance.

The present analysis of the narrative function of negation in the poem begins with an examination of the repetition of negatives leading to the formation of negative strings (a convenient label for cases when the negative occurs four or more times within a stanza or three or more times in one line). This is followed by sections on the use of particular emphatic constructions involving the negative, namely litotes and antithesis (constructions that may of course also be repeated in strings).

Negative strings

Strings of negatives can be seen to emphasize and enliven the content of lists through variation. (This was suggested by Muzio's use of negation to achieve variation and novelty, quoted above). For example, in the twenty-first stanza of a series of twenty-nine describing the Christian parade in the *Gerusalemme liberata*, the poet confesses that he is 'di numerar già lasso'. He then changes temporarily from a positive to a negative mode of expression. In so doing, he also uses a device which takes the opposite form of *reticentia*, but with the same emphasizing function:

> Né Guasco né Ridolfo a dietro lasso,
> né l'un né l'altro Guido, ambo famosi,
> non Eberardo e non Gernier trapasso
> sotto silenzio ingratamente ascosi (I, 56, 1–4).[3]

---

[3] The edition of the *Gerusalemme liberata* used in this book is by L. Caretti.

Reticentia itself occurs together with another negative string in the following example:

> Non cala il ferro mai ch'a pien non colga,
> né coglie a pien che piaga anco non faccia,
> né piaga fa che l'alma altrui non tolga;
> e piú direi, ma il ver di falso ha faccia (IX, 23, 1–4).

In conjunction with an invocation to the Muse, another emphatic device drawing attention to what follows, the negative is also repeated to achieve greater semantic impact in a series of superlatives describing the first battle between Tancredi and Argante:

> Or qui, Musa, rinforza in me la voce,
> e furor pari a quel furor m'inspira,
> sí che non sian de l'opre indegni i carmi
> ed esprima il mio canto il suon de l'armi (VI, 39, 5–8)

and:

> né fu di corso mai, né fu di salto,
> né fu mai tal velocità di penne,
> né furia eguale a quella ond'a l'assalto
> quinci Tancredi e quindi Argante venne (VI, 40, 3–6).

Again to highlight a battle scene, negatives are repeated following another invocation by the poet, this time to Night:

> Notte, che nel profondo oscuro seno
> chiudesti e ne l'oblio fatto sí grande,
> piacciati ch'io ne 'l tragga e 'n bel sereno
> a le future età lo spieghi e mande (XII, 54, 3–6)

and:

> Non schivar, non parar, non ritirarsi
> voglion costor, né qui destrezza ha parte.
> Non danno i colpi …
> … il piè d'orma non parte (XII, 55, 1–3, 6).

A further example occurs in the following extended simile:

> Come pari d'ardir, con forza pare
> quinci Austro in guerra vien, quindi Aquilone,
> non ei fra lor, non cede il cielo o 'l mare,
> ma nube a nube e flutto a flutto oppone;
> cosí né ceder qua, né là piegare

> si vede l'ostinata aspra tenzone (IX, 52, 1–6).

Action scenes therefore form one particular narrative situation to be emphasized using negative strings. Another typical narrative area to be emphasized in this way concerns attributes of character, such as the following hyperbolic description of Alcasto's temerity:

> che non avria temuto orribil fèra,
> né mostro formidabile ad uom forte,
> né tremoto, né folgore, né vento,
> né s'altro ha il mondo piú di violento (XIII, 24, 5–8).

Or the description of Solimano's bravery in death:

> ... pur mentre more,
> già non oblia la generosa usanza:
> non fugge i colpi e gemito non spande,
> né atto fa se non se altero e grande (XX, 107, 5–8).

Many of the negative strings in the poem occur in speech. There they tend either to stress the persuasive function of passages uttered in order to convince an addressee to act in a certain way, or to heighten the effect of an emotional dialogue or monologue. Instances of the persuasive role of negative strings are the following words of Pluto persuading his spirits to fight:

> Ah! non fia ver, ché non sono anco estinti
> gli spirti in voi di quel valor primiero ...
> Fummo, io no 'l nego, in quel conflitto vinti,
> pur non mancò virtute al gran pensiero (IV, 15, 1–2, 5–6)

and the didactic speech of the Mago to Rinaldo:

> Signor, non sotto l'ombra in piaggia molle
> tra fonti e fior, tra ninfe e tra sirene,
> ma in cima a l'erto e faticoso colle
> de la virtú riposto è il nostro bene.
> Chi non gela e non suda e non s'estolle
> da le vie del piacer, là non perviene (XVII, 61, 1–6).

A heightening of emotional effect with negative strings can be observed in Erminia's monologue as she longs for Clorinda's lifestyle and freedom:

> quant'io la invidio! e non l'invidio il vanto
> o 'l feminil onor de l'esser bella.
> A lei non tarda i passi il lungo manto,

> né 'l suo valor rinchiude invida cella,
> ma veste l'armi, e se d'uscirne agogna,
> vassene e non la tien tema o vergogna (VI, 82, 3–8)

and:

> Ah perché forti a me natura e 'l cielo
> altrettanto non fèr le membra e 'l petto …
> Ché sí non riterrebbe arsura o gelo,
> non turbo o pioggia il mio infiammato affetto,
> ch'al sol non fossi ed al notturno lampo,
> accompagnata o sola, armata in campo (VI, 83, 1–2, 5–8).

Tancredi's emotional account to Goffredo of his experience in the forest also depends on the repetition of negatives for its effect:

> No, no, piú non potrei (vinto mi chiamo)
> né corteccia scorzar, né sveller ramo (XIII, 49, 7–8),

as does Argante's impassioned self-reproof at the news of Clorinda's death:

> Che non feci o non dissi? o quai non porsi
> preghiere al re che fèsse aprir le porte? (XII, 102, 5–6).

These elements of repetition and emphasis characteristic of the negative string are also rhetorical devices in their own right, typifying the way in which rhetorical categories overlap, and indicating the virtual impossibility of establishing watertight divisions.[4]

Litotes

The study of litotes is particularly beset by such complications of overlap. Even 'standard' definitions of this figure appear not to coincide. The *Oxford English Dictionary* concentrates on the element of

---

[4] See Quintilian's *Institutio oratoria* for an account of *repetitio*: IX. i. 33; IX. ii. 4; IX. iii. 29, and emphasis: VI. iii. 69; VIII. ii. 11; VIII. iii. 83, 86; VIII. iv. 26; IX. ii. 64; IX. iii. 57; and the *Rhetorica ad Herennium* for a description of *repetitio*: IV. xiii. 19, and emphasis: IV. xliii. 67. Tasso mentions *repetizione* as a figure in his discussion on style in the later *Discorsi*: 'Ma le figure de la forma graziosa possono più agevolmente esser ricevute dal poema eroico e mescolate con quelle de la magnificenza e con l'altre. Una fra l'altre è la repetizione, o la replica che vogliam dirla, la quale, come che sia attissima ad irritar gli animi, può esser nondimeno usata per acquistar grazia' (*Discorsi*, 231). For the figure of emphasis in the Renaissance period, see Trissino in Weinberg 1970–4, ii. 79.

affirmation: 'A figure of speech, in which an affirmative is expressed by the negative of the contrary', and cites as an example 'a citizen of no mean city'. The *Grande dizionario della lingua italiana*, on the other hand, singles out the element of attenuation: 'Figura retorica mediante la quale si tende ad attenuare un enunciato negando il contrario di esso', and cites examples whose implied meaning is also given, such as 'io non ti odio' for 'io ti amo', and 'ingegno non comune' for 'bell'ingegno' (Battaglia 1975, ix. 158).

Classical treatises on rhetoric, from which these definitions are ultimately derived, present a situation that is also far from straightforward. As Lausberg points out, even the names given to this figure are manifold. He also gives Quintilian's description of a figure corresponding to litotes, but not named as such. Lausberg's own, more extensive definition of litotes appears to hinge on the periphrastic combination of emphasis and irony (Lausberg 1960, 304). He explains that the superlative degree of the intended meaning is indicated by denial of the opposite. Here irony is not total, but gradual. 'Not small', taken as straightforward irony, would suggest 'small'. As an instance of litotes, it suggests not just 'of ordinary size' or 'big', but 'very big'. The superlative degree (very big), although not incompatible with the denial of the opposite of its ordinary degree (not little), is not acceptable as its ordinary meaning and is here introduced through the mechanism of irony. The function of irony is in fact quite crucial, and will prove important not only in pinpointing examples of litotes, but also in ascertaining their narrative function in the *Gerusalemme liberata*.

A brief glance at the role of litotes in rhetorical theory from classical times to the Renaissance will help to illuminate the difficulties in defining this figure. There emerges a picture of fluctuation as the actual scope of litotes widened. This is particularly the case in the thirteenth century, when it appears categorized as part of larger rhetorical units such as *oppositio*, *correctio*, *deminutio* and *amplificatio*. These rhetorical units, especially *amplificatio*, were themselves undergoing expansion, a fact that would help to account for the changing role of the figures contained within them.

The *Rhetorica ad Herennium* deals with *amplificatio* under invention in judicial and epideictic speeches. There it appears as a form of embellishment (along with similes, examples and previous judgements) constituting one of the five parts of the argument (the other four being proposition, reason, proof of reason and summary).

Amplificatio was also present in the conclusion of the speech, together with the summing-up and the appeal to pity (II. xxx. 47). In addition, *amplificatio*, together with *deminutio*, was considered a general rhetorical principle. Cicero says in his *De oratore*:

> But the highest distinction of eloquence consists in amplification by means of ornament, which can be used to make one's speech not only increase the importance of a subject and raise it to a higher level, but also to diminish and disparage it (III. xxvii. 104).

Quintilian similarly says in his *Institutio oratoria*: 'But the real power of oratory lies in enhancing or attenuating the force of words' (VIII. iii. 89).

Quintilian's four methods of amplification (*incrementum*, *comparatio*, *ratiocinatio* and *congeries*) were expanded to eight in the thirteenth century (*interpretatio*, *circumlocutio*, *comparatio*, *apostrophatio*, *prosopopeia*, *digressio*, *descriptio* and *oppositio*), partly under the influence in late antiquity of school exercises such as Priscian's *Praeexercitamina* (III. iv).[5] On the other hand, his care in excluding tropes, such as hyperbole, as a means of amplification, was not reflected in medieval treatment of the subject, which dealt with it primarily in terms of figures (III. iv. 29). However, he does provide a basis for a stylistic elaboration on how to amplify by dealing with it in his section on style (VIII. iv).

The medieval expansion of the means of *amplificatio* included litotes as part of the eighth figure, *oppositio*. This figure was considered a type of antithesis that amplified and emphasized discourse by means of periphrasis, stating what was *not* meant, as well as what was.[6] Litotes was also advocated as a means of *deminutio*.[7] This use of the same figure in both amplification and its opposite, diminution, highlights the plurality of functions attributed in rhetorical theory to certain figures. This is particularly characteristic of figures used in *amplificatio* and *deminutio*. Quintilian even points out, after dealing with amplification, that 'Attenuation is effected by the same method since there are as many degrees of descent as ascent' (VIII. iv. 28).

Renaissance rhetoric in part returned *amplificatio* to its position in classical times.[8] It also retained the medieval predilection for listing figures, and it is in such lists that litotes is to be found. Gilio da

---

[5] See Curtius 1944, 273, Faral 1962, 204 ff., and Gallo 1971, 167.

[6] See Geoffroi de Vinsauf in Faral 1962, 218 and Arbusow 1963, 28, 87.

[7] See Geoffroi de Vinsauf in Faral 1962, 236 and Arbusow 1963, 86.

[8] For amplification as a part of the speech, see Denores, *Breve trattato dell'oratore* (1574) and Lionardi, *Dialogi della inventione poetica* (1554) (Weinberg 1970–4, iii. 126, ii. 241). For amplification by figures and other means, see Minturno, *L'arte poetica* (1564), p. 37.

Fabriano writes in his *Topica poetica* (1580) under *figure delle parole*: 'LIPTOTES. Si forma questa figura quando con due negative si fa una affermativa, come vuol Servio Virgilio: "Nec candida cursum / luna negat" ... Il Petrarca: "Negar non posso, che l'affanno / che va innanzi al morir non doglia forte, / Ma piú la tema de l'eterno danno"' (p. 52). Gilio does not deal with amplification in terms of figures, as was the medieval practice, but in terms of *inventio*. Tasso himself does not mention litotes in his *Discorsi*, but *oppositio* does appear as a source of *diletto*, in conjunction with *contraposti*. *Correzione* also occurs, as a means of producing *gravità* (*correctio* being a figure linked to *oppositio*, in that its latter half corrects, or opposes, the former).[9]

The situation regarding litotes is therefore by no means straightforward. In order to arrive at a working definition, two major facets of litotes can be isolated. The first relates to the meaning of the original Greek adjective for simple, plain, or meagre, and can most conveniently be seen in terms of semantic function, that is, understatement. The second concerns the actual mechanics of this figure, which involves the use of the negative of the contrary of what is meant. Examples of litotes quoted to illustrate the figure almost invariably contain this element of negation. Strictly speaking, of course, this corresponds to the figure antenantiosis, in which a positive statement is made in a negative form. Antenantiosis, or *exadversio*, is, in fact, one of the terms used by Lausberg for litotes, although two separate figures are involved (Lausberg 1960, 304). The situation is further complicated by Trissino, who in his *La poetica* (1529) illustrates the figure antiphrasis with what is in fact a litotes: 'l'antifrasi è la parola che significa e dinota il contrario o vero quello che a esso contrario è propinquo, come è: ... "non si allegrò", cioè "si dolse"' (Weinberg 1970–4, ii. 79). The element of negation itself appears in two forms. In addition to the form in which the contrary is negated, there is another type of litotes (as indicated in Gilio's definition) in which the contrary is itself also a negative, for example 'nec negat'.[10]

In examining the *Gerusalemme liberata* for examples of litotes, the following two types will be distinguished, based on the preceding survey of definitions. First, litotes in which the contrary is negated, as in *non picciole proposte* (VI, 14, 8). Second, litotes in which the contrary

[9] *Discorsi*, 233. See Lausberg 1960, 391 and Weinberg 1970–4, i. 298.
[10] See the entry for litotes, 2, 'duo negativa unum adfirmant' in the *Thesaurus linguae latinae* 1972, vii, co. 1514.

is also a negative, as in *no 'l neghi* (V, 11, 3). A third type, possible in the light of thirteenth-century interpretation, in which litotes appears as the first part of an opposition, such as *non fatto, ma nato* (XIV, 48, 8), will not be differentiated here. Negation in general as part of the *non* + *ma* form of antithesis will be dealt with in the next section.

In order to identify correctly instances of litotes in the poem, attention must be paid to the presence or absence of irony (in the form of an intended superlative degree of meaning expressed by a denial of the opposite of the ordinary degree). The litotes must, in other words, make its meaning, and so its *voluntas*, clear. Context is essential for this, as implied by the way examples (excerpts without a context) illustrating the figure are as a rule accompanied by an explanation of their meaning. Line position, to indicate whether the litotes is placed emphatically, such as at the beginning or end of a line, will be made clear in the following examples by placing a vertical line | before or after the litotes, signifying either the beginning or end of a line. Such positions frequently coincide with a high ironic content. Two-thirds of the examples found in the poem are in one or other of these emphatic positions.

Instances of the first type of litotes to be analysed (negation of the contrary which is not itself a negative) amount to around seventy-five examples. One particularly effective form of irony to be found here is dramatic irony, which occurs when the reader is aware of something of which a character is ignorant. When Alcandro sees '| la non vera Clorinda' (VI, 112, 2), he believes her to be the real Clorinda, whereas we know that it is in fact Erminia in Clorinda's armour. Tancredi's very last moment of blissful unawareness before realizing that he has killed Clorinda is expressed in a powerful example of dramatic irony via litotes when he uncovers 'la fronte | non conosciuta ancor' (XII, 67, 4). The reader, on the other hand, has known her identity throughout the duel. When an angel appears in order to heal Goffredo's arrow wound, he is *non veduto* (XI, 73, 7) as far as the characters are concerned, while the reader is given full details of the apparition. *Non veduto* recurs as an example of dramatic irony when Solimano, hidden from the pagan council but not from the reader, listens to patently unfounded speculations on his fate: '| non veduto rimira e spia d'intorno / e ode' (X, 35, 2). There is additional play on the juxtaposition of verbs of sight, as Solimano is unseen, but himself sees (see Ch. 6).

Moving away from dramatic irony as a product of litotes in third-person narrative to the ironic effect of litotes in direct speech, Solimano, after revealing his presence to the council, retorts with remarks made pointed by the use of litotes. He prefaces what he has been called ('timido e fugace' X, 47, 5) with a negative, declaiming that he is ' | non fugace e non timido' (X, 50, 2). Contrary to the meagre expectations he has heard voiced about himself, he believes he will be of 'non poco aiuto' (X, 52, 8). Argante, vaunting intentions similarly expressed in this heavily ironic form, asks the herald to announce to the Christians his 'non picciole proposte | ' (VI, 14, 8).

Another use of litotes involves the prefiguring of some future event. The ominous notion of physical disfigurement central to Dudone's 'non brutte ferite' (I, 53, 8), mentioned as a positive feature in the description of the Christian parade, foreshadows his 'acerba morte' later on (V, 13, 2). Armida's belief as she expresses her desire for Rinaldo's death 'che non invano | soglion portarne ogni saetta i venti' (XVII, 47, 1), is belied by future events as her arrows fail to wound him and an ironic reversal in fact takes place: 'mentre ella saetta, Amor lei piaga' (XX, 65, 8). Reference to the past is implied when her face is 'del non suo pianto or lagrimosa' (XX, 129, 6). She has shed many tears for Rinaldo, and now her face is wet not with her own tears, but with those he now sheds for her.

The relationship between the meaning of a litotes and a preceding word can highlight the underlying and all-important implication. When Argante meets Goffredo, the former's attitude of 'uom ... non curante | ' (II, 60, 8) is preceded and qualified by *in guisa d'*, the resulting picture being that of a deliberate, rhetorical understatement of concern, indeed of extreme nonchalance, implying actual intensity of involvement. The additional element of dramatic irony is also present, as the reader is told that his behaviour is feigned, but there is nothing to suggest that any of the characters are aware that he is anything but *non curante*. In another example of litotes linked significantly to a preceding word, Goffredo's apparently spontaneous concession to Guelfo to recall his nephew Rinaldo, expressed as 'cosa non pensata in pria' (XIV, 25, 4), is prefaced by 'quasi egli pieghi / la mente a', indicating that, on the contrary, the idea is not a new one. In fact the reader and Goffredo (but none of the other characters) already know this, since Rinaldo's reacceptance into the Christian camp, and even the precise manner in which this should take place, was suggested to Goffredo in a dream by Ugone. This type of dramatic irony is also present in Vafrino's comment that he will be a 'non conosciuta spia |' (XVIII, 58, 6). This says more than at first glance appears, for Vafrino obviously cannot spy successfully if he is *conosciuto*. There is also, therefore, an element of pleonasm present. Another instance of litotes overlapping with a different rhetorical figure is '| Non io … narrar potrei …' (IX, 92, 3), an instance of *praeteritio*.

Finally, this first type of litotes in which the contrary is negated, but is not itself a negation, is used to emphasize an emotion. For example, 'cor non lieto |' (VI, 80, 3) expresses the extreme state of Erminia's unhappiness in her unrequited love for Tancredi. It can also be used to emphasize an opinion, such as that of Pindoro who, as night falls, halts the duel between Tancredi and Argante with the admonition that 'generoso cor non molto cura | notturno pregio che s'asconde e tace' (VI, 52, 3). *Non molto cura* suggests that the magnanimous soul would greatly despise a victory won in darkness. And when Raimondo sees Goffredo donning the lightweight armour of a foot soldier, he expresses his extreme unease with the words: 'Io già non lodo | che vada con sí debili difese' (XI, 21, 5), an understatement presumably prompted by respect for a social superior.

In conjunction with this first group of around seventy-five diverse examples of the first type of litotes, there is a separate group of around twenty-five examples of *non lunge* or *non lontano*. The regularity with which this recurs may indicate that it is, in fact, a fixed, conventional way of signifying *vicino*, and is consequently of little significance, its rhetorical function as litotes having been diminished by use as a fixed expression. Its role in the poem may therefore simply be that of a metrical variant of *vicino*. About one half the instances convey no more than the spatial notion of 'nearby'. Three examples are: '| Non lunge a l'auree porte ond'esce il sole / è cristallina porta in oriente' (XIV, 3, 1), '| Non lunge un sagacissimo valletto / pose' (XIV, 55, 1), and 'una colonna eretta / vede, e un picciol battello indi non lunge |' (XIV, 57, 6).

In other cases, however, an additional significance is apparent. For instance, after an entire octave devoted to describing the stealthy approach of Ormondo disguised as a Christian in the plan to kill Goffredo, the words 'non lontano al fianco | del pio Goffredo il fer pagan si mise' (XX, 45, 1) convey that the Christian leader is in imminent danger. When Lesbino is slain by Argillan, Solimano is 'non molto lunge |' (IX, 85, 1). Nonetheless, despite being near, Solimano is powerless to save him. Solidarity among the Christians is also emphasized by *non lunge*, as in the example 'gli eroi compagni, i quai non lunge | erano sparsi, a ragunarsi invita Goffredo' (I, 19, 1). It is also underlined in the position of the heroic Dudone's grave, which is '| non lunge a gli steccati' (III, 72, 5). On other occasions, the spatial proximity of the pagans, expressed using litotes, can clearly be interpreted as emphasis on the threat they pose. Examples of this are the nearness of the forest symbolizing an evil, pagan threat, 'Sorge non lunge a le cristiane tende / tra solitarie valli alta foresta' (XIII, 2, 1), and Carlo's account of the massacre of Sveno's army, a disaster that closely follows the ill-placed encampment of the army 'ove i confini | non lunge erano omai de' Palestini' (VIII, 13, 8).

The discussion of litotes has so far concentrated on deliberate rhetorical use classifiable in terms of figures and functions. There are also, however, examples in which this type of negation can be seen to have another, perhaps more involuntary motivation and significance. One such example occurs in Arsete's account to Clorinda of her mother's fears about her father's reaction to her birth: 'ch'egli avria dal candor che in te si vide / argomentato in lei non bianca fede |' (XII, 24, 8). On one level *non bianca fede*, or infidelity, is a homonymic play on words based on several meanings of 'white', such as 'purity' and 'colour', particularly skin colour. However, in conjunction with the description of the mother a few stanzas before, in which the pejorative association of dark skin with ugliness is introduced through its negation in another litotes ('che bruna è sí, ma il bruno il bel non toglie |' (XII, 21, 8), the subsequent litotes (*non bianca fede*) acquires an additional level of significance which links infidelity (also pejorative) directly with dark skin. Racism is further present in the emphasis on Clorinda's whiteness, despite her parentage, implying the unsuitability of dark skin for a female warrior of her prominence.[11] Racial values provide a further dimension to these examples, surfacing via the mechanism of negation as a vehicle for the covert transmission of ideological reinforcers. This additional role of litotes, over and above its ironic function, also extends to other ideologically meaningful areas, such as gender portrayal and maintenance of the socio-religious hierarchy, as will be seen shortly.

[11] On the racial implications of the portrayal of the Moslem as enemy, see Connelly 1977.

Other instances of litotes point towards a 'return' of the 'repressed', and appear to correspond more closely to Freudian negation. For example, when the Christian army follows its leaders in a religious procession, it is described in the following terms: 'e non confuso | seguiva il campo in lor difesa armato' (XI, 6, 3). Freud said: 'In our interpretation, we take the liberty of disregarding the negation and of picking out the subject-matter alone of the association' (Freud *SE* xix. 235). According to his theory, it is possible to see the notion of confusion essential to the litotes *non confuso*, as the 'repressed' returning. In other words, the unbounded energies of the *id* in the shape of an absence of order represent paganism returning against the super-ego or (social) order, equated with Christianity. Through excessive denial of confusion in the Christian army, then, the notion of confusion itself is introduced into the text, and is brought into direct association with the epitome of its opposite, namely the ordered Christian procession. This opposition between Christian order and pagan disorder is a recurrent theme in the poem. A few stanzas later, for instance, the regularity of the Christian *melodia soave* is contrasted with the discordant pagan *stride, bestemmie, onte* and *gridi* (XI, 12 and 13). And when Rinaldo, the main representative and hope of the Christian army and society, is reclaimed in order to fulfil his obligations, his exit from the centre of the island of libidinous, pagan temptation is described as 'e de la *torta / confusione* uscí del labirinto' (XVI, 35, 1).

The second type of litotes, namely cases where the negated word is itself a negative, poses questions of a similar nature to those encountered with the *non lunge* or *non lontano* group. Many examples of the double negative are too formulaic to produce the full ironic impact of which litotes is capable. The production of a weaker or stronger form of irony appears to correspond to whether the negated word is more or less predominantly negative in character; in other words, whether or not it contains any other important semantic variables. For instance, double negations with *negare* and *meno* are less ironic in significance than, say, *vietare*, which contains richer semantic elements. In some cases, moreover, there is a higher incidence of the same examples of the former group (*non negare* appears nine times, *non meno* fifteen times), whereas double negatives from the latter group often occur on a less frequent basis (*non vietare* appears only three times, and *non rifiutare* only twice). This would seem to reveal a more idiosyncratic and less formulaic usage which is consequently higher in ironic content.

Non negare represents the most purely negative of the double negatives forming the second type of litotes. Of the nine instances in the poem, eight occur in direct speech. Their predominant function appears to be the basic rhetorical one pertaining to the speech and its reasoning processes. For example, in the line 'Fummo, io no 'l nego, in quel conflitto vinti' (IV, 15, 5), *no 'l nego* serves to impart a concessionary tone to this part of Pluto's speech. This induces his hearers to feel at ease after he has previously bombarded them with a series of rhetorical questions (IV, 12–14), and ensures their receptivity to subsequent commands that form the actual high point of the speech and bring it to a close (IV, 16–17). Armida's long speech attempting to win back Rinaldo similarly makes use of *no 'l nego*, together with other concessionary phrases: 'Giusto a te pare, *e siasi. Anch'io* le genti / cristiane odiai, *no 'l nego ...*' (XVI, 45, 3). *Non di negare* appears in Goffredo's speech (V, 3, 3) in order to temper a decision that he knows will be unpopular, namely postponing aid for Armida. Guglielmo's *no 'l nego* (X, 60, 3) is an attenuated, and therefore all the more guilty, form of admission to having followed her nevertheless. Lastly, *no 'l nego* occurs in the reasoning process in Clorinda's debate with herself about the advantages and disadvantages of the type of fighting to which she feels restricted (XII, 3, 7). Technically speaking, then, examples of *non negare* are classifiable as litotes. However, the actual function of these examples shows that *non negare* is less similar to litotes than to other rhetorical devices. None of these examples, moreover, occurs in an emphatic line position.

Like *negare*, the term *meno* is also characterized by a negative element, this time of a comparative nature. Instances of *non meno* can therefore be categorized as litotes of the second type. *Non meno* functions in the poem to emphasize the equal importance of one thing in relation to another, thereby implying the possibility of this not being the case (in the manner of a Freudian negation). Also implicit is the presence of another person (character/reader) who does not believe it and who needs to be convinced. Some ironic content is thus always present in this implication of another possibility. It does, however, vary in degree, and is not usually as intense as in examples of litotes where the negated word is characterized by more than the neutral negative marker.

The following two examples of *non meno* illustrate the greatest ironic content of which this particular double negative is capable. First, Tancredi's reaction to Armida in comparison with that of Goffredo: 'Ma contra l'arme di costei non meno | si mostrò di Tancredi invitto il core' (V, 65, 1). The implication is that it would, in fact, be highly plausible for Tancredi to have been won over by her. He is much younger, and so more susceptible, than Goffredo, and no one, other than Rinaldo, is 'più bel di maniere e di sembiante' than he (I, 45, 3). A powerful reason for Tancredi's invincibility despite the odds is given immediately afterwards, also using a negation: 'però ch'altro desio gli ingombra il seno, / né vi può loco aver novello ardore' (V, 65, 3). The second example concerns Carlo's instructions to Rinaldo on giving him Sveno's sword. In using it, the youth should be 'giusto e pio non men che forte' (XVII, 83, 6). The implication is that Rinaldo needs to be persuaded, as he may otherwise not display the former two qualities. Carlo perhaps considers these more common in older men, while Rinaldo is more likely to use the sword to win glory in battle (a possibility that appears justified in view of his impetuous behaviour earlier on).

Other instances of *non meno* are merely used for emphasis through understatement in order to stress the parity of one particular element with another. For instance, Orcano underlines Argante's heroism by stating that his deeds match his words:

> però se 'l buon circasso a te per uso
> troppo in vero parlar fervido sòle,
> ciò si conceda a lui che poi ne l'opre
> il medesmo fervor *non meno* scopre (X, 40, 8).

Sveno's longing for heroic stature is emphasized by the equal weight he gives to his willingness to achieve it through death and his desire to attain it through victory:

> corona o di martirio o di vittoria!
> L'una spero io ben piú, ma *non men* bramo
> l'altra ove è maggior merto e pari gloria (VIII, 15, 3).

When Ismeno tells Aladino that he has successfully enchanted the forest to thwart the Christians, he draws attention to the fact that something else (an impending drought) has also given him satisfaction: 'Or cosa aggiungo a queste / fatte da me ch'a me *non meno* aggrada' (XIII, 13, 2).

Irony is also very low key in another use of *non meno*. The following instance shows an intensification of ferocity and tumult everywhere on the battlefield, in an attempt to produce vividness: '| *Non meno* intanto son feri i litigi / da l'altra parte, e i guerrier folti e densi' (IX, 53, 1). Other instances produce an effect similar to that of the simile. The extent of Aletto's influence over Argillano is emphasized by the lines: 'Ma fu stupor ch'Aletto al cor gl'infuse | *non men* che morte sia profondo e grave' (VIII, 59, 4). In like vein, Arsete's estimation of his relationship with Clorinda, he wishes her to realize, has been akin to that of a servant and father:

> ... e qual tua vita
> sia stata poscia tu medesma il sai;
> e sai *non men* che servo insieme e padre
> io t'ho seguita ... (XII, 38, 7).

The further function of persuasion is also served by this particular example, in that Arsete draws attention to his care for her, and by implication her reciprocal responsibility towards him. His aim here is to predispose her favourably towards his design, which is to dissuade her from going into battle, particularly in armour different from her own.

The basic rhetorical function of persuasion, rather than irony, is also uppermost in the following three examples. First, as part of Armida's attempt to enlist Goffredo's aid by emphasizing that *pietà*, in the form of helping her, is as important as victory: '| *né meno* il vanto di pietà si prezza / che 'l trionfar de gl' inimici sui' (IV, 41, 5). Second, the demon trying to persuade Gernando to challenge Rinaldo to a duel does so partly by stressing that such a heroic action is exactly what is expected of him: 'ma già *non meno* esso da te n'attese' (V, 20, 7). And third, the Mago instructing Rinaldo on the duties he must perform emphasizes the greatness of his family line, the Italian branch of the Este, in comparison with the German branch, thereby underlining the young descendant's responsibility to it:

> un gran ramo estense ...
> ... già mezza ingombra
> la gran Germania, e tutta anco l'adombra.
> Ma ne' suoi rami italici fioriva
> bella *non men* la regal pianta a prova (XVII, 80–1).

Some instances of *non meno* are of particular interest in their implications for gender portrayal, yet another area of ideological reinforcement. The scene in which a bathing nymph on Armida's island lets down her hair is described in terms that, first of all, fragment the woman's body by isolating her *mammelle* and other erotic areas as objects for the male gaze. Carlo and Ubaldo have stopped to look ('fermarsi a riguardarle'), as too, by implication, has the reader, consequently also assumed to be male:

> Una intanto drizzossi, e le mammelle
> e tutto ciò che più la vista alletti
> mostrò, dal seno in suso, aperto al cielo;
> e 'l lago a l'altre membra era un bel velo (XV, 59, 5–8).

The letting down of the nymph's hair is described in terms that identify certain parts of her body as spectacle: 'Oh che vago spettacolo è lor tolto!' (XV, 61, 5). Also at stake is the alienation of aspects of the woman's body from the rest of her identity by the separation of the spectacle from the woman who provides it: 'ma *non men* vago fu chi loro il tolse' (XV, 61, 6). What at first glance appears as a sort of pleonastic vacuum set up in this second line by an apparently superfluous repetition of the woman's identity, in fact functions to provide a space that is filled by the ideological substructure subtending the poem (in this case woman as body and as spectacle for the male gaze).

Another example of *non meno* forms part of a similar instance of ideological surfacing. This concerns the description of Clorinda's prowess in battle, which is immediately introduced in terms of that of Argante: 'Non lontana è Clorinda, e già *non meno* | par che di tronche membra il campo asperga' (IX, 68, 1). In other words, her valour is measured in relation to that of a man, by the use of relative comparative, rather than independent superlative, values. *Non meno* thereby introduces into the text the idea of her being less proficient than Argante. This limiting notion precedes, and so diminishes, the subsequent account of her feats, an effect which even the culminating note of indomitability ('l'indomita guerriera' IX, 71, 1) fails to dispel.

Gildippe is similarly described, this time in terms of Clorinda: 'non fa d'incontra a lei Gildippe altera / de' saracini suoi strage *men fella*' (IX, 71, 3). Both female warriors are finally relegated to a sub-male position: they are never allowed to fight each other, but are each to be reserved for a greater (male) enemy. This is in accordance with the

social rules, represented by the inevitable and conveniently unques-
tionable *fato*: 'Ma far prova di lor non è lor dato, / ch'a nemico maggior le serba il fato' (IX, 71, 7). Clorinda will ultimately be slain by
Tancredi, and Gildippe by Solimano. In other words, the ability of
these female warriors, although great, must not be seen to exceed
that of their male counterparts. As a result, female valour is described
essentially in terms of negative comparatives. This culminates in male
supremacy over a femininity that is already fragmented, and in an act
characterized by sexual overtones. In the case of Tancredi and
Clorinda, an erotic subtext precedes the final, sexualized death blow:
'Spinge egli il ferro nel bel sen di punta / che vi s'immerge … la
trafitta / vergine minacciando incalza e preme' (XII, 64, 65).
Solimano despatches Gildippe, for whom no such subtext exists, in a
slightly less sexualized fashion: 'drizzò percossa … ch'osò … entrar
nel seno' (XX, 96, 2).

Other forms of double negative litotes using *mancare* and *cessare*
have little ironic content, their purpose being that of emphasis. This
effect is enhanced in many cases by emphatic line positioning. *Non
mancare* is used in the following examples as an emphatic way of say-
ing 'there were' and 'there will be' respectively: '| *Non mancar* qui
cento ministri e cento / che accorti e pronti a servir gli osti foro'
(XIV, 49, 1), and 'già *non mancherà* chi là vi scòrga' (XIV, 71, 7). The
other three cases of *non mancare* emphasize the presence of *virtú*: 'pur
non mancò virtute al gran pensiero' (IV, 15, 6), 'ché per vecchiezza in
lei virtú *non manca* |' (XVII, 86, 8), and 'Virtú ch' a' valorosi unqua
non manca |' (XX, 84, 1).

Non cessare similarly performs an emphatic function, this time
highlighting an action or an effect actually in process. For instance,
Armida persists in trying to distract the Christians: 'Di procurare il
suo soccorso intanto | *non cessò* mai l'ingannatrice rea' (V, 60, 2).
The enduring impression made on both Christians and pagans by
the duel between Tancredi and Argante is described as: 'un'alta
meraviglia ed un orrore / che per lunga stagione in lor *non cessa* |'
(VI, 54, 4). Argante's relentlessness in seeking out Raimondo on the
battlefield, despite all obstacles, is underlined as follows: '| *Non
cessa*, non s'allenta, anzi è piú fero / quanto ristretto è piú da que'
gagliardi' (VII, 107, 5). And the Christians continue their advance,
despite Argante's taunts: 'per suo dir *non cessa* | la gente occulta'
(XI, 37, 1).

One characteristic that these four double negatives (*non negare, non meno, non mancare* and *non cessare*) have in common, and that contributes to their low ironic content in comparison with other examples of litotes, is that they cannot stand on their own. Another semantic ingredient is necessary in each case to complete the sense: it is necessary to know *what* is negated, ceasing, lacking, etc. This particular type of double negative is formulaic in nature, with a fixed meaning, and necessarily occurs in combination with other words providing the salient semantic variable. The sort of emphasis through understatement that is produced in this way is essentially one of degree, with the double negative acting as qualifier. The low-key ironic effect of this type of double-negative litotes is clearly different from the first type of litotes, such as *non timido*.

However, other forms of double-negative litotes are capable of producing a full ironic effect. In these cases the negated word itself provides the salient semantic variable, as well as containing a negative element. This is illustrated by instances of *non tacere*. When Gernando, under the influence of an evil spirit, busily spreads slanderous rumours about Rinaldo, this is expressed as 'a suo disnor *non tace* |' (V, 23, 6). Irony is also evident in the pleonasm 'la garrula fama omai *non tace* |' (XII, 84, 3). Tancredi, communicating Goffredo's highly explicit resolve to punish Rinaldo, says: 'a quel ch'io scerna / nel capitan ch'in tutto anco *no 'l tace* |' (V, 41, 6). In all these examples, more than the mere opposite of *tacere* (*parlare* or *dire*) is implied, and all occur in an emphatic position at the end of a line. Instances of *non rifiutare* (also found at the end of a line) similarly suggest much more than *accettare*. Aggression and sarcasm, for instance, are suggested by Argante's words to Tancredi:

> Tardi riedi, e non solo; io *non rifiuto* |
> però combatter teco e riprovarmi,
> benché non qual guerrier, ma qui venuto
> quasi inventor di machine tu parmi (XIX, 3, 1)

and by the words of Clorinda, also addressed to Tancredi:

> − Guerra e morte avrai; − disse − io *non rifiuto* |
> darlati, se la cerchi (XII, 53, 1).

Instances of *non vietare* and *non disdire* are of particular interest. They appear to function not so much as examples of double-negative litotes, but as a means of underlining the possession of power implied by the verbs. This is suggested by the exclusive nature of their use. They are spoken by Goffredo ('a te Tancredi l'uscir *non vieto* |' VI, 25, 3), and used by King Aladino with reference to the highest authority ('se 'l Ciel *no 'l vieta*' X, 53, 7). The divine Ugone, spokesman of the wood, says of Rinaldo: 'A lui sol di troncar *non fia disdetto* | il bosco' (XIV, 14, 1). These three examples are clear cases in which the negated element is of paramount significance, and they function very much as vehicles for transmitting and reinforcing the ideological status quo in relation to the highest levels of the socio-religious hierarchy. It is also worth noting that the double negation constituting this second type of litotes results, as has been seen, in the positive meanings of either 'more' or 'equal'. However, examples with *non mai* (and its equivalent *non più*) produce a negative sense, as in "l non mai stabil regno' (IX, 99, 4), 'ove alcun legno / rado, o *non mai*, va de le nostre sponde' (XIV, 69, 6), 'e miràr quinci e quindi anco inalzarsi / *non più* veduta una ed un'altra mole' (XVIII, 64, 6), and 'arte di schermo nova e *non più* udita / a i magnanimi amanti usar vedresti' (XX, 36, 1).

Antithesis

The next negative construction to be dealt with is the *non* or *né* + *ma* (or occasionally *pur* or *anzi*) type of antithesis, namely *oppositio*. This is, of course, only one form of antithesis, which can also exist without a negative element, for example 'tra viva e morte' (XVI, 62, 2).[12] The *non* + *ma* construction is an emphatic, and in the poem at times heavily normative, form of amplification. Its frequent appearance in the *Gerusalemme liberata* (it occurs about 200 times, on average once every seventy lines) is in itself not surprising, the epic being a genre dominated, as has already been observed, by the emphatic and the superlative. It is also to be found in the *Orlando furioso* with the same frequency, and in the *Aeneid*, although to a lesser extent (fifty-two times, on average once every 190 lines).[13]

[12] For a detailed breakdown of the various types of antithesis to be found in the poem, see Lepschy 1983.

[13] The Latin expression takes the form of *non/ne/nec/ni* + *sed*, and is found in the following lines of the *Aeneid*: I, 60, 139, 675; II, 101, 288, 315, 541, 788; III, 173, 261, 586; IV, 98, 229, 366, 620, 697; V, 195, 531, 734; VI, 48, 95, 171, 511, 564, 675; VII, 104, 440, 525, 704, 806; VIII, 131, 318; IX, 57, 312, 378, 519, 705; X, 292, 308, 411, 435, 510, 664, 713, 735, 856; XI, 149, 181, 874, 881; XII, 765, 811.

The varying contexts in which this construction is to be found indicate its fundamental nature as a rhetorical device with a variety of functions. As indicated above, this construction became a focal point of interest for medieval theorists, who were the first to name it *oppositio* or *oppositum*, the eighth part of *amplificatio* (Curtius 1944, 273). The increased popularity of *oppositio* in medieval times, which saw the expansion of methods of amplification (a feature reflected in school exercises of the period), no doubt helped to lay the foundations for its extensive use thereafter. Amplification itself is discussed frequently in Renaissance treatises, which tend to stress its importance as a common ingredient in various types of writing, namely poetry, history and oratory. Daniello, for instance, says in his *Della poetica* (1536): 'Sono così dell'uno [istorico] come dell'altro [poeta] proprie l'amplificazioni, le digressioni, la varietà' (Weinberg 1970–4, i. 254). Amplification is also considered a means of producing vividness in poetry. Salviati says in his *Parafrasi e commento della Poetica d'Aristotile* (1586): 'ovunque comparando, diminuendo, *accrescendo*, partitamente recitando, ci si fanno le cose trovate dal poeta quasi toccar con mano, quasi nella lor forma verisimile visibilmente apparire' (Weinberg 1961, 613).

Tasso himself in his later *Discorsi* includes *oppositio* as a source of *diletto* in the *forma graziosa*, a form suitable for the epic poem: 'Ma perché in questa forma bella e ornata si ricerca principalmente il diletto, e 'l diletto nasce dalle metafore, dall'efficacia e dall'opposizione, tutte tre son proprie di questa figura' (*Discorsi*, 233). He goes on to specify *contraposti*, in the form of the *non + ma* construction, as a particularly successful type of *oppositio*: 'e particolarmente mi paion belli i contraposti, come son quelli del Bembo: "… or non pur ardo, / secco già e fral, ma incenerisco e pero"' (p. 233). His attitude towards *contrarietà* and *contradizione* is also positive: 'Bellissimi ancora sono e ornatissimi gli aggiunti i quali implicano contrarietà e contradizione' (p. 234). In the earlier *Discorsi*, however, he had advocated care in the use of antithesis, warning that over-precise attention to an exact correspondence between all elements of the figure may lead to a sense of affectation and pomposity (the latter in particular being a fault which the poet aiming at *gravità* could easily commit):

Per non incorrere nel vizio del gonfio, schivi il magnifico dicitore certe minute diligenze, come di fare che membro a membro corrisponda, verbo a verbo, nome a nome; e non solo in quanto al numero, ma quanto al senso.

Schivi gli antiteti come: tu veloce fanciullo, io vecchio e tardo; ché tutte queste figure, ove si scopre l'affettazione, sono proprie della mediocrità, e sì come molto dilettano, così nulla movono (*Discorsi*, 45).

In identifying instances of *non* + *ma* in the *Gerusalemme liberata* (composed, it will be remembered, between the writing of the earlier and the later *Discorsi*), it is useful to note that two types of *ma*, the second half of the construction, can be discerned. The first type, type I, links up with the preceding phrase to complete the construction. Type II (thus labelled in examples), despite its position immediately after a negative, performs the different function of introducing a new section, or development, in the narrative (usually after a full stop or a semicolon). The latter type of *ma* is illustrated by the following examples:

> Da le notti inquiete il dolce sonno
> bandito fugge, e i languidi mortali
> lusingando ritrarlo a sé no 'l ponno;
> ma pur la sete è il pessimo de' mali (XIII, 58, 1–4)

and:

> Egli alza il ferro, e 'l suo pregar non cura;
> ma colei si trasmuta (XVIII, 35, 1–2).

Underlining the *non* + *ma* unit is an important feature involving form and content. While its basic structure is clearly antithetical, on the semantic level the degree to which the latter half of the construction opposes the former is variable.[14] Tasso touches on this point in his aforementioned phrase warning against too precise a correspondence between the two parts of an antithesis 'non solo in quanto al numero, ma in quanto al senso' (itself an instance of *oppositio*). An antithesis can, in effect, be considered to link two things by bringing them together in one construction.

Analysis of instances of the *non* + *ma* antithesis in the poem reveals two fundamental types of semantic relationship between the constituent halves. The first, which can be described as *contrasting*, follows the pattern: *not a but b*, where *b* is the opposite of *a*. Examples of this pattern are: 'Non *venir* seco tu, ma *resta*' (I, 70, 1), and 'né *seguir* le cale, / ma co' suoi fuggitivi *si ritira*' (III, 31, 49). The second type, which involves the notion of gradation and can be described as *complementary* or *contiguous*, follows the pattern: *not a but a^1*, where a^1 is

---

[14] See Lepschy 1983.

complementary or/and contiguous to *a*. Examples of the second type are: 'in atto / non pur di *rea*, ma di *dannata*' (II, 27, 6) (complementary) and 'sí veloce / ch'uom non li vede *uccidere*, ma *uccisi*' (XX, 77, 4) (contiguous).

Both *a* and *a*¹ may each consist of more than one part. These are invariably parallel in function, as in the examples: 'non pur le *merci* e i *legni*, / ma intere inghiotte le *cittadi* e i *regni*' (I, 43, 7) (contiguous) and 'non si *vede* pur, né pur *s'intende* / *picciol cenno* fra tanti o *bassa voce*, ma se ne sta ciascun *tacito e immoto*' (VI, 49, 4) (complementary or contiguous). On the other hand, some examples of the contrasting type (*not a but b*) are made more complicated in cases where more than two parts are involved in the construction; in other words, when some are contrasted, while others are in a complementary or contiguous relationship. In the following example (with *ma* type II), Ercole and Ulisse are contrasted, whereas their actions are in a contiguous relationship: 'Ercole ... non osò di tentar l'alto oceano: / segno le mète ... / ma quei segni sprezzò ch'egli prescrisse, / di veder vago e di saper, Ulisse' (XV, 25).

Instances of the contrasting type of *non* + *ma* construction outnumber the complementary or contiguous variety by about 2:1 (*c.*150:70). The contrasts, which show a simpler semantic relationship, lend themselves to broad semantic grouping. The largest group (around sixty-five) can be seen to concern, not surprisingly, the field of actions. Examples of this group are: *edifica* vs. *move ruine* (I, 25) and *venir* vs. *resta* (I, 70).[15] The next largest group (around forty-five) is that of attributes, mostly in the sense of qualifier (adjective), but also in the sense of quality (noun); for instance, *minor* vs. *doppio* (III, 59), *pietà* vs. *util* (IV, 66), and *timor* vs. *santa voglia* (V, 47).[16] Another, small-

---

[15] Other examples in the field of actions are: *celi* vs. *riveli* (II, 15), *seguir* vs. *si ritira* (III, 31), *aspettàr* vs. *volando uscian* (IV, 18), *serba* vs. *cangia* (IV, 87), *bada* vs. *si rivolge altrove* (V, 31), *si ritenne* vs. *volse* (V, 40), *in ritirarsi tarda* vs. *si raccoglie e si ristringe* (VI, 43), *aspetta* vs. *s'affretta* (VI, 89), *seguir* vs. *s'è ritenuto* (VI, 112), *rifiuti* vs. *è chiesta* (VII, 66), *si stanca* vs. *si rinforza* (VII, 91), *s'allenta* vs. *è piú fero* (VII, 107), *s'allenta* vs. *noce* (VIII, 23), *cade* vs. *oppone* (IX, 52), *v'entra* vs. *passa* (XIII, 3), *resista* vs. *in fuga è mosso* (XV, 52) and *s'invia* vs. *schiva* (XVI, 72).

[16] Other examples in the field of attributes are: *turbati e rotti* vs. *con securezza e con quiete* (VI, 4), *basso* vs. *eccelse* (VII, 9), *le solite sue* vs. *dal re* (VII, 51), *nostri in parte* vs. *tutti loro* (VIII, 65), *umile* vs. *insuperbito* (IX, 46), *atti* vs. *paventosi* (IX, 77), *feroci* vs. *di pietate e d'umiltà* (XI, 6), *morte* vs. *vivaci* (XII, 97), *magno* vs. *bassa . . . e breve* (XIV, 10), *sotterranei* vs. *aerea* (XIV, 43), *fatto* vs. *nato* (XIV, 48), *vera* vs. *magica* (XIV, 61), *vote* vs. *feconde* (XV, 27), *oscuro* vs. *illustre* (XVIII, 41), *lento* vs. *intrepido e invitto* (XVIII, 75), *furtive e torte* vs. *dritto* (XIX, 59), *vago* vs. *con arte* (XIX, 69), *certo* vs. *varia* (XX, 49), *espresso* vs. *indistinto* (XX, 51) and *saldo* vs. *caduti* (XX, 121).

er group (around seventeen) concerns people, and frequently has hierarchical implications; for example, *Tancredi* vs. *ignoto campion* (VII, 84), *il forte vulgo e gli assoldati* vs. *fanciulli e vecchi* (XI, 26), *guerrier* vs. *inventor di machine* (XIX, 3), and, of special interest in terms of gender portrayal, Argante's taunt 'o *Franchi* no, ma *Franche*' (XI, 61).

The semantic structure of the complementary/contiguous group is more complicated, due to the oblique and adjacent, rather than direct and opposite, relationship between the two parts. The complementary examples can be divided into two closely related groups. The first group consists of complementary aspects or stages which together form a complete unit. For example, guilty and condemned ('in atto / non pur di *rea*, ma di *dannata* ei scorse' II, 27, 4), soul and body ('non pur l'*alma* e la vita, / ma la forma del *corpo* anco e del volto' XVIII, 69, 3), city walls and gates ('per le *mura* non sol, ma per le *porte*' XVIII, 105, 2), identity, both personal and social ('Indarno chiedi / quel c'ho per uso di non far palese. / Ma *chiunque io* mi sia, tu inanzi vedi / *un di quei due che la gran torre accese*' XII, 61, 2) (*ma* type II).

The second complementary group consists of similar aspects of one thing. For instance, earthly desire is seen to concern possessions, power and honour ('non cupidigia in lui d'*oro* o d'*impero*, / ma d'*onor* brame immoderate, ardenti' I, 10, 5). Time is made up of future and present ('Né sol la tema di *futuro danno* / con sollecito moto il cor le scote, / ma de *le piaghe ch'egli avea* l'affanno' VI, 66, 1), and of present and past ('Né sol l'estrane genti avien che mova / *il duro caso e 'l gran publico danno*, / ma *l'antiche cagioni*' VIII, 73, 1). Physical needs include those of food and sleep ('*Cibo* non prende già ... / ma 'l *sonno*, che de' miseri mortali / è co 'l suo dolce oblio posa e quiete, / sopí co' sensi i suoi dolori' VII, 4, 1) (*ma* type II). Sensory perceptions can be visual and auditory ('né d'entrar *s'avede*, / ma *sente* poi che suona a lui di dietro / la porta, e 'n loco il serra oscuro e tetro' VII, 45, 6). Cures can be achieved with herbs and magic words ('*Dittamo e croco* non avea, ma *note* / per uso tal sapea potenti e maghe' XIX, 113, 3) (*ma* type II). Warfare can take the form of attack and siege ('piú non s'assaglia, / ma *si stringa* la torre' XIX, 128, 2), surrounding and blockading the enemy ('non avria potuto / (cotanto ella volgea) *cingerla* a pieno; / ma le vie tutte ond'aver pote aiuto / tenta Goffredo d'*impedirle* almeno' III, 65, 3) (*ma* type II).

Contiguous examples are those which are adjacent on the same paradigm, often presenting an ascending degree leading to the cumulative effect of a graded climax, or sometimes expressing a descending degree. Some of the following examples can also be regarded as complementaries showing similar aspects of one thing. Examples of an ascending order resulting in a cumulative effect (frequently involving the additional use of *solo* or *pur*) are as follows.

Instances in which numbers or quantities are involved:

> Colpo che ad *un* sol noccia unqua non scende,
> ma *indiviso* è il dolor d'ogni ferita (I, 57, 5–6) (*ma* type II)
>
> né solo i *diece* a lei promessi aspetta
> ma di furto menarne *altri* confida (V, 1, 3–4) (*ma* type II)
>
> e che non solo è di pugnare accinto
> e con *uno* e con *duo* del campo ostile,
> ma dopo il *terzo*, il *quarto* accetta e 'l *quinto* (VI, 16, 1–3) (*ma* type II)
>
> né già soli *costor*, ma in altre guise
> *molti* piagò di loro e *molti* uccise (IX, 90, 7–8)
>
> Clorinda fui, né *sol* qui spirto umano
> albergo in questa pianta rozza e dura,
> ma *ciascun altro ancor*, franco o pagano
> astretto è qui da novo incanto e strano (XIII, 43, 1–4) (*ma* type II)
>
> Né *quelli* pur, ma *qual* piú in guerra è chiaro
> la lingua al vanto ha baldanzosa e presta (XVII, 53, 1–2)
>
> ... e pur non *questo* solo,
> ma di Guasconi *ancor* lascia *uno stuolo* (XX, 6, 7–8)
>
> ... *squadra* non pare
> ma un'*oste immensa* ... (XVII, 17, 1–2).

Instances using the concept of size:

> l'ocean che non pur le *merci* e i *legni*,
> ma intere inghiotte le *cittadi* e i *regni* (I, 43, 7–8)
>
> ... e par che crolli
> non pur le *quercie* ma le *rocche* e i *colli* (VII, 115, 7–8)
>
> Costui non solo incominciò a comporre
> *catapulte, balliste* ed *arieti* ...
> ma fece *opra maggior* : mirabil *torre* (XVIII, 43, 1–2, 5) (*ma* type II).

Examples denoting intensity or degree, as of colour:

> e smarrisce il bel volto in un colore
> che non è *pallidezza*, ma *candore* (II, 26, 7–8)

reaction:

> … dal mio re con *istupore* accolte
> sono non sol, ma con *diletto* insieme (II, 63, 3–4)

materials:

> … ancor che fina
> fosse e d'*acciaio* no, ma di *diamante* (VIII, 22, 5–6)

unconsciousness:

> né già fu *sonno* il suo quieto e soave,
> ma fu *stupor* ch'Aletto al cor gl'infuse (VIII, 59, 2–3)

and suffering:

> Ei come gli altri in *lagrime* non solve
> il duol …
> ma i bianchi crini suoi d'*immonda polve*
> *si sparge e brutta, e fiede il volto e 'l petto* (XII, 101, 3–6).

Instances showing a descending degree are less frequent. For example, in relation to the result of a blow:

> l'elmo non *fende* già, ma lui ben *scote* (VII, 42, 3)
> l'elmo fatal (ché non si può) non *fende*,
> ma lo *scote* in arcion con piú d'un crollo (XX, 103, 3–4)
> Non è *mortal*, ma *grave* il colpo e 'l salto (XI, 36, 1)

the social order:

> … promisi in voto
> non pur l'opera qui di *capitano*,
> ma d'impiegarvi ancor, quando che fosse,
> qual *privato guerrier* l'arme e le posse (XI, 23, 5–8)

and the manner of achieving fame:

> e li guida Arontèo cui nulla onora
> *pregio* o *virtú*, ma i *titoli* il fan chiaro (XVII, 16, 3–4)

A closer look at a few of these examples further clarifies the mechanics of this complementary/contiguous construction. One example of special interest is that involving colour: 'e smarrisce il bel volto in un colore / che non è *pallidezza*, ma *candore*' (II, 26, 7–8). This is often related by editors of the poem to a line in Petrarch's

Trionfi mortali: 'Pallida no ma piú che neve bianca' (I, 166). Tasso's antithesis, however, has additional resonance, due partly to the homonymic quality of *candore*, which refers both to a colour (whiteness) and to a moral quality (forthrightness). On the one hand, this colour reference is in a contiguous relationship to the tone reference in *pallidezza*, while on the other hand forthrightness contrasts with the connotation evoked by *pallidezza*, that of faintheartedness. The dual presence of contiguity and contrast, in themselves contrasting, leads to a certain tension leading to the poetic effect achieved by this particular antithesis.

Another example showing the presence of both contiguity and contrast in each of the two key words is the following: 'Cosa vedi, signor, non pur *mortale*, / ma già *morta* a i diletti ...' (IV, 36, 3–4). *Mortale*, referring to limited lifespan, is in a contiguous relationship with *morta*, in an expression of ascending degree. However, the two words are also brought into contrast in that *mortale* is used to refer to the still-living, in opposition to *morta*, the already dead. The contiguous elements of personal and social identity in the following example can also be seen to operate in a complex way. A disguised Clorinda replies scornfully to Tancredi:

> ... Indarno chiedi
> quel c'ho per uso di non far palese.
> Ma *chiunque io mi sia, tu inanzi vedi*
> *un di quei due che la gran torre accese* (XII, 61, 1–4).

The effect on Tancredi of this revelation by Clorinda of her actions in battle, in other words, of her social identity, is to infuriate him, thereby precipitating the final, fatal stage of the duel that culminates with her death. Disclosure of her personal identity, which would have answered his actual question ('che 'l tuo nome e 'l tuo stato a me tu scopra'), would have inspired the opposite reaction. A strong element of dramatic irony is therefore present, which serves to heighten the narrative tension at this point. This example also performs the straightforward rhetorical function of a taunt, aimed in a duel by one participant at the other.

One fundamental function that has been posited for the *non* + *ma* construction and which, it has been suggested, may even account for its existence in the first place, is a purely metrical one. Gallo, quoting the medieval rhetorician Tibino, believes that:

It is conceivable that *oppositio* arose as a rhyme-finding device: 'The eighth way of finding suitable rhymes is called *contrarii positio*, it is when the writer cannot find the riming word; let him use then the phrase of the contrary meaning with the negative sign' (Gallo 1971, 188 n. 125).

It is certainly reasonable to assume that any means of amplification provides access to a further fund of rhyming opportunities. Metrical considerations aside, this construction appears to fulfil a variety of functions that may, on the whole, be described as rhetorical or narrative in nature.

The key to the narrative functions, which can be seen at work mainly in the third-person narrative (and also in direct speech when a character is the narrator of events), is to be found in the way the narrative progresses. This happens in gradual stages, step by step, as opposed to presenting only the actions themselves. The narrative is constructed along amplificatory lines, exploring areas related to, or preceding, action, such as possibility or motivation. The entire narrative may, indeed, be regarded as a form of amplification of one action, the liberation of Jerusalem. The narrative depicts not only the action itself, the result of which is already known at the onset from the title, but also the complex of stages contributing to that action.

The *non* + *ma* unit forms a fundamental part of this amplificatory procedure, a role with which, as has been noted, it was associated in medieval and Renaissance poetics. The way this construction amplifies is repetitive in nature, portraying what did not/could not/might not happen, as well as what did. Many instances attract attention to what someone does not do, before showing what they then do, as in the following examples:

> l'intrepido Soldan che il fero assalto
> sente venir, no 'l fugge e no 'l declina;
> ma se gli spinge incontra … (IX, 49, 3–5)
>
> Né pose indugio al suo desir, ma ratto
> d'elmo s'armò … (XX, 74, 5–6)
>
> né poi, ciò fatto, in ritirarsi tarda,
> ma si raccoglie e si ristringe in guarda (VI, 43, 7–8).

An extended version of this, with the mere addition of *piú*, shows action that is in the process of happening and then ceases, together with the following action:

> né pote l'ira omai tener *piú* chiusa,
> ma grida … (V, 26, 6–7)
> … né sovra lui *piú* bada;

> ma si rivolge altrove … (V, 31, 6–7)
>
> … *più* fra lor non si ritenne,
> ma vèr Rinaldo immantinente volse
> un suo destrier … (V, 40, 2–4)
>
> … *più* non aspetta,
> ma da quella a la sua stanza congiunta
> l'arme involate di portar s'affretta (VI, 89, 2–4)
>
> *più* non osò por la vittoria in forse,
> ma fermò i giri … (XX, 108, 6–7)
>
> … e *più* non bada,
> ma giú se 'n viene … (XX, 84, 8; 85, 1).

The spanning of two stanzas by the last quotation further heightens the sense of speed with which the action takes place.

The use of *però* helps to portray an action that took place despite the circumstances, and so heightens the heroism of the action, as in the following examples:

> … a vòto batte
> e spande senza pro l'ire e le posse;
> non si stanca *però*, ma raddoppiando
> va tagli e punte … (VII, 91, 5–8)
>
> Né perché senta inacerbir le doglie
> de le sue piaghe, e grave il corpo ed egro,
> vien *però* che si posi e l'arme spoglie,
> ma travagliando il dí ne passa integro (X, 5, 1–4)
>
> non s'accheta ei *però*, ma 'l suono e 'l moto
> ritien de l'onde anco agitate e grosse (XII, 63, 3–4)
>
> … ascolta
> quel che da lei novo rimbombo uscia,
> né *però* il piede audace indietro volta,
> ma securo e sprezzante è come pria (XIII, 26, 3–6).

The inclusion of *forse* similarly amplifies the action by prefacing what happened with the possibility of what might have happened:

> che *forse* il velocissimo Aquilino
> non sottraggeasi e rimaneane oppresso;
> ma l'aiuto invisibile vicino
> non mancò … (VII, 92, 3–6)

and:

> né *forse* colà dentro era il Soldano
> dal fatal suo nemico assai securo;
> ma già suona a ritratta il capitano (XIX, 50, 3–5).

Sometimes emotional and mental processes are also detailed by the *non* + *ma* construction (in the form of *né* + *pur*, and *né* + *ma* in the following examples). This provides amplificatory details in the form of motive and reason for the action that takes place in the latter half of the construction:

> ... né vide fuga o scampo
> da la presente irreparabil morte;
> pur, tutto essendo testimonio il campo,
> fa sembianti d'intrepido e di forte (V, 27, 3–6)

and:

> Né creder può che l'uomo a fere imprese
> avezzo sempre, or lento in ozio stia;
> ma, d'averlo aspettando aspro nemico,
> parla al fedel suo messaggiero Enrico (I, 67, 5–8).

As well as playing an important part in narrative progression, the *non* + *ma* construction also fulfils the closely related function of producing narrative precision, particularly where description is concerned. When what is being described also happens to be an action, both narrative progression and precision are involved. Precision is achieved by means of a build-up leading to a climax that can result, for instance, in the cumulative effect discussed above. The first half of the construction states what something is not, while the second is able to define all the more precisely what it *is*, due to the preceding exclusion. This also has the effect of prolonging attention already secured for the object of the description, thereby emphasizing it. This form of emphasis can be seen as a characteristic feature of the construction. For example:

> che non armento od animal lanuto,
> né preda simíl, ma ch'è seguita
> dal suo german Clorinda impaurita (VI, 112, 6–8)

> mai non si scorge a se stessa simile,
> ma in diversi colori al sol si tinge (XV, 5, 3–4)

> non d'incanti terribile né lieta,
> piena d'orror ma de l'orror innato (XVIII, 38, 3–4)

> e cerca il ferro no, ma il corpo averso (XIX, 12, 4)

> Non lascia il desir vago a freno sciolto,
> ma gira gli occhi cupidi con arte (XIX, 69, 3–4) (*ma* type II)

> Non v'è silenzio e non v'è grido espresso,
> ma odi un non so che roco e indistinto (XX, 51, 5–6) (*ma*
>   type II)
>
> Pugna questa non è, ma strage sola (XX, 56, 7).

A particular variation of narrative precision occurs with the use of *pur*, which sometimes modifies the first half from what is *not*, to what is *not only*, with the second half detailing what is additional and note-worthy. For example:

> Né *pur* l'umana gente or si rallegra
> e dei suoi danni a ristorar si viene,
> ma la terra ...
> la pioggia in sé raccoglie e si rintegra (XIII, 78, 1–5)
>
> né *pur* n'ode Rinaldo il romor solo,
> ma d'un messaggio ancor nova piú certa (XX, 101, 3–4)
>
> ch'ivi non *pur* fra gli uomini si pugna,
> ma le machine insieme anco fan pugna (XVIII, 79, 7–8)
>
> e non si vede *pur*, né *pur* s'intende
> picciol cenno fra tanti o bassa voce,
> ma se ne sta ciascun tacito e immoto (VI, 49, 5–7).

The use of *sol* and analogous forms has a similar effect. For instance:

> Né *solamente* discacciò costoro
> la spada micidial dal dolce mondo,
> ma spinti insieme a crudel morte foro (XX, 40, 1–3)
>
> Né *sol* non v'è chi la tenzon rifiuti,
> ma ella omai da molti a prova è chiesta (VII, 66, 5–6)

and:

> Né *sol* la tema di futuro danno
> con sollecito moto il cor le scote,
> ma de le piaghe ch'egli avea l'affanno
> è cagion che quetar l'alma non pote (VI, 66, 1–4).

This last example also serves to refer forward to future events in the narrative, in a foreshadowing of the occasion when Erminia's present fears of a *futuro danno* will be realized as she discovers Tancredi seriously wounded in Canto XIX. The function of narrative progression is also at work here, in that her worries about present time, in the latter half of the construction, prompt her to leave the city and join Tancredi, thereby precipitating a series of events that will include

Tancredi's departure from the Christian camp.

The function of producing narrative precision is closely linked with the creation of vividness, bearing in mind that the Renaissance saw *amplificatio* in general as a means of creating *enargeia* in poetry. One particularly effective example is: 'sí veloce / ch'uom non li vede uccidere, ma uccisi' (XX, 77, 3–4), which vividly portrays the speed with which Solimano despatches his opponents. Emphasis on the reaction of the spectators in turn highlights the drama of the spectacle, in this case the first duel between Tancredi and Argante, in the lines: 'e non si vede pur, né pur s'intende / picciol cenno fra tanti o bassa voce, / ma se ne sta ciascuno tacito e immoto' (VI, 49, 5–7).

Finally, the use of *già* in providing both narrative precision and progression further emphasizes the negative element, as in the following instances:

> Giacea, prono non *già*, ma come vòlto
> ebbe sempre a le stelle il suo desire (VIII, 33, 1–2)

> né *già* fu sonno il suo queto e soave,
> ma fu stupor ch'Aletto al cor gl'infuse (VIII, 59, 2–3)

> né 'l celò *già*, ma con enfiate labbia
> si trasse avanti al capitano … (II, 88, 3–4)

> ma *già* no 'l mostra, anzi la voce alzando (VIII, 21, 5)

> *Già* non mira Tancredi ove il circasso
> la spaventosa fronte al cielo estolle,
> ma move il suo destrier con lento passo,
> volgendo gli occhi ov'è colei su 'l colle (VI, 27, 1–4).

Turning now to the rhetorical functions performed by this construction when used in direct speech, the basic function is that of persuasion itself, as in the following examples:

> … È mio parer ch'a i novi albori,
> come concluso fu, piú non s'assaglia,
> ma si stringa la torre … (XIX, 128, 1–3)

> Cedi! non fia timor, ma santa voglia,
> ch'a questo ceder tuo palma si serba (V, 47, 3–4)

and:

> Pure io femina sono, e nulla riede
> mia morte in danno a la città smarrita;
> ma se tu cadi (tolga il Ciel gli augúri),

or chi sarà che piú difenda i muri? (XII, 8, 5–8) (*ma* type II).

The rhetorical nature of this last example, the purpose of which is to dissuade Argante from stealing Clorinda's limelight by going out to burn the tower with her, is made patently clear in the light of her real feelings expressed in her soliloquy a few stanzas previously, when she complains of her role as archer: 'Dunque sol tanto a donna e piú non lice?' (XII, 3, 8). Reasoning processes feature prominently in some cases, as in Tancredi's debate with himself when confronted with the city of fire in the enchanted wood:

> Non mai la vita, ove cagione onesta
> del comun pro la chieda, altri risparmi,
> ma né prodigo sia d'anima grande
> uom degno; e tale è ben chi qui la spande (XIII, 34, 5–8)
>   (*ma* type II).

The figure of *negatio*, which consists of pretending to deny what is really affirmed (the deliberate, rhetorical equivalent of Freudian negation) is present on some occasions in the first half of the construction as part of the attempt to persuade. Goffredo, for instance, communicates his decision regarding Armida in terms that attempt to mollify his refusal to help her

> Stata è da voi la mia sentenza udita,
> ch'era non di negare a la donzella,
> ma di darle in stagion matura aita (V, 3, 2–4).

The overt contradiction posited between 'to deny' and 'not to deny' is betrayed, however, by the qualifier *in stagion matura* in the latter part, in conjunction with what is obviously a *negatio* in the first. The actual relationship here is not that of two contradictories ('to deny' and 'not to deny'), but, rather, of two complementaries ('to deny in principle' and 'to deny at present'). Both halves, in other words, signify denial.
A similar case is that of Orcano's comment to the King about Argante's enthusiasm:

> … O signor, già non accuso
> il fervor di magnifiche parole …
> Ma si conviene a te, cui fatto il corso
> de le cose e de' tempi han sí prudente,
> impor colà de' tuoi consigli il morso
> dove costui se ne trascorre ardente (X, 40, 1–2; 41, 1–4)
>   (*ma* type II).

The *negatio* in the first part is laid bare as the construction progresses, resulting not in the contradiction 'to criticize' vs. 'not to criticize', but in the complementary pair 'to criticize' and 'to persuade someone else to do likewise', with unqualified criticism as the core of the message.

While persuasion is at the root of all the rhetorical functions, certain subdivisions are also discernible, such as didacticism, giving orders, incitement to action, taunt, praise, flattery and request. Didacticism and giving orders occur in speeches by superiors to inferiors. Examples of the *non* + *ma* construction which serve as orders now follow.

Goffredo to Enrico:

> Non venir seco tu, ma resta appresso
> al re de' Greci a procurar l'aiuto (I, 70, 1–2)

Spirit to Gernando:

> ... né già soffrirlo déi,
> ma ciò che puoi dimostra e ciò che sei (V, 22, 7–8)

the now-divine Ugone to Goffredo:

> Però non chieder tu ...
> ma richiesto concedi ... (XIV, 16, 5–7)

the Mago to Carlo and Ubaldo:

> né le vivande poste in verde riva
> v'allettin poi, né le donzelle infide ...
> ma voi, gli sguardi e le parole accorte
> sprezzando, entrate pur ne l'alte porte (XIV, 75, 3–8) (*ma*
>   type II)

the Mago to Rinaldo:

> Or odi i detti miei, contrari al canto
> de le sirene, e non ti sian molesti,
> ma gli serba nel cor ... (XVII, 60, 5–7)

Piero to Rinaldo:

> Deh! né voce che dolce o pianga o canti,
> né beltà che soave o rida o guardi,
> con tenere lusinghe il cor ti pieghi,
> ma sprezza i finti aspetti e i finti preghi (XVIII, 10, 5–8).

Didacticism is present in the following examples:

Ugone to Goffredo:

> nulla eguale a tai nomi ha in sé di magno,
> ma è bassa palude e breve stagno (XIV, 10, 7–8)

Fortuna to Carlo and Ubaldo:

> né già d'abitator le terre han vòte,
> ma son come le vostre anco feconde (XV, 27, 3–4)

the Mago to Rinaldo:

> Signor, non sotto l'ombra in piaggia molle
> tra fonti e fior, tra ninfe e tra sirene,
> ma in cima a l'erto e faticoso colle
> de la virtú riposto è il nostro bene (XVII, 61, 1–4).

Incitement to action is the rhetorical function of the following examples:

Argante to Aladino:

> A lor né i prandi mai turbati e rotti,
> né molestate son le cene liete,
> anzi egualmente i dí lunghi e le notti
> traggon con securezza e con quiete (VI, 4, 1–4)

> non di morir pugnando ed onorato,
> ma di vita e di palma anco avrei speme (VI, 6, 3–4)

Argillano to the Christians:

> nostri in parte non son, ma tutti loro
> i trionfi, gli onor, le terre e l'oro (VIII, 65, 7–8)

Emireno to Ormondo:

> Non fia – l'altro dicea – che 'l re cortese
> l'opera grande inonorata lasse:
> ben ei darà ciò che per te si chiede,
> ma congiunta l'avrai d'alta mercede (XIX, 64, 5–8) (*ma* type II).

The construction is also used as part of a taunt when the aim is to persuade the addressee that he is in an inferior position:

Argillano to the Arabs:

> Non regger voi de gli elmi e de gli scudi
> sète atti il peso, o 'l petto armarvi e il dorso,

> ma commettete paventosi e nudi
> i colpi al vento e la salute al corso (IX, 77, 1–4)

Argante to the Christians:

> Non gioveranvi le caverne estrane,
> ma vi morrete come belve in tane (XI, 36, 7–8)
> … o Franchi no, ma Franche? (XI, 61, 8).

Praise is the function of the following examples:

Erminia of Goffredo:

> e non minor che duce è cavaliero,
> ma del doppio valor tutte ha le parti (III, 59, 3–4)

Carlo of Sveno:

> Ripercote percosso e non s'allenta,
> ma quanto offeso è piú tanto piú noce (VIII, 23, 3–4).

Flattery, in other words praise with an ulterior motive (in this case to help ensure that Erminia does not betray him), is the purpose of the antithesis in Vafrino's remark to her:

> Non t'ho (che mi sovenga) unqua veduto,
> e degna pur d'esser mirata sei (XIX, 80, 5–6).

Lastly, the *non* + *ma* unit serves the function of a request in Guelfo's words to Goffredo:

> né soffrir ch'egli torpa in vil riposo,
> ma rende insieme la sua gloria ad esso (XIV, 24, 3–4).

Some examples are of particular rhetorical interest in that they maximize the emphatic potential of the construction to produce a normative statement that can present its message not once, but twice, by stating both what *should be* and what *should not*. This provides a useful vehicle for ideological reinforcement. The subordination of earthly (personal) desires to religious (social) duty is frequently stressed in this manner. This is firmly established at the beginning of the poem, when Goffredo, in an almost figurative litotes, is shown laudably setting aside worldly aspirations, while Baldovin, Tancredi and Boemondo are criticized for nurturing them:

> vide Goffredo che scacciar desia
> de la santa città gli empi pagani,

e pien di fé, di zelo, ogni mortale
gloria, imperio, tesor mette in non cale (I, 8, 5–8)

Ma vede in Baldovin cupido ingegno,
ch'a l'umane grandezze intento aspira:
vede Tancredi aver la vita a sdegno,
tanto un suo vano amor l'ange e martira:
e fondar Boemondo al novo regno
suo d'Antiochia alti princípi mira (I, 9, 1–6)

e cotanto internarsi in tal pensiero,
ch'altra impresa non par che piú rammenti (I, 10, 1–2) (*ma*
type II).

The fact that this is all seen through the eyes of God justifies and so
further reinforces the message, which is repeated at various points.
For instance, with reference to Goffredo:

Non che 'l vedersi a gli altri in Ciel preporre
d'aura d'ambizion gli gonfi il petto,
ma il suo voler piú nel voler s'infiamma
del suo Signor, come favilla in fiamma (I, 18, 5–8)

Goffredo to Alete:

ché non ambiziosi avari affetti
ne spronaro a l'impresa, e ne fur guida . . .
ma la sua [God's] man ch'i duri cor penètra
soavemente, e gli ammollisce e spetra (II, 83, 1–2, 7–8)

Carlo, speaking of Sveno:

ma piú ch'altra cagione, il mosse il zelo
non del terren ma de l'onor del Cielo (VIII, 7, 7–8).

As well as underlining the dominance of social duty over individual fulfilment, the structure of the social hierarchy itself is also reinforced by means of the *non* + *ma* construction. A *guerrier* is thus seen
to be superior in status to an *inventor di machine* in Argante's taunting
of Tancredi:

benché non qual guerrier, ma qui venuto
quasi inventor di machine tu parmi (XIX, 3, 3–4).

Clorinda's success in battle is expressed in terms of class, as she stains
her arrows 'non di sangue plebeo ma del piú degno' (XI, 41, 7). The
obedience of an inferior towards a superior, which is basic to the

maintenance of social order, is also shown using this type of antithesis. The dynamics of obedient behaviour are indicated as Carlo and Ubaldo do not ask further questions, in other words challenge or imply the insufficiency of their superior's words, words inspired in turn by a higher power. On the contrary, they show their acceptance of their inferior position by remaining silent:

> ... e più da lui [Piero] non chiese
> Carlo o l'altro che seco iva messaggio,
> ma furo ubidienti a le parole
> che spirito divin dettar gli suole (XIV, 31, 5–8) (*ma* type II).

The negative construction in the *Gerusalemme liberata* can be seen to fulfil a wide range of functions. These range from the overtly rhetorical and poetical, to the overtly and covertly ideological. Rhetorical and poetic use of figures such as *oppositio* and *negatio* took place in the sixteenth-century context of rules and assumptions whose roots were clearly situated in ancient rhetoric, and which still figure in language use today. The process of ideological reinforcement inherent in some of the examples discussed also continues as part of the wider western philosophical and logical framework governing methods of communication. As such, ideological tendentiousness is inscribed in both the spoken and the written word, as well as in gesture. That denial signified by negation can be seen to function at times on an involuntary, and what might be termed unconscious, level, has been signalled in this chapter. The following chapter pursues this line of argument further by exploring the narrative fulcrum of the *Gerusalemme liberata* from a psychoanalytical perspective.

CHAPTER 5

The Mirror Episode

On its most obvious level, the *Gerusalemme liberata* is an account of deeds performed by exemplary heroes who successfully complete their quest despite various obstructing factors.[1] However, although pagans provide the apparent obstacle to Christian heroes, it is one that is patently surmountable, as the title of the poem immediately suggests, and the frequent intervention of God leads one inevitably to assume. In effect, the essential nexus of opposition is not located at the level of two hostile societies in combat, or even of individuals of different religions pitted against each other, although this clearly provides the overt framework conforming to the dominant ideology of the time. It is to be found, rather, in the conflictual nature of the relationship between the individual and the external world, the latter especially, but not exclusively, represented by the social group.

The notion of the individual in the context of society is particularly important in the epic genre, and it is the problematic nature of this relationship between the individual and the group that is foregrounded in this poem. Hence it is the conflict taking place within, and almost contrary to, the overt framework, that is actually given prominence in the narrative. As a result, a pagan such as Solimano appears in the same sympathetic light as the central Christian heroes, and the final taking of Jerusalem is an anti-climax instead of the high point. Emphasis on the individual, and the resulting prevalence of certain antithetical elements, particularly those of pleasure as opposed to duty, have, indeed, become a critical commonplace as the distinguishing characteristics of the poem.

The relationship between the individual and society, as portrayed by Tasso's text, acquires an additional resonance when assimilated with a possible third narrative level which emerges in the light of an

[1] An earlier version of this chapter appeared as 'The Mirror Episode in Canto XVI of the *Gerusalemme liberata*', *The Italianist*, 3 (1983), 30–46.

insight of the French psychoanalyst Jacques Lacan.[2] This takes the
form of a study of the significance of the mirror in the psychological
development of the infant, entitled 'The Mirror Stage as Formative
of the Function of the *I*' (Lacan 1985).[3] The mirror itself, definable
as any substance (water, glass, metal) used to cast a reflection, performs a distinctly social function, being one of the means whereby
the individual observes and checks the outer self, and it appears, not
surprisingly, throughout the ages and in a variety of contexts as a literary commonplace. In so doing, the mirror invariably retains its
essential, dynamic duality, inherent in the basic phenomenon of an
object being reflected and therefore repeated and duplicated, yet
different. This may be in the form of two mutually antagonistic but
inexorably interdependent forces, as in the theme of the double, or,
on the other hand, in the form of a duality of which one part desires
to be unified with the other, with fatal results, as in the Narcissus
theme (Rank 1979). As well as being part of such larger, stock
themes, the mirror is used in the expression of a multitude of contrasting, conflictual pairs, such as truth vs. falsehood, present vs.
future, inner self vs. outer self. As regards the relation of the self to
the self and, by extension, of the self to the outer world, a psychoan-
alytic elaboration of the significance of the perception of a dual self,
effected by means of a visual reflection, may uncover certain of the
motivating forces behind the function of the mirror as a fundamental
literary commonplace, and, consequently, reveal a further dimension
of the text.

Lacan's mirror stage

The basic tenet in the notion of the mirror stage, as expounded by
Lacan, is that it represents a step forward in the psychological
development of the infant aged between six and eighteen months.
This occurs in the form of a distinction made by the infant, on rec-

[2] In his article 'Armida allo specchio', Sempoux comments that, with the figure of
Armida, 'zone pericolose della psicologia del profondo' are touched. He quotes
Lacan's phrase 'al posto dell'altro' in this context, but does not expand this notion
further, restricting his treatment of the mirror episode to the themes of magic and
inversion (Sempoux 1978).

[3] The notion of the mirror stage was first presented by Lacan at the International
Congress of Psychoanalysis in 1936 and elaborated in 1949 under the title 'Le Stade
du miroir comme formateur de la fonction du *Je* telle qu'elle nous est révélée dans
l'expérience psychanalytique' (Lacan 1966).

ognizing its reflection in a mirror, between the self of the *Innenwelt* (the self as it has been felt to be until this moment) and the self in the context of an *Umwelt* (perception of the self in a new relationship). Lacan explains: 'I am led, therefore, to regard the function of the mirror stage as a particular case of the function of the *imago*, which is to establish a relationship between the organism and its reality—or, as they say, between the *Innenwelt* and the *Umwelt*' (Lacan 1985, 4). A transformation then takes place as the result of an identification of the pre-existing, unconscious, instinctual representation of the self (the *imago*) with the reflection of that self perceived in the mirror (the 'counterpart'):

We have only to understand the mirror stage *as an identification*, in the full sense that analysis gives to the term: namely, the transformation that takes place in the subject when he assumes an image—whose predestination to this phase-effect is sufficiently indicated by the use, in analytic theory, of the ancient term *imago* (Lacan 1985, 2).

This new awareness of an additional, contextual facet in the existence of the self opens up the possibility of a dialectic. The self, no longer able to be completely self-oriented, moves towards a new phase marked by interaction (most notably through language) with the world outside, and in particular with other members of society: 'This moment in which the mirror-stage comes to an end inaugurates, by the identification with the *imago* of the counterpart ... the dialectic that will henceforth link the *I* to socially elaborated situations' (Lacan 1985, 5).

The transformation undergone in the mirror stage, namely the process of recognition that takes place as the *imago* is identified with the counterpart of the reflection, is a pleasurable experience, described with words denoting play (*ludiquement*) and jubilation (*jubilatoire*) (Lacan 1966, 90). The particular type of libidinal energy engaged at this moment is that of primary narcissism: 'the term primary narcissism, by which analytic doctrine designates the libidinal investment characteristic of that moment' (Lacan 1985, 6). This is a stage representing total freedom for the *I*, which is still in the primordial, ideal form, and as yet unhampered by the inevitably restrictive dialectic of social interaction characterizing the new phase, of which this joyful mirror stage, ironically, is the precursor. Lacan says:

This jubilant assumption of his specular image by the child at the *infans* stage ... would seem to exhibit in an exemplary situation the symbolic matrix in which the *I* is precipitated in a primordial form, before it is objectified in the dialectic of identification with the other, and before language restores to it, in the universal, its function as subject (Lacan 1985, 2).

By recognizing an image of itself, and thereby rupturing the *Innenwelt* from the *Umwelt*, the presence of an 'outer self' takes shape. This outer self is the self perceived from the outside as part of a larger structure, within the bounds of which, necessarily, it must act. The outer self is accepted in addition to, and potentially in conflict with, the more familiar 'inner self'.

The dynamic tension latent in this duality is heightened as movement towards the new phase on completion of the mirror stage (the 'deflection of the specular *I* into the social *I*') entails the process of 'normalization'. This may be understood in terms of repression; in other words, the imposition of restraint on the libidinal energy of the primordial *I* by means of socioculturally determined structures. Lacan explains this important moment as follows:

It is this moment that decisively tips the whole of human knowledge into mediatization through the desire of the other, constitutes its objects in an abstract equivalence by the co-operation of others and turns the *I* into that apparatus for which every instinctual thrust constitutes a danger, even though it should correspond to a natural maturation—the very normalization of this maturation being henceforth dependent, in man, on a cultural mediation as exemplified, in the case of the sexual object, by the Oedipus complex (Lacan 1985, 5–6).

Conflict is already present at birth in the form of primordial discord (related by Lacan to the anatomically premature birth of the infant) (Lacan 1985, 4). This initial discord is temporarily appeased by the pleasures of primary narcissism and identification, of which the mirror stage signals both the climax and the culmination. This stage also sets in motion a desire for a reunified perception of the self, and for a homogeneous identity. This succeeds on the purely physical level, progressing from 'the succession of phantasies that extends from a fragmented body-image to a form of its totality that I shall call orthopaedic' (Lacan 1985, 4). It is thwarted in other ways, however, as the 'inner self' is constrained by, and therefore potentially or actually in conflict with, the 'outer self'. This is because the outer self is characterized by its interaction and interdependency with forces which are *outside*, and whose motivatory direction is, quite simply, *other*.

An endless situation of tense duality ensues ('to break out of the circle of the *Innenwelt* generates the inexhaustible quadrature of the ego's verifications') (Lacan 1985, 4). This is dynamized by anticipation that is not stilled by the compromise of 'the assumption of the armour of an alienating identity which will mark with its rigid structure the subject's entire mental development' (p. 4). Conflictual elements thus prevail. Lacan often speaks of the *I* in terms of alienation, and of the subject resolving as *I* the discord experienced with its own reality (p. 2). The result is an essentially non-unified state. Temporary states of oneness obtain, presumably, when either the 'inner' or the 'outer self' gains total control, at which point there can be a correspondence of desires. However, the inexorable force of external, social pressures dictates the general predominance of the latter, contextual part of the duality, while domination by the free, instinctual drives of the 'inner self' can only ever be short-lived.

In its function as a precursory stage to this eventual state of dynamic duality, epitomized by potential or actual conflict, the mirror stage can be regarded as a significant and ambiguous turning point. It encapsulates both the unifying moment of pleasurable identification by the 'inner self' with a hitherto unperceived 'outer self', and the crucial premonitory awareness of the essential duality simultaneously present in that recognition. This 'internal' drama gives rise to the possibility of the 'external' drama of 'the dialectic that will henceforth link the *I* to socially elaborated situations' (Lacan 1985, 5). This displaces the gravitational centre of action from within the static, closed circle of inward-oriented self-absorption, and outwards along a dialectical, open-ended chain of social *inter*actions in which 'mediation by the desire of the other' and 'competition from the other' suddenly predominate. The result is an unbalancing and normalizing, or repression, of the instinctive drive, which is denied any natural development. Ideologically determined sociocultural structures belonging to the Other (*l'autre*) impose themselves via the 'outer self', and pressure is brought to bear on the potentially anti-social energies of the 'inner self' to align themselves with social desires, or be channelled into an area of de-fusion.

Awareness of a dual self brought about during the internal drama of perceiving a mirror image is therefore significant in a variety of ways. Apart from its importance as an ambivalent, precursory stage in psychological development, the recurrence of this particular awareness acts as a reminder of the permanence of dynamic tension in the potential or actual conflict inherent in duality. This takes place both within the individual ('inner' vs. 'outer self') and between the individual and the world outside ('inner self' vs. exterior elements controlling the 'outer self').

It is these specific areas of conflict with which the *Gerusalemme liberata*, on its most profound level, concerns itself. This can be illustrated by an analysis both of the mirror episode in Canto XVI and eruptions of this level into other levels of the text. In a study entitled 'The Opposing Mirrors', Corrigan emphasizes the importance of the mirror ritual as one of the climaxes of the poem, especially in comparison with equivalent episodes in the *Achilleid* by Statius and Ariosto's *Orlando furioso*. Corrigan argues that Tasso retains, and gives even greater emphasis to, Statius' theme of self-recognition in the shield, while also adding the further theme of the mirror. While Renaissance connotations attributed to the mirror were those of Vanity and Lust, the shield, on the other hand, is interpreted by Corrigan as a possible symbol for Divine Grace leading to self-knowledge. As a consequence, Rinaldo undergoes a character change, unlike either Achilles or Ruggiero. A further link is postulated between the mirror ritual and the shield episode by considering the former in terms of painting, or descriptive narration, and the latter in relation to moral philosophy or dramatic narration (Corrigan 1956).

The context of the mirror episode is crucial to an appreciation of its function as a precursory stage and an important turning point in the narrative. The main protagonist of the episode, Rinaldo, is an exemplary individual whose positive qualities are described in terms that are both superlative and hyperbolic.[4] He is therefore prime social material. However, his usefulness to society is hampered by his impulsive behaviour. This first reveals itself in his hasty eagerness to avenge

---

[4] Rinaldo is described using the following superlatives: 'Rinaldo, il piú magnanimo e il piú bello, / tutti precorre ('III, 37, 3–4); 'Eccoti il domator d'ogni gagliardo' (III, 37, 8); 'Questi ha nel pregio de la spada eguali / pochi, o nessuno' (III, 38, 1–2); 'ché nulla teme la secura testa / o di sasso o di strai nembo o tempesta' (III, 51, 7–8); 'il giovenetto a cui / il pregio di fortezza ogn'altro cede' (VIII, 38, 3–4); 'il pregio e 'l fior de la latina gente' (VIII, 70, 6); 'il qual piú sempre essalta / la gloria sua con opre eccelse e nove' (X, 71, 3–4); 'de' tuoi consigli essecutor soprano' (XIV, 13, 4). His hyperbolic qualities are as follows: 'Ed è men ratto il lampo' (III, 37, 4); 'Se fosser tra' nemici altri sei tali, / già Soria tutta vinta e serva fôra; / e già dómi sarebbono i piú australi / regni, e i regni piú prossimi a l'aurora' (III, 38, 3–6); 'e la sua destra irata / teman piú d'ogni machina le mura' (III, 39, 1–2).

the death of Dudone: 'Or qual indugio è questo? e che s'aspetta? / poi ch'è morto il signor che ne fu guida, / ché non corriamo a vendicarlo in fretta?' (III, 50, 4–6). His zeal is censured as excessive ('il troppo ardire', III, 53, 1) and inopportune ('ch'a le vostr'ire / non è loco opportuno o la stagione', III, 53, 3–4) by the messenger who is sent to restrain him ('sopravien chi reprime il suo talento', III, 52, 6; 'e incontinente il ritornar impone', III, 53, 2). The instinctual element in Rinaldo is subjugated resentfully to the will of *altrui* (the equivalent of Lacan's *autre*), in other words, the will of society as represented by the emissary of its head:

> 'Goffredo il vi comanda'. A questo dire
> Rinaldo si frenò, ch'*altrui* fu sprone,
> benché dentro ne frema, e in piú d'un segno
> dimostri fuore il mal celato sdegno (III, 53, 5–8).

At the next critical point, when he is goaded by Gernando, Rinaldo is unable to hold back his characteristic impulse of anger: 'Né pote l'ira omai tener piú chiusa' (V, 26, 6). Nor can it, this time, be controlled by *altrui*: 'Ma per le voci *altrui* già non s'allenta / ne l'offeso guerrier l'impeto e l'ira' (V, 29, 1–2). His unrestrained, instinctual reaction culminates in a fatal attack on Gernando: 'E con la man, ne l'ira anco maestra, / mille colpi vèr lui drizza e comparte' (V, 30, 1–2). This action has grave consequences for him. His uncontrolled behaviour is criticized as excessive: 'troppo trascorre, ov'ira il cor gli sprone' (V, 54, 4). It is also censured as a violation of sacred social discipline: 'or se a violar l'editto / e de la disciplina il sacro onore / costretto fu' (V, 55, 5–6). This climax to his anti-social impetuousness, condemned as *errore* (XIV, 17, 2), *fallo* (XIV, 22, 8) and *peccato* (XIV, 21, 6), results in his exile.

It is during his *lontano essilio* that Rinaldo's mock death occurs. For the purposes of the social group he has left behind, he is as good as dead. He has abandoned his duty, with the result that his absence signifies social death. This is highlighted by the fact that it is from the remains of his armour that Rinaldo's 'death' is primarily deduced. His military armour, including his *vóto elmetto* and coat of arms, in other words, the outer casing signalling his social belonging, can be equated with Lacan's rigid 'armour (*armure*) of an alienating [i.e. other] identity' (Lacan 1985, 4):

> un guerrier morto in riva a l'onde.

> A l'*arme* ed a l'*insegne* ogn'uom si mosse,
> che furon conosciute ancor che immonde (VIII, 52, 4–6).

However, his identity cannot actually be verified beyond doubt from these social tokens or from the remains of the corpse, because the head and right sword arm are missing. Rinaldo's fragmented body recalls the *corps morcelé* of Lacan's infant prior to the mirror stage. This is linked to what Lacan refers to as 'a real *specific prematurity of birth* in man' detectable, for instance, in the lack of motor coordination. This feeds into the mirror stage:

> The *mirror stage* is a drama whose internal thrust is precipitated from insufficiency to anticipation—and which manufactures for the subject, caught up in the lure of spatial identification, the succession of phantasies that extends from a fragmented body-image to a form of its totality that I shall call orthopaedic (Lacan 1985, 4).

The incomplete, fragmented, infantile body preceding the mirror stage may recur in dreams (Lacan 1985, 4). It may also lie at the heart of popular patriarchal fantasies of the fragmented female body discernible in cultural production (particularly cinema), including the *Gerusalemme liberata* itself, where it can be read as a desire to disempower femininity by returning it to its uncoordinated state prior to the mirror stage (see Ch. 6).

In order to identify Rinaldo from his *corps morcelé*, recourse has to be made to a witness, whose description of a youthful head ('d'uom giovenetto e senza peli al mento', VIII, 54, 8) is accepted as final proof. However, the identification is false on several counts. On an overt narrative level, this is a mock death engineered by pagan forces to demoralize the Christian troops. On a Lacanian level, Rinaldo is by definition incapable of bearing a genuine social identity because at this point he is still in an infantile state and has yet to experience the mirror stage. Considerable emphasis is given throughout the poem to the characteristic youthfulness of Rinaldo, which is linked to what is perceived as socially destructive ('a' danni nostri' V, 45, 8) lack of self-control ('quel suo indomito ardimento' V, 56, 4). Tancredi, addressing him as *giovene invitto*, invokes civil society and the Christian brotherhood of which they are both part:

> Dimmi, che pensi far? vorrai le mani
> del *civil* sangue tuo dunque bruttarte?
> e con le piaghe indegne de' *cristiani*

trafigger Cristo, ond'ei son membra e parte? (V, 46, 1–4).

He is later told by Goffredo to take his destructive behaviour else-where ('porti risse altrove' V, 59, 6). Rinaldo's youth is highly signif-icant in relation to the psychological change effected by the mirror stage as formulated by Lacan. The young warrior is called *fanciullo*, *garzon, giovene* and *giovenetto*,[5] and references are made to his *giovenetto cor* (V, 13, 7), *vita giovanetta acerba* (X, 74, 7), *fanciulleschi affanni* (X, 75, 1) and *giovenili errori* (XVIII, 9, 4).

The mirror episode occurs during Rinaldo's exile, in other words, at a point in the narrative when he is separated from his social group. He is not taking part in its activities, which take the form of a reli-gious duty (the quest to liberate Jerusalem from the pagans). Instead, he is in a place of pleasure, in Armida's garden on the *Isole fortunate*. The description of these islands contains elements of disapproval that serve to counterbalance its positive aspects: 'Ben son elle feconde e vaghe e liete, / ma pur molto di falso al ver s'aggiunge' (XV, 37, 5–6). The relationship of Rinaldo and Armida in this place is described in a similarly negative fashion, as observed through the eyes of Carlo and Ubaldo who have been sent to reclaim Rinaldo for society and its tasks. There is criticism in the form of a comment on the unsuitabil-ity of the mirror hanging from his waist (*estraneo arnese* XVI, 20, 1) and in the definition of his role in the relationship, which is one of *servitú* (XVI, 21, 1) entailing his confinement to one place: 'Egli riman, ch'a lui non si concede / por orma o trar momento in altra parte' (XVI, 26, 5–6). Rinaldo is therefore in a situation of isolation from society, and instead of forming part of a group, he is a *romito amante* (XVI, 26, 8).

The mirror ritual as primary narcissism

When considered in context, particularly in relation to subsequent events, and bearing in mind Rinaldo's characteristics of youth and instinctual impulsiveness, two episodes in the poem together consti-tute a mirror episode which corresponds strikingly to Lacan's mirror stage involving the socialization of the *I*. These are the mirror ritual

[5] The term *fanciullo* is used in relation to Rinaldo as follows: I, 58, 1; III, 38, 2; V, 21, 8; XVII, 91, 1; *garzon*: V, 51, 2; V, 58, 2; VIII, 47, 1; XIV, 17, 2; XVI, 29, 1; XVI, 34, 1; XVII, 86, 2; *giovene*: V, 45, 3; V, 53, 1; XIV, 17, 5; XIV, 26, 8; *giovenetto*: V, 9, 2; VIII, 38, 3; VIII, 46, 4; VIII, 54, 8; XIV, 65, 1; XIV, 71, 4; XVII, 54, 5; XVII, 59, 5; XVII, 95, 2; XIX, 126, 1.

between Rinaldo and Armida, and the shield-as-mirror episode that follows shortly afterwards. The mirror ritual can be seen as an aspect of the mirror stage in that it represents the pleasurable primary narcissism in play at this time ('primary narcissism, by which analytic doctrine designates the libidinal investment characteristic of that moment') (Lacan 1985, 6). Primary narcissism involves an exclusive interest in the self, a self-absorption that is reflected in a type of concentricity. The circuit is, as it were, closed and complete, and the situation is one of stasis rather than dialectical movement.

This concentric pattern is reflected in the description of Rinaldo: 'ch'egli è in grembo a la donna, essa a l'erbetta' (XVI, 17, 8). He is enclosed (*rinchiuso* XV, 40, 3; 'un breve angolo *serra*' XVI, 32, 6) and static ('fra cibi ed ozio … *torpe*' XV, 44, 3–4; *sopito* XVI, 29, 6; 'da cupo e grave sonno *oppresso*' XVI, 31, 1; *in ozio* XVI, 32, 6; 'Qual sonno o qual letargo ha sí *sopita*' XVI, 33, 1). This condition is one of detachment, of being 'fuora / del mondo' (XVI, 32, 5–6) and unmoved by its requirements ('te sol de l'universo il moto nulla / move', XVI, 32, 7–8). Energies are concentrated in an inward direction, rather than responding to the exigencies of the outer world.

The self-oriented direction of Rinaldo's libidinal energies characterizing this phase is typified by Armida, whose function in the narrative requires close scrutiny. Her attention, directed exclusively towards herself, is an extension of Rinaldo's desires. When she watches him as he sleeps, her reaction is described as self-absorbed and reference made to the mythical Narcissus himself: 'e 'n su la vaga fronte / pende omai sí che par Narciso al fonte' (XIV, 66, 7–8). As this line implies, Armida is attracted ultimately by herself in Rinaldo, as she is later by the image of her own reflection in the mirror held up by him. She is the sole object of attention for both of them:

> mirano in vari oggetti un solo oggetto:
> ella del vetro a sé fa specchio, ed egli
> gli occhi di lei sereni a sé fa spegli. (XVI, 20, 6–8)

> L'uno di servitú, l'altra d'impero
> si gloria, ella in se stessa ed egli in lei (XVI, 21, 1–2).

Her first words to him when she learns of his imminent departure reveal her predominant concern that a part of herself will depart with him: 'O tu che porte / parte teco di me' (XVI, 40, 1–2). She is interested only in herself, and in others merely as a reflection of herself:

'sé gradí sola, e fuor di sé in altrui / sol qualche effetto de' begli occhi sui' (XVI, 38, 7–8). According to Rinaldo, she is reflected even more completely in his desires than in the mirror itself:

> ché son, se tu no 'l sai, ritratto vero
> de le bellezze tue gli incendi miei;
> la forma lor, la meraviglia a pieno
> piú che il cristallo tuo mostra il mio seno (XVI, 21, 5–8).

If she were to look at him, instead of at the mirror he holds, she would in fact see herself: 'ché il guardo tuo ... / gioirebbe felice in sé rivolto' (XVI, 22, 3–4).

However, Armida does not need to look at him. She is self-absorbed, self-contained, and gratified by herself alone, or by herself in others. She is the embodiment of his love, rather than its object. She does not function as a proper character involved in a two-way exchange with Rinaldo, but as the external manifestation of the libidinal energy of his primary narcissism. The pleasurable nature of this phase is indicated by the enjoyment which is expressed during the process of self-gratification: 'Con luci ella *ridenti* ... / Ella del vetro a sé fa specchio' (XVI, 20, 5, 7) and '*Ride* Armida, ma non che cesse / dal vagheggiarsi' (XVI, 23, 1–2). Armida is a part of Rinaldo, like his *ira*, which he at first indulges and allows to govern him. His repression of this particular manifestation of his *id*, as was the case in his subjugation of his *ira*, is only achieved with some difficulty:

> ... a freno
> può ritener le lagrime a fatica.
> Pur quel tenero affetto entro restringe,
> e quanto può gli atti compone e infinge (XVI, 52, 5–8),

and is accompanied by il *pianto amaro* (XVI, 61, 3) and *sospiri* (XVI, 61, 6). It is significant and appropriate that it should be Armida who is responsible for engineering Rinaldo's mock death, in other words his demise in social terms. He has been rendered socially ineffectual (and even harmful, in the case of Gernando), because his actions are dictated by the uncontrolled impulses of his self-oriented *id*, of which Armida is the external manifestation. Both Armida and his *ira* are eventually normalized/socialized in Rinaldo. On the surface level of the narrative Armida is finally saved from suicide and converted to Christianity by Rinaldo. In effect, Rinaldo is sublimating his affective, sexual desires on to a religio-social plane, thereby ensuring their survival in some form, while placing his *ira* under the control and in the services of his religion/society by directing it against the pagans.

Armida's conversion is accompanied by sudden, uncharacteristic meekness and obedience. This not only goes counter to the portrayal of her throughout the poem, but also contradicts the Aristotelian rule forbidding any change in character:

Fourthly, it [a character] should be consistent. Even if the original be inconsistent and offers such a character to the poet for representation, still he must be consistently inconsistent (*Poetics* 1454ª xv. 6, trans. Hamilton Fyfe).

Tasso was well aware of this rule. In the *Discorsi del poema eroico* he says: 'Ma si ricerca appresso Aristotele ne' costumi … che sian eguali' (*Discorsi*, 149). Another rule of composition is broken in relation to Armida, in that Rinaldo is never enlightened as to the falsity of her story claiming the throne of Damascus as the daughter of its king, which he still believes to be the truth at the end of the poem, when he says: 'Nel soglio, ove regnàr gli avoli tuoi, / riporti giuro' (XX, 135, 3–4). This amounts to the outwitting of a male character by a female character, which does not comply with the Aristotelian rule that a woman, being of a different, inferior class, should not be given manly attributes (including cleverness), as this would be unsuitable:

the character will be good, if the choice is good. Even a woman is 'good' and so is a slave, although it may be said that a woman is an inferior thing and a slave beneath consideration. The second point is that the characters should be appropriate. A character may be manly, but it is not appropriate for a woman to be manly or clever (*Poetics* 1454ª xv. 3–4, trans. Hamilton Fyfe).

This is reiterated by Tasso in the later *Discorsi*: 'molte fiate i costumi … non sono convenienti, come la fortezza alla donna' (*Discorsi*, 149–50). These contraventions of the rules for epic composition may be the result of modelling Armida on the tradition of Circe and Medea (IV, 86), mythical women renowned for their power over men. However, they may also underline the fact that Armida indeed functions more as an externalization of a facet of Rinaldo, than as a complete character in her own right.

The shield-as-mirror stage

The mirror ritual is the expression, on the narrative level of the text, of the pleasurable, uncontrolled libidinal energies at play in the self-absorbed/Armida phase in Rinaldo's development, a process equivalent to primary narcissism. This is closely followed in the poem by the shield-as-mirror episode, the mirror stage itself, with the particular type of libidinal energy accompanying it having already emerged in the narrative. The joyful self-orientation of the *id* involved exclusively with its own reflection is at this point joined by another, more disturbing aspect of self-recognition. Rinaldo sees himself reflected in the shield in his entirety, in a delimited form, as opposed to one facet of him mirroring itself in self-perpetuating, concentric isolation. As a consequence he is transformed by a new awareness of a hitherto unglimpsed perception of himself from the outside, a self that is firmly situated in, and part of, a context. He immediately views this new self in qualitative and quantitative terms, that is, in relation to a norm, to a certain set of rules that are external to him, yet nevertheless inexorably applicable to him: 'Egli al lucido scudo il guardo gira, / onde si specchia in lui *qual* siasi e *quanto*' (XVI, 30, 1–2).

His reappraisal of himself is highly critical, with pejorative observations on the emasculating effects of the *lascivie* that have rendered him *effeminato* and *inutile* for the purposes of his social task. This is signified in unmistakably phallic terms by the condition of his social tool, his sword, which has lost its fierceness and now hangs idly:

> e 'l ferro, il ferro aver, non ch'altro, mira
> dal troppo lusso effeminato a canto:
> guernito è sí ch'inutile ornamento
> sembra, non militar fero instrumento (XVI, 30, 5–8).

The isolated, static self-indulgence of primary narcissism is abruptly contextualized and put in its place at the moment of identification with the reflection in the shield:

> Qual uom da cupo e grave sonno oppresso
> dopo vaneggiar lungo in sé riviene,
> tal ei tornò nel rimirar se stesso (XVI, 31, 1–3).

Rinaldo experiences dissatisfaction with this prior state, and can no longer bear to look at his reflection: 'ma se stesso mirar già non sostiene; / giú cade il guardo' (XVI, 31, 4–5). This is accompanied by the reactions of shame and self-effacement: 'e timido e dimesso, / guardando a terra, la vergogna il tiene' (XVI, 31, 5–6). A crucial change has been dictated. This momentous transformation opens up a dialectical frequency of interaction and communication that is in diametric opposition to the closed-circuit concentricity of Armida's garden. He now accepts the reminder of his inferiority, implicit in Ubaldo's evocation of the Lacanian *Nom-du-père* ('o figlio di Bertoldo' XVI, 32, 5) and represses the uncontrolled, self-oriented energies of the *id*, externalized in the narrative in the character of Armida. The newly perceived and Other-infiltrated 'outer self' of the youth (*garzon*) now violently rejects all signs connoting the dominating presence of these forces, as represented by Armida's arrangement of Rinaldo's outer garb:

> Ma poi che diè vergogna a sdegno loco ...
> squarciossi i vani fregi e quelle indegne
> pompe, di servitù misera insegne (XVI, 34, 3, 7–8).

He then leaves the 'torta / confusione ... del labirinto' (XVI, 35, 1–2), the geographically twisted and confusing labyrinth that acts as a metaphor for the now-surpassed psychological stage that was 'twisted' (*torta*) and may also suggest, paronymically, the notion of 'wrong' in social terms.

The socialization of Rinaldo's *I* has now been successfully inaugurated, and with his exit from the labyrinth there is a change in narrative direction. His transformation has occurred, significantly, during a period of inactivity and 'absence' of the *id*, in other words, unbeknown to Armida, who becomes aware of the change only upon her return. During their encounter, which takes place *outside* the labyrinth, Rinaldo clarifies Armida's new position. He stipulates that this is one of subordination to the religio-social duty to which he will now divert his energies: 'sarò tuo cavalier quanto concede / la guerra d'Asia e con l'onor la fede' (XVI, 54, 7–8).

His social reintegration continues with another shield episode during which he acquires a new social skin in the form of a new set of armour. These *armi novelle* (XVII, 58, 1), together with the sword of Sveno, replace the armour discarded during his mock death, and initiate the period of Rinaldo's usefulness to his social group. The shield in particular has the function of inserting him even deeper into a social context. In contrast to the image of the self alone in the mirror episode—self-perpetuating and static in the mirror ritual, progressing to the delimited self-image in the adamantine shield—this shield shows the deeds of Rinaldo's ancestors. These are members of the renowned Este family, a well-defined social group of which he is inescapably a part: 'e in questo scudo affissa gli occhi omai, / ch'ivi de' tuoi maggior l'opre vedrai' (XVII, 64, 7–8).

The description of the shield is a dense network of references to family relationships and uninterrupted lineage: 'Del sangue d'Azio, glorioso, augusto / l'ordin vi si vedea, nulla interrotto' (XVII, 66, 3–4).[6] Rinaldo is successfully drawn into this web of family ties, which arouse in him the concomitant social sentiment *par excellence*, that of honour: 'Rinaldo sveglia, in rimirando, mille / spirti d'onor da le natie faville' (XVII, 81, 7–8). His reaction is one of being taken over ('è rapito' 82, 2). The final outcome is his acceptance of his social role, as he eagerly dons the armour: 'e s'arma frettoloso, e con la spene / già la vittoria usurpa e la previene' (XVII, 82, 7–8).

Rinaldo's position within a family unit is further reinforced by reference to his role in its future. Having seen on the shield 'i rami e la vetusta alta radice' of his 'stirpe altera' (86, 3–4), Rinaldo's attention is drawn, in a hyperbole, to the continuation of that line through him:

> Non fu mai greca o barbara o latina
> progenie, in questo o nel buon tempo antico,
> ricca di tanti eroi quanti destina
> a te chiari nepoti il Cielo amico (XVII, 89, 3–6).

By now, with the distance between himself and the *Isole fortunate* ever increasing, Rinaldo is totally receptive:

> … e le parole
> lietamente accoglieva il giovenetto,
> che del pensier de la futura prole
> un tacito piacer sentia nel petto (XVII, 95, 1–4).

The stage is now set for him to fulfil the particular social role dictated by his birthright. He is now one of a group of *cavalieri*: 'Quinci i tre cavalier su 'l lito spose' (XVII, 56, 1). References to him in this

---

[6] Many other references in Canto XVII indicate the importance of family and lineage: 'Ecco l'erede / del padre grande il gran figlio Acarino' (70, 2–3); 'suo fratel' (72, 2); 'l'orme del padre' (73, 2); 'il nipote' (74, 6); 'co' cinque figli Ottone' (74, 8); 'Alberto il figliuolo' (76, 1); 'genero il compra Otton con larga dote' (76, 4); 'Non si vedea virile erede a tanto / retaggio a sí gran padre esser successo' (77, 3–4); 'in piú felici rami / germogliava la prole alma e feconda' (79, 3–4); 'Guelfo il figliuol, figliuol di Cunigonda; / e 'l buon germe roman con destro fato / è ne' campi bavarici traslato' (79, 6–8); 'Là d'un gran ramo estense ei par ch'inesti / l'arbore di Guelfon' (80, 1–2); 'Ma ne' suoi rami italici fioriva / bella non men la regal pianta a prova' (81, 1–2); 'qui Azzo il sesto i suoi prischi rinova' (81, 4).

role, together with that of *guerriero*, increase considerably hereafter.[7] He performs this function superlatively well, and is described as *vincitor* (XVIII, 38, 5; XIX, 37, 8; XX, 107, 1), *vincitor guerriero* (XVIII, 39, 4), *fero vincitore* (XX, 54, 7) and *vincitor veloce* (XX, 57, 7), culminating in *italico eroe* (XX, 115, 6). Rinaldo also furthers the cause of his social group by serving as an inspiring example for others to emulate:

> L'essempio a l'opre ardite e pellegrine
> spinge i compagni: ei non è sol che monte,
> ché molti appoggian seco eccelse scale (XVIII, 76, 5–7)

and:

> Dièr sovra gli altri i suoi compagni egregi,
> che d'emulo furor l'essempio accese (XX, 56, 3–4).

The socialization of his *I* and his consequent fulfilment of the role allotted to him are made to seem inevitable. His sword is described as *l'inevitabile tua spada* (XVI, 33, 8). Particular recourse is taken to the notion of fate: *per leggi … fatali* (X, 77, 6), *fatal nave* (XIII, 51, 3), *fatal guerriero* (XVI, 33, 5), *la destinata spada* (XVII, 83, 3), *l'elmo fatal* (XX, 103, 3) and the will of God: 'la vita giovenetta acerba / a piú mature glorie il Ciel riserba' (X, 74, 7–8). Rinaldo effectively has no choice. Interestingly Solimano is in a similar position, despite the fact that he is part of an opposing religio-social group. At one point, alone and distanced from his social context, he glimpses the powerlessness (and terror) of the human condition:

> e mirò, benché lunge, il fer Soldano;
> mirò, quasi in teatro od in agone,
> l'aspra tragedia de lo stato umano:
> i vari assalti e 'l fero orror di morte,
> e i gran giochi del caso e de la sorte (XX, 73, 4–8).

During this brief moment of solitude, away from the masses and standing outside the social group, his critical faculties, previously held in abeyance by immersion in the masses, come into play. This phenomenon is noted by Freud in his 'Group Psychology and the Analysis of the Ego' (1921) as follows:

---

[7] Rinaldo is described as a *cavalier/o* in the following lines: XVI, 21, 3; XVIII, 4, 1; 11, 1; 19, 1; 33, 7; 37, 5; XIX, 34, 1; 36, 5; XX, 62, 1; 65, 2; 115, 2; 127, 3; and as *guerrier/o*: XV, 40, 3; XVI, 33, 5; XVIII, 21, 1; 26, 1; 28, 3; 39, 4; 40, 5; XIX, 46, 8.

The most remarkable and also the most important result of the formation of a group is the 'exaltation or intensification of emotion' produced in every member of it ... The greater the number of people in whom the same affect can be simultaneously observed, the stronger does this automatic compulsion grow. The individual loses his power of criticism, and lets himself slip into the same affect (Freud *SE* xviii. 84).

Solimano's subsequent realization of the true nature of the individual's predicament, of which he was hitherto unaware, stuns and stupifies him: 'Stette attonito alquanto e stupefatto / a quelle prime viste' (XX, 74, 1–2). However, the many preceding years of performing a particular role outweigh this moment of awareness, and in an instant, as if by automatic response, he springs into action and becomes part of it again: 'e poi s'accese, / e desiò trovarsi anch'egli in atto / nel periglioso campo a l'alte imprese' (XX, 74, 2–4).

Rinaldo's effectiveness upon reinsertion into his social context affirms his successful social reintegration, set in motion by the conflictual mirror episode. He now employs his redirected *id* in a positive manner for the purposes of society (*a pro de' nostri* XVIII, 2, 7), rather than contrary to its interests, as was the case previously. This diversion of his energies is seen as making amends for past misdeeds: 'in ammenda / del fallo, in pro comune il sangue spenda' (XIV, 22, 7–8). He is then allotted the task of conquering the enchanted wood, specifically for the common good, in addition to his usual heroic feats:

> E per emenda io vorrò sol che faccia,
> quai per uso faresti, opre famose;
> e 'n danno de' nemici e *'n pro de' nostri*
> vincer convienti de la selva i mostri (XVIII, 2, 5–8).

The wood itself, providing an obstacle to social enterprise, functions as an externalization of the desires and fears preoccupying the individual mind which is as yet insufficiently disciplined and controlled for the purposes of society. Rinaldo, who is in the process of achieving the high status of exemplary social member, is the only one capable of conquering the wood. This is because of the successful socialization of his *I*, accompanied by the corresponding repression, sublimation and redirection of the self-oriented, self-preoccupied energies of his *id*. The wood is represented as insuperable by others:

> ... la gran selva orrenda
> tentata fu ne' tre seguenti giorni
> da i piú famosi; e pur alcun non fue
> che non fuggisse a le minaccie sue (XIII, 31, 5–8).

It is emphasized that Rinaldo alone will be victorious:

> E chi sarà, s'egli non è, quel forte
> ch'osi troncar le spaventose piante? (XIV, 23, 1–2)
>
> A lui sol di troncar non fia disdetto
> il bosco ch'ha gli incanti in sua difesa (XIV, 14, 1–2).

His success, considered inevitable after his return to society, is fundamental to the outcome of the Crusade itself, which, although never
in doubt, is reiterated at this point:

> ... altri conviene
> che de le piante sue la selva spoglie.
> Già già la fatal nave ...
> già, rotte l'indegnissime catene,
> l'aspettato guerrier dal lido scoglie;
> non è lontana omai l'ora prescritta
> che sia presa Sion, l'oste sconfitta (XIII, 51, 1–3, 5–8)
>
> A lui sol di troncar non fia disdetto
> il bosco ch'ha gli incanti in sua difesa;
> e da lui il campo tuo ...
> prenderà maggior forza a nova impresa;
> e i rinforzati muri e d'Oriente
> supererà l'essercito possente (XIV, 14, 1–3, 6–8).

However, Rinaldo will only conquer the wood, in other words,
continue to repress and redirect the instinctual energies of his *id*
sufficiently for the needs of society, if there is no lapse in the socialization process undergone by his *I*: 'Vincerai ... / pur ch'altro folle
error non ti ritardi' (XVIII, 10, 3–4). This process, characterized by
the continual conflict, potential or actual, between the self-oriented
id of the 'inner self' and the restrictive, contrary pressures of the
Other-infiltrated 'outer self', needs to be constantly reinforced in
order to continue to be effective. The warning received here by
Rinaldo performs the function of such a reinforcement. The advice
accompanying it ('ma sprezza i finti aspetti e i finti preghi' XVIII, 10,
8) is duly followed when he reaches the wood:

> Rinaldo guata, e di veder gli è aviso
> le sembianze d'Armida e il dolce viso (XVIII, 30, 7–8)
>
> ma il cavaliero, assorto sí, non crudo,
> piú non v'attende, e stringe il ferro ignudo (XVIII, 33, 7–8).

He successfully disenchants the wood, which can consequently be used to ensure the victory of the Christian army. The final, decisive battle then ensues. His combative skills are placed enthusiastically in the service of the Christians: 'ma, intrepido ed invitto ad ogni scossa, / sprezzaria, se cadesse, Olimpo ed Ossa' (XVIII, 75, 7–8); 'con quella man cui nessun pondo è grave' (XIX, 36, 6); 'Non l'ariete di far piú si vanti, / non la bombarda, fulmine di morte' (XIX, 37, 5–6); 'Desio di superar chi non ha pari / in opra d'arme' (XIX, 49, 5–6).

Once the Christian victory is assured, and his social duty done, then Rinaldo may redirect his attention to that area of himself which has been subjugated to it:

> Allor si ferma a rimirar Rinaldo
> ove drizzi gli assalti, ove gli aiuti,
> e de' pagan non vede ordine saldo,
> ma gli stendardi lor tutti caduti.
> Qui pon fine a le morti, e in lui quel caldo
> disdegno marzial par che s'attuti.
> Placido è fatto, e gli si reca a mente
> la donna che fuggia sola e dolente (XX, 121).

He may now concern himself with Armida again:

> Ben rimirò la fuga; *or* da lui chiede
> pietà che n'abbia cura e cortesia,
> e gli sovien che si promise in fede
> suo cavalier quando da lei partia (XX, 122, 1–4).

However, his concern is not only the conditional one indicated during their encounter outside the labyrinth ('sarò tuo cavalier quanto concede / la guerra d'Asia e con l'onor la fede' XVI, 54, 7–8). The self-oriented drive of Rinaldo's *id*, having been repressed during the mirror episode and again in the wood, now undergoes a final sublimation. This takes the form of the conversion of Armida to Christianity (XX, 136, 7–8), which can be seen as the real climax of the poem. There follow a mere eight more stanzas culminating in the anti-climactic line 'Cosí vince Goffredo' (XX, 144, 1) that provides the overt, surface climax matching the title of the poem. In effect, the socialization process inaugurated by the mirror episode has been successfully sustained and completed. In accordance with epic tradition, from Achilles onwards, the errant hero has returned to the fold.

Fathers of the mirror stage

At this point it is of interest to return to the particular reinforcement procedure that accompanies this socialization process. This is the admonition received by Rinaldo prior to his confrontation with the enchanted wood, in other words, the second occasion on which he must subjugate and redirect the self-oriented energies of his *id*. The nature of its source ('il ministro del Ciel' XVIII, 9, 5) significantly underlines the manner in which religious elements bolster the socialization process throughout the poem. The predominating figure in this context is Piero the hermit, who is both aged (*veglio* I, 32, 1, *vecchio* XI, 4, 1) and socially respected (*venerabile* X, 73, 4). He is not only the promoter (*autor primiero* I, 29, 4) of the entire social enterprise represented by the Crusade, but acts as an invaluable fount of knowledge for the social group. *Il saggio Piero* (X, 78, 1) is characterized by a divine gift of knowing: "l vostro Piero, a cui lo Ciel comparte / l'alta notizia de' secreti sui, / saprà' (XIV, 18, 1–3). His knowledge is specifically useful in relation to the whereabouts of Rinaldo ('saprà drizzare i messaggieri' XIV, 18, 3) and in terms of the hero's future contributions to society. Piero prophesies a glorious, and therefore socially useful, destiny for Rinaldo, as well as foretelling his return to conquer the wood and the subsequent taking of the Holy City (X, 74–77, XIII, 51).

Most significantly, he instigates the mirror episode itself. It is he who sends Carlo and Ubaldo to the Mago of Ascalona, another aged, sage and socially revered figure who has been converted and baptized by Piero himself. The Mago acts as the instrument of Piero, who gives him knowledge of the future:

> Ma l'arte mia per sé dentro al futuro
> non scorge il ver che troppo occulto giace (XVII, 88, 1–2)
> ch'io l'intesi da tal che senza velo
> i secreti talor scopre del Cielo (XVII, 88, 7–8).

It is at the hands of this socially respected religious figure that the underlying process of the socialization of the *I* receives its most overt formulation in Canto XVII, and so comes nearest to being transported from the position of deep psychic structure to the surface plot. As the mouthpiece of social interest, he expresses the instinctual energies of the *id* in terms of *ire* which should not be employed in an aggressive, anti-social manner: 'non perché l'usi ne' civili assalti'. Nor should they be used to further any sexual-affective desires: 'né perché sian di desideri ingordi / elle ministre'. On the contrary, these self-oriented, impulsive drives should be redirected outwards to become socially contextualized and useful: 'ma perché il tuo valore, armato d'esse, / piú fero assalga gli aversari esterni'. The concept of repression is even used by the Mago in relation to the drive of desire: 'e sian con maggior forza indi *ripresse* / le cupidigie, empi nemici interni'). These drives are, moreover, opposed to reason (*a ragion discordi*), a formulation that also appears elsewhere in the poem, when the drives of the *id* are translated variously as *ira*, *sensi* and *Amor*:

> ... oltra ogni segno
> di ragione il trasporta ira e disdegno (V, 17, 7–8)
>
> cosí ragion pacifica reina
> de' sensi fassi, e se medesma affina (XVI, 41, 7–8)
>
> Non entra Amor a rinovar nel seno,
> che ragion congelò, la fiamma antica (XVI, 52, 1–2).

Performing the function of an extension of Piero, the Mago of Ascalona is the source of the adamantine shield which Ubaldo, on behalf of society, holds up to Rinaldo, thereby precipitating the shield-as-mirror stage. It is also the Mago who shows Rinaldo the shield portraying the glorious deeds of the young warrior's ancestors, to reinforce the socialization process already initiated, and further reintegrate Rinaldo with his social group. The shield, in itself an essentially social object denoting role, is therefore provided by a religious patriarch in both the crucial shield-as-mirror stage and in the subsequent reinforcement scene, thereby establishing a strong link between religion and the socialization process. The final sublimation of the self-oriented energies of Rinaldo's *id* takes place in the same vein with the conversion of Armida to Christianity.

The forces countering Christian religion, society and, most importantly, the socialization process which it is seen to underpin, are clearly those of the opposing and therefore 'evil' pagan religion and social group. They are described with terms such as *maligno* (V, 18, 1), *iniquo* (IV, 22, 8) and *empi* (XIII, 7, 8). These forces work to obstruct the socialization process by encouraging the anti-social, self-oriented energies of the *id*, particularly on three key occasions. First, 'evil' forces infuse Gernando with *ira*:

> Tal che 'l maligno spirito d'Averno,

> ch'in lui strada sí larga aprir si vede,
> tacito in sen gli serpe ed al governo
> de' suoi pensieri lusingando siede.
> E qui piú sempre l'ira e l'odio interno
> inacerbisce, e 'l cor stimola e fiede (V, 18, 1–6).

This provokes the impulsive, uncontrolled, aggressive aspect of Rinaldo's *id* into action, which in turn results in his departure and consequent social ineffectiveness. Second, it is an 'evil' spirit which prompts Idraote, who is pondering on how to weaken Christian power, to use Armida, his niece, as a distraction:

> in questo suo pensier il sovragiunge
> l'angelo iniquo, e piú l'instiga e punge (IV, 22, 7–8)

> Esso il consiglia, e gli ministra i modi
> onde l'impresa agevolar si pote.
> Donna a cui di beltà le prime lodi
> concedea l'Oriente, è sua nepote (IV, 23, 1–4).

The entire episode of Armida betokening the temporary domination of Rinaldo by the sexual-affective energies of his *id* is thus instigated by these anti-social, anti-Christian forces.

Third, summoned by Ismeno, they are responsible for the enchanted wood, in other words, for the apparent concretization of the desires and fears of the *id* which proves an insurmountable challenge to all but Rinaldo:

> cittadini d'Averno, or qui v'invoco,
> e te, signor de' regni empi del foco (XIII, 7, 7–8)

> Prendete in guardia questa selva, e queste
> piante che numerate a voi consegno (XIII, 8, 1–2).

One effect of this incantation is to prompt irrational, unfounded fears that spring from none other than the instinctual impulse of fear itself:

> cosí temean, senza saper qual cosa
> siasi quella però che gli sgomenti,
> se non che 'l timor forse a i sensi finge
> maggior prodigi di Chimera o Sfinge (XIII, 18, 5–8).

The image of a child is used, significantly, to open this description of an instinctual reaction that is uncontrollable by a mind as yet insufficiently developed:

> Qual *semplice bambin* mirar non osa

> dove insolite larve abbia presenti,
> o come pave ne la notte ombrosa,
> imaginando pur mostri e portenti (XIII, 18, 1–4).

Another effect of the enchanted wood is to project the sexual-affective instinct on to an illusory plane which appears to present an incarnation of the desired person (Armida, in the case of Rinaldo, and Clorinda in that of Tancredi); or, rather, which generates a powerful intensification of these particular energies of the *id*.

Rinaldo, in whom the socialization process set in motion by the mirror episode can be seen to progress smoothly towards a satisfactory climax, successfully controls these drives. He remains unmoved by 'le sembianze d'Armida', and releases the wood from its spell. Tancredi, on the other hand, fails in his attempt to conquer the wood, a feat which only seems possible for those who have passed a certain stage of development. Yet he, together with Rinaldo, would seem to be the most likely to conquer the wood, and his case deserves special attention.

He is second only to Rinaldo, with whom he is linked in terms of exemplary, hyperbolic qualities:

> Vien poi Tancredi, e non è alcun fra tanti
> (tranne Rinaldo) o feritor maggiore,
> o piú bel di maniere e di sembianti,
> o piú eccelso ed intrepido di core (I, 45, 1–4).

Only he and Rinaldo are equal to Goffredo in battle:

> Sol Raimondo in consiglio, ed in battaglia
> sol Rinaldo e Tancredi a lui s'agguaglia (III, 59, 7–8).

However, the condition with which Tancredi is predominantly associated is that of stasis and immobility. This state results from his *vano amor* for Clorinda and closely resembles Rinaldo's behaviour in Armida's garden:

> ... or lei veggendo impètra (III, 23, 2)

> move il suo destrier con lento passo,
> volgendo gli occhi ov'è colei su 'l colle;
> poscia immobil si ferma, e pare un sasso (VI, 27, 3–5)

> Si scote allor Tancredi, e dal suo tardo
> pensier, quasi da un sonno, al fin si desta (VI, 30, 5–6)

> La vide, la conobbe, e restò senza
> e voce e moto ... (XII, 67, 7–8)

> e l'imperio di sé libero cede ...

> Già simile a l'estinto il vivo langue
> al colore, al silenzio, a gli atti, al sangue (XII, 70, 3, 7–8)
>
> pallido, freddo, muto, e quasi privo
> di movimento ... (XII, 96, 3–4).

As a result, Tancredi's social task takes second place:

> Sol di mirar s'appaga, e di battaglia
> sembiante fa che poco or piú gli caglia (VI, 27, 7–8)

and:

> Or veggendo sue voglie altrove intese
> e starne lui quasi al pugnar restio (VI, 29, 5–6).

He even acts counter to the enterprise of his social group when he protects Clorinda, a formidable member of the opposing army, from death at the hands of a Christian warrior, described pejoratively as *uomo inumano* and *villano* (III, 29, 3; 30, 8). This description takes place in third-person narration, indicating Tasso's sympathy with Tancredi's plight. Tancredi, succumbing to an impulse of *ira*, pursues *quel villan* (III, 36, 2) and is carried far away from his allotted place: 'si mira a dietro, e vede ben che lunge / troppo è trascorsa la sua audace gente' (III, 36, 3–4). He absents himself for an even longer period on a later occasion when he follows Erminia, believing her to be Clorinda. As a result, he fails to fulfil his obligation to continue the duel with Argante, depriving Goffredo of the services of 'il fior de' suoi guerrier gagliardi' (VII, 58, 5).

The high point occurs in Tancredi's unwitting slaying of Clorinda. The performance of socio-Christian duty (the continued socialization of his *I*) is in direct conflict here with the sexual-affective drives of his *id* in the form of Clorinda. Clorinda, like Armida, can be seen to function as a pagan obstacle forming part of the overt narrative framework. At the same time, the patently sexual connotations of the final struggle between Tancredi and Clorinda (including references to her *bel sen* and *mammelle*, and culminating in the phrase *trafitta / vergine* XII, 64, 3, 6, 1–2) indicate the return of the repressed energies of the *id*. This intrudes into the surface plot (Christians vs. pagans) by virtue of its sheer irrelevance. There then follows the sublimation of these energies by means of the surface narrative expedient of conversion to Christianity. This performs a similar function in the case of Rinaldo, when the subjugatory *ancella* or *ancilla* is also used (XII, 65, 8; XX,

136, 7).

However, the socialization process is not as complete in Tancredi as in Rinaldo, the conqueror of the enchanted wood. Tancredi's reaction when confronted by the apparent voice and blood of Clorinda reveals that he is still basically an *amante*. Despite some initial wavering, he is ultimately dominated by his instinctual drives: 'tal il timido amante a pien non crede / a i falsi inganni, e pur ne teme e cede' (XIII, 44, 7–8). The struggle that takes place within him heightens when he drops his sword. His instinctual urges then take over completely ('Va fuor di sé' 45, 5) and the symbol of his social function disappears irrevocably: 'Il suo caduto ferro intanto fore / portò del bosco impetuoso vento' (46, 5–6). Although he performs his social role to the best of his abilities thereafter, his deeds are not bathed in glory, as are those of Rinaldo. He is, moreover, presented yet again in a static, inactive condition. While he is victorious against Argante, and therefore successfully completes the important social task he had originally undertaken and then abandoned for Clorinda, he does not achieve this with the ease of Rinaldo. On the contrary, he returns to his characteristic, basically immobile state punctuated by occasional activity, a state from which he never fully emerges. Tancredi appears to remain in a state of limbo, with his *I* only partially socialized, while in Rinaldo the process is markedly more complete.

Rinaldo's involvement in the mirror ritual and the shield-as-mirror scene denotes the repression of his *id* and the successful socialization of his *I*, processes that are central to the *Gerusalemme liberata*. The Lacanian perspective of the mirror stage exposes these processes covertly at work in the text. It is at this covert level that the essential nexus of opposition, and therefore the major obstacle to plot progression, is located. This level not only gives resonance to and supports, but also intrudes into, the overt, surface plot ostensibly dominating the poem (Christians vs. pagan). In the following chapter another covert facet of the poem is explored, a facet that similarly reinforces the ideological framework of the narrative.

CHAPTER 6

❖

The Ideology of the Look

This chapter aims to discover some of the ways in which the faculty of sight functions in the *Gerusalemme liberata*.[1] One main consideration is whether the act of looking can be seen to operate as an *ideologically closed text-procedure*. The term *closed* is used here in the sense of indicating a univocal function, while *ideologically* refers specifically to value assumptions and their underlying power structures. Closed text-procedures are a possible, if not inevitable, component in the cultural production of any period. The authoritarian context of the Counter-Reformation within which this poem was written gives special relevance to this type of analysis. Given this normative context, and the overtly religious tendency of the *Gerusalemme liberata* itself, it would seem reasonable to examine the poem for ideologically closed text-procedures which would act as vehicles for the transmission of univocal, unambiguous units of meaning, structured and underpinned by the social order.

The notion of *closed* (as well as *open*), taken from semiotics, refers to systems of relations between Reader and text. In the case of *open* systems, this relationship becomes dialectical (Eco 1967, 20, 25). According to Barthes, it is also without finality: 'hors de toute finalité imaginable ... Aucun alibi ne tient, rien ne se reconstitue, rien ne se récupère' (Barthes 1973, 83). This absence of finality, with an 'extrême toujours déplacé, extrême vide, mobile, imprévisible', generates Reader pleasure in the text: 'Cet extrême garantit la jouissance' (p. 83). An open text, Eco argues, is also *non-ideologico*. In other words, it is not closed and univocal, but allows for the contestation of meaning by communicating 'la natura contraddittoria del proprio spazio semantico a cui si riferisce' (Eco 1982, 363).

---

[1] Excerpts from a previous version of this chapter appeared in '"Donna liberata"?: The Portrayal of Women in Italian Renaissance Epic', in Z. Barański and S. Vinall (eds.), *Women and Italy: Essays on Gender, Culture and History* (London: Macmillan, 1991), 173–208.

Ideologically closed text-procedures, on the other hand, include a *dispositio ideologica*:

una argomentazione che, mentre sceglie esplicitamente una delle possibili selezioni circostanziali del semema quale premessa, non rende esplicito il fatto che esistono altre premesse contraddittorie o premesse apparentemente complementari che portano a una conclusione contraddittoria, pertanto occultando la contraddittorietà dello spazio semantico' (Eco 1982, 364).

By virtue of not acknowledging 'le multiple interconnessioni dell'universo semantico', they obscure 'anche *le ragioni pratiche* per cui certi segni sono stati prodotti insieme coi loro interpretanti'. As a result they produce false consciousness: 'Così l'oblio produce falsa coscienza' (Eco 1982, 369). Closed text-procedures can therefore be seen as ideological sub-codes which transmit presuppositions in an untold, or covert manner (Eco 1981, 22).

The poem makes much use of the semantic field of sight (acts of looking and seeing), which lends itself particularly well to an analysis involving the concept of closed text-procedures. The choice of visual acts for this analysis was not motivated simply by numerical considerations, but by the fact that the look is not as readily associated with power relations as are other types of action (such as acts of physical violence or verbal acts). This situation is reflected by the fact that interest in the role of the look in power relations is relatively recent. The use of non-verbal means in general as part of the technique of persuasion played only a minor role in classical treatises on rhetoric. It is present as a small part of *pronuntiatio* or *actio*, the division of rhetoric dealing with delivery. There it appears as *corporis motus*, together with *vocis figura*, and consists of the deliberate striking of poses, such as *acer aspectus*, at appropriate points in the speech (*Rhetorica ad Herennium* III. xi. 19, xv. 27). Quintilian too mentions *actio decora* as part of the combination of oratorical skills that impress the hearer (X. i. 17). However, this acknowledgement of the power of non-verbal communication was not developed further, and *pronuntiatio*, along with *memoria*, was discarded by the Middle Ages.

It is the post-Freudian era, with its interest in the unconscious, that heralds a significant stage in the study of the implications behind non-verbal (as well as verbal) acts. In the words of Sapir, writing in 1927:

another field for the development of unconscious cultural patterns is that of gesture ... an elaborate and secret code that is written nowhere, known by none, and understood by all. And this code is by no means referable to simple organic responses. On the contrary, it is as finely certain and artificial, as definitely a creation of social tradition, as language or religion or industrial technology ... the laws of gesture, the unwritten code of gestural messages and responses, is the anonymous work of an elaborate social tradition (Sapir 1958, 556).

Sapir's use of the term 'certain' in relation to the code of gestures prefigures the notion of *closed* with reference to a particular system in the transmission of meaning (indeed, major elements of semiotics are already apparent in this passage, especially in the concept of a socially determined, yet covert code).

The specific relationship between non-verbal communication and power, however, has become a focal point of attention only in relatively recent times. This has meant a growing interest in the actual dynamics underlying the establishment and maintenance of hierarchical power structures. The notion of body language as a comparatively unconscious (for both subject/sender and object/addressee) but indisputable means of communication, and thence potential power nexus, has not occupied a prominent position in literary studies. However, film theory from the 1970s onwards has included discussion of this concept.[2] One prime area of investigation has been the act of looking itself, both on the part of the characters on screen and of the spectator in the auditorium.

A central notion here has been the function of the look in maintaining structures of difference in cinema whose closed text-procedures support the dominant ideology. Analysis of this process has concentrated on the position of the spectator as voyeur in relation to each side of the difference. Consideration has been given to issues such as whether the spectator or camera eye looks exclusively with the looker and at the object, while never occupying the position of the person being looked at; and, when the spectator participates as subject of the look, how the object is presented. The body-as-object may, for instance, be fragmented by the look which dismembers it by focusing on one body-part after the other.

It is not surprising that the analysis of body language, or body politics, has come to the forefront in studies based on the specific cultural form represented by the film, which in itself is especially reliant on physical movement (this having preceded the use of talking in the development of cinematic language). However, this type of investiga-

---

[2] See Cohan & Hark 1993, Doane 1991, Kuhn 1982, Mulvey 1989, Neale 1983.

tion, in itself involving a variety of disciplines, need not necessarily be exclusive to the field of film studies. Cultural forms are very much interlinked and, as the theory of semiotics has shown, there is a clear common denominator in the relationship between Spectator and Reader as Interpreter of a Text.

In a genre such as the epic poem, characterized by overt conflictual bodily activity, analysis of one aspect of physical interaction operating on a covert level may be particularly revealing. The results may also have interesting implications for other interlocking and equally covert closed text-procedures reinforcing existing power relations. One major issue in the following analysis, then, concerns the nature of the relationship between subject and object of the look; in particular, whether the subject of the act of looking differs in terms of power position from the object being looked at. If the relationship between subject and object of the same type of look invariably entails the same power differential, then the act of looking can be considered to function as a closed text-procedure reinforcing dominant hierarchical relations.

Examples of the look in the *Gerusalemme liberata* are considered first in the light of two particular types of look:

A   the look of a (would-be) superior used to establish or maintain power.

B   the look of an inferior, sometimes at the direct instigation of a (would-be) superior, used to monitor, reiterate or show acceptance of an inferior position.

The criteria used to determine look type A are any of the following:

1. The terms used to describe the look and to express its subject and object suggest that the former is superior and the latter inferior.
2. The look is used as part of a pattern of behaviour aimed at maintaining or reasserting power.
3. The subject looks but is not seen by the object, and therefore enjoys an advantage.
4. The object, aware of being looked at, reacts in a manner which determines the look as related in some way to the establishment or maintenance of power, a reaction that may be either positive or negative.

The criteria used to determine look type B are any of the following:

1. The terms used to describe the look and to express its sub-

ject and object suggest that the former is inferior and the latter superior.

2. The look occurs at the instigation of someone attempting to establish or maintain power.
3. The subject of the look is anonymous or generalized.
4. The reaction of the subject after looking shows the looker to be inferior to the object of the look.

The precise nature of the power relationship is then established by examining the terms in which, for example, the superior subject and inferior object of the look are expressed (italicized in the examples below). The superior is often presented in terms that:

(i) denote superior social status and function:

> Ma poi ch'ebbe di questi e d'altri cori
> scorti gl'intimi sensi *il Re del mondo* (I, 11, 1–2)

> *Il capitan* rivolse gli occhi in giro
> tre volte e quattro, e mirò in fronte i suoi (II, 80, 5–6).

(ii) refer to the family name, which, in a context that is patrilineal, evokes the notion of the superior family member denoted by the *Nom-du-père*:

> Mira intanto *il Buglion* d'eccelsa parte
> de la forte cittade il sito e l'arte (III, 54, 7–8)

and, *Nom-du-père* par excellence:

> quando da l'alto soglio *il Padre eterno* ...
> gli occhi in giú volse, e in un sol punto e una
> vista mirò ciò ch'in sé il mondo aduna (I, 7, 3, 7–8).

(iii) are qualified by an epithet of praise relating to a specialized code, such as the religious:

> ... il *pio* Buglione ...
> ... 'n lui pensando alquanto fisse
> le luci ebbe tenute ... (III, 67, 6–8)

and the chivalric:

> Il *magnanimo* eroe ...
> già veggendo il nemico a piè venire (VII, 37, 1, 4).

The inferior may be expressed in terms denoting:

(i) gender differentiation, at its most extreme in the use of the term *vergine*:

> Vergine era fra lor di già matura
> verginità …
> e de' vagheggiatori ella s'invola
> a le lodi, a gli sguardi, inculta e sola (II, 14, 1–2, 7–8).

(ii) a part of the body which thereby becomes isolated, either directly, as in Altamor's look:

> volge un guardo a la mano, uno al bel volto,
> talor insidia piú guardata parte (XIX, 69, 1, 5–6)

or by means of a metaphor, as in the look of Amor:

> tu per mille custodie entro a i piú casti
> verginei alberghi il guardo altrui portasti (II, 15, 5, 7–8).

Lastly, account is taken of who possesses which type of look, and whether a pattern can be seen to emerge. Sometimes the object of a look is not another person, but is non-human, such as a thing, an animal, or a place. In such a case, the look may still retain its ideological significance. In other words, if the non-human object is regarded as symbolic in some way, or as an extension of a facet of a particular person, it may be seen to function in favour of one or other of the poles in a power-determined relationship. Situations in which the look is used to establish and maintain power include those of conflict, when dominance is the main issue. Conflict of one sort or another is central to the poem: the title itself indicates that the main plot concerns the establishment of superiority by the Christians over the pagans prior to the reclaiming of Jerusalem, the very symbol of power.

Particular situations of conflict in which the look is used to establish and maintain power fall into two categories, namely physical and psychological combat. Physical combat takes the form of fighting between Christians and pagans, and fighting among Christians (usually instigated by forces supporting the pagans). Psychological combat takes more varied forms: aggressive verbal interchanges; debilitating forces put into play by the pagans against the Christians, such as the enchanted wood and the charms of Armida's island; the woman's look used as a dangerous weapon; and attempts to gain knowledge, particularly concerning the plans of the opposition. Of special interest is the fact that other, rather less apparent areas of conflict are also discernible in the light of an analysis revealing the existence of certain types of look which lie outside the main plot.

The position of the Reader is also of importance in relation to the ideological function of the act of looking. The Reader is obviously present in some way as the look takes place, if only by virtue of setting the act in motion by reading it. Sometimes, however, the Reader is specifically invited to participate in a particular manner in the look, either alone or along with the subject (in which case an additional element of voyeurism may be present). It is noteworthy in this regard that the Reader is never invited to share the vision of the person being looked at, a device that further consolidates the pattern of superiority established by the dynamics of the act of looking in the poem. On at least one occasion didacticism, in the form of an exemplum, provides the vehicle for ideology to surface, as the Reader is openly instructed to learn, as well as look. (This occurs, for instance, at the death of Ismeno in Canto XVIII, 89, and follows an impersonal verb of seeing, *si vedea* 88, 3, which directly involves the Reader in that act.)

Attention is paid not only to the purely ideological function of the look, but also to the way in which the act of looking operates as a narrative unit. Some examples of the look can be seen to serve both an ideological and a narrative function. Others illustrate one of the functions more clearly than the other. Three key narrative functions have been chosen as a basis for this examination: plot movement, plot obstruction and plot retardation (Propp 1979, 21). Looking sometimes plays an important part in plot movement, leading to an action or reaction, and thereby becomes instrumental in moving the plot forward towards resolution and closure. On other occasions a look may lead to the opposite, namely plot obstruction. Alternatively, it may serve the related function of plot retardation as a delaying device. For instance, Tancredi's immobility on looking at Clorinda when he is about to fight Argante (a key figure on the pagan side) provides the opportunity for an additional narrative episode to take place. As a result of Tancredi's inaction, another Christian knight, who is of lesser importance, takes up the challenge unsuccessfully in his stead, so that the subsequent encounter between Tancredi and Argante is postponed. This, in turn, is not conclusive, and again the obstacle involves looking, as impaired vision due to failing light obstructs resolution.

The decisive encounter is thus both delayed and highlighted, taking place towards the end of the poem in Canto XIX, rather than early on in Canto VI. In this way plot retardation by means of devices depending on the look successfully prevents the premature killing and disappearance of a major character from the plot.

Again in the context of narrative function, the act of looking often operates as a vehicle for providing the Reader with plot information, rather than having any particular bearing on the relationship between the seeing subject and its object. This is often the case when the subject looks at the object to see it performing certain actions. Past actions, for instance, can be narrated by a character who has seen them take place. Additionally, as part of a conventional rhetorical attempt to make the narrative appear as vivid and lifelike as possible, the Reader is at times directly addressed by the poet in an exhortation to look.

The first stage in the analysis is to locate references to the act of looking and seeing in the poem. These amount to a total of about 1,500. In a poem of some 15,000 lines, the incidence of this particular semantic field appears quite high, although perhaps not surprisingly so. The epic form is characterized by action, which is necessarily accompanied by looking and seeing. These references fall into seven major semantic sections. The sections are not totally independent of each other. They can also, in some cases, be further divided. This is especially true of the first section, which contains 50 per cent of all examples of the look in the poem. An examination of the syntax of expressions of the look concludes the analysis. The semantic sections are as follows:

1. Looking and seeing
2. Not looking and not seeing
3. Appearing and not appearing
4. Directing the look of another
5. Seeming
6. Seeing as knowing
7. The Reader and the look

1. Looking and seeing

A distinction must first of all be made between the act of looking, staring and admiring, and the act of seeing and perceiving. A verb of looking constitutes a deliberate act of looking and is consequently more meaningful in the context of the politics of the look in which the look is used to establish or maintain a position of superiority over the person looked at. The act of seeing, on the other hand, does not necessarily constitute an intentional act, although it may do so on occasion, as well as functioning as precursor or follower to a look. The relative passivity of the act of seeing, in comparison with that of looking, is apparent particularly in cases when the subject sees the object as a result of the object presenting itself within the subject's field of vision (sect. 3). In such a case, the object may be regarded as determining the direction of the subject's look, and thereby attains a superior status with respect to the looker (e.g. God in I, 8).

When seeing has wider connotations of knowing, for instance in the case of God, the ultimate Seer, another dimension comes into play, namely that of knowledge (through sight) as power. Words of seeing in themselves already possess the dual meaning of cognitive as well as purely visual perception (instances of seeing which specifically denote knowledge will be dealt with in sect. 6). Of particular interest is whether any character has exclusive possession of this kind of sight or power. Numerically, instances of looking correspond roughly to those of seeing (341:370). However, varieties of verbs and verbal constructions of looking exceed those of seeing by a ratio of 5:1 (96:18). Instances of looking can be divided into the following groups: (a) looking, (b) directing the look, (c) staring, (d) spying, (e) looking and state of mind, (f) the woman's look as dangerous, (g) the penetrating or fragmenting look.

A. Looking

This type of look is the simple, standard look which is more numerous than any other in this section. The other groups consist of different ways of looking and prove to be more interesting. This is reflected by the greater variety of verbs occurring in these groups (and even at times, within the span of one single group). Although *looking* forms by far the largest group, it is expressed by only two verbs, predominantly *mirare* (sometimes *rimirare*) and, less frequently, *guardare* (or *ri(s)guardare*).

Leaving aside, for reasons of space, the not inconsiderable number of looks in which the object is non-human (almost 50%), and turning to the remaining examples, a pattern can be discerned when these are examined according to the type of analysis outlined above. Certain examples of the look conform to what has been defined as look type A, in that the terms used to describe the look, and to express its subject and object, suggest that the former is superior to the latter. For instance, in the following example: 'Il capitan ... / ... mirò in fronte i suoi' (II, 80, 5–6), the look is described as one which is directed fully into the face of the object (*in fronte*). The subject is expressed by a term of high military rank, while the objects are denoted by the possessive pronoun deriving from the subject, and are therefore inferior. This look is also part of a pattern of behaviour brought about by verbal conflict in which Goffredo reasserts his leadership, as well as maintaining a position of strength in response to the pagan challenge.

Other examples show the subject of a voyeuristic act of looking to be unseen by the object, who is consequently placed in a vulnerable position, the inferiority of which is confirmed by the actions carried out subsequently by the looker. For instance, Vafrino, unnoticed by the pagans, spends his time in their camp looking ('I guerrier, i destrier, l'arme rimira', XIX, 60, 3; 'Vafrin vi guata e par ch'ad altro intenda', XIX, 61, 7). As a result, he is able to thwart the pagan plot to kill Goffredo, thereby helping to ensure a Christian victory. Carlo and Ubaldo watch unseen from behind a bush ('Ascosi / mirano i duo guerrier gli atti amorosi', XVI, 19, 7–8), in a gratuitous act of voyeurism which precedes their subjugation of the lovers. Another instance is the temporarily dominant Armida, who 'senz'esser vista e ode e vede' (VII, 36, 8), and so ensures Tancredi's capture.

The reaction of the object to being looked at can also be an indication of whether the look is being used (or considered to have been used) as a means of asserting power. When Tancredi looks at Clorinda for the first time ('Egli mirolla', I, 47, 5), her reaction is aggressive ('ben l'assaliva', 48, 2). The warlike context in which the look takes place (both are armed) automatically gives it an overtly power-oriented connotation, and Clorinda reacts accordingly (even though this look is in reality one of love). In other cases, the look signifying and helping to reinforce power over inferiors is welcomed and indeed desired by the latter. This is typified by the positive attitude of the pagan king and the Christian commander to the looks of their superiors, Allah and God respectively (XII, 10, 7–8; V, 91, 3–4).

Other examples of *looking* can be seen to correspond to look type

B. In the following cases, it is the manner of the look, and sometimes also the way in which the looker is described (italicized in the following examples) which suggest that the subject of the look is inferior to the object: 'la donna ... / ... gli atti ... mira; / ... *ne teme e ne sospira*' (IV, 67, 3–4, 6); 'il piú giovin Buglione, il qual rimira / *con geloso occhio* il figlio di Sofia' (V, 8, 1–2); 'io miro *timido e confuso*' (XII, 31, 5) (the object being a tigress); '*Stupido* lor riguardo' (VIII, 29, 1); 'giovenetto, il qual *tacito e muto* / il riguardava' (XVII, 59, 5–6). The last two examples illustrate a recurring feature concerning the superior status of age over youth. Various *vecchi* in the poem, in the form of either *mago* or *eremita*, are seen to wield authority of a religious and social nature, especially over those younger than themselves.

The following two examples illustrate a look which has been instigated by a power superior to that of the looker, resulting in the manipulation of the subject of the look. In the first example, the Mago of Ascalona makes Rinaldo look at a shield displaying the heroic deeds of his ancestors, thereby precipitating the desired reaction: 'Rinaldo sveglia, in rimirando, mille / spirti d'onor da le natie faville' (XVII, 81, 7–8). In the next example, the Christian knights are obliged to look at the wood, which has been bewitched by Ismeno, if they are to use materials from it for the building of siege machines. This leads to the debilitating reaction planned by Ismeno: 'Ben ha tre volte e piú d'aspro diamante / rincinto il cor chi intrepido la guata' (XIII, 23, 5–6).

Both these examples perform a clearly discernible narrative, as well as ideological, function. In the former, the look instigated in an inferior by a superior leads to a reaction in which the sentiments of family honour and social duty are aroused. This is important in predisposing Rinaldo to divert all his energies into securing victory for his religion and society, thereby helping to move the plot forward towards resolution and closure. In the latter example, the movement of the plot towards closure is obstructed as the result of a reaction to a look instigated in the looker, once again, by a superior power. When the subject of the look is anonymous or generalized, and so de-individualized, in contrast to the object, it is again the subject that is inferior to the object. This is further emphasized when the object is expressed in positive terms, as in the following examples (with the subject capitalized and the positive object term italicized):

dolcemente feroce alzar vedresti

la *regal* fronte, e in lui mirar sol TUTTI …
se 'l miri fulminar ne l'arme avolto,
Marte lo stimi; *Amor*, se scopre il volto (I, 58, 3–4, 7–8)

gran TURBA scese de' fedeli al piano
d'ogni età mescolata e d'ogni sesso:
portò suoi doni al *vincitor* cristiano,
godea in mirarlo e in ragionar con esso (I, 77, 3–6)

… il *pio* Goffredo
… le GENTI averse
d'alto il miraro, e corse lor per l'ossa
un timor freddo (XI, 75, 5; 76, 5–7).

The last example also shows a typical reaction of an inferior subject looking at a more powerful object, namely fear. Another reaction of this type is to imitate the object, as in the example of Clorinda and the pagan women:

e mirando la vergine gagliarda,
vero amor de la patria arma le donne.
Correr le vedi e collocarsi in guarda (XI, 58, 3–5).

Other examples of the look in this group also perform a narrative function. The look of Erminia at Vafrino, for example, heralds another stage in the movement of the plot towards resolution, as it confirms her recognition of him. This in turn leads to their prevention of a possible plot obstruction by defusing the plan to kill Goffredo ('l'udí, guardollo, e poi gli venne a lato', XIX, 79, 4).

B. Directing the look

Directing the look is a slow-motion version of looking that contributes to the static, highly visual and picture-like quality of the poem. At times this process of slow motion can be taken to almost ridiculous extremes, as in the following example, which forms part of an attempt to emphasize the religious zeal of Piero:

… l'Eremita intanto
volgeva al cielo l'una e l'altra luce.
Non un color, non serba un volto: oh quanto
piú sacro e venerabile or riluce! (X, 73, 1–4).

The distinction between *directing the look* and *looking* in this context is therefore one of narrative function regarding intensity of effect, or vividness. Other features in this second group have both narrative and ideological implications. The directional element characterizing this group often lays special emphasis on the spatial dimension. The look can be directed upwards, downwards, or all around, and in each case the direction is significant. Looking around is indicated by the adverbial *intorno* and *in giro* in conjunction with words of looking, or by the verbs *volgere* or *rivolgere gli occhi* or *lo sguardo* and, in one instance, simply by *girare gli occhi*:

(1)   Il capitan *rivolse gli occhi in giro*
           tre volte e quattro, e mirò in fronte i suoi (II, 80, 5–6).

(2)   ... 'l capitano,
           poi ch'*intorno ha mirato*, a i suoi discende (III, 64, 1–2).

(3)   Goffredo *intorno* gli occhi gravi e tardi
           volge con mente allor dubbia e sospesa,
           né, perché molto pensi e molto guardi,
           atto gli s'offre alcuno a tanta impresa.
           Vi manca il fior de' suoi guerrier gagliardi (VII, 58, 1–5).

(4)   Sol con la faccia torva e disdegnosa
           tacito si rimase il fer circasso,
           a guisa di leon quando si posa,
           girando gli occhi e non movendo il passo (X, 56, 1–4).

(5)   ... al cavalier giacente, ...
           Stupido *intorno* ei *guarda*, e i servi e 'l loco
           al fin conosce ... (XII, 74, 2, 7–8).

(6)   Rinaldo ... (XIV, 57, 2)
           ... ei sol ... (58, 8)
           Come è là giunto, cupido e vagante
           volge intorno lo sguardo ... (59, 1–2).

(7)   Rinaldo intanto irresoluto bada,
           ché quel rischio di sé degno non era,
           e stima onor plebeo quand'egli vada
           per le comuni vie co 'l vulgo in schiera.
           E *volge intorno gli occhi*, e quella strada
           sol gli piace tentar ch'altri dispera (XVIII, 72, 1–6).

(8)   il buon Tancredi ...
           Dal letto il fianco infermo egli solleva,
           vien su la vetta e *volge gli occhi in giro*;
           vede, giacendo il conte, altri ritrarsi,
           altri del tutto già fugati e sparsi (XX, 83, 4–8).

The look around emerges from these examples as a look in the exclusive possession of a superior subject in the process of establishing or maintaining a position of power over an inferior, either directly or indirectly (look type A). In nos. 1 and 2, the subject is expressed by the superior military term *capitan*, while the *possessive* pronoun *suoi* is used for his military inferiors who are the object of his look in no. 1. He *descends* to his soldiers in no. 2, having ascended alone to the heights (physical/religious/political) of Jerusalem in order to survey the terrain and plan a strategy of attack for his army. In no. 1, the visual survey of *i suoi* by *il capitan* follows an aggressive address by Alete challenging the Christian army to abandon the campaign, and precedes Goffredo's reply, thereby appearing to function as a preliminary in re-establishing and reinforcing his leadership and superiority. This in turn is followed by an emphatically direct look into the faces of those he 'possesses' ('e mirò in fronte i suoi') prior to fixing his opponent with a stare ('e poi nel volto di colui gli affisse / ch'attendea la risposta') and finally replying verbally. Three different looks, beginning with looking around, are used here by Goffredo in an attempt to emphasize his superior position in relation both to his own men and to the opposition.

In no. 3, the subject of the look is not called *capitan*, but *Goffredo*. However, the object is yet again expressed using the notion of possession, this time in the form of the possessive adjective ('suoi guerrier gagliardi'). At this point Goffredo is looking around at his knights to induce one of them to take up Argante's challenge. But the tacit hope expressed by his look is not satisfied ('né, perché ... molto guardi, / atto gli s'offre alcuno a tanta impresa'). In this case, looking around is used as a means both of reasserting dominance and of exerting pressure on an inferior to act in a certain way, but is not successful, and Goffredo has to resort to verbal exhortation.

Nos. 6 and 7 show Rinaldo looking around. In no. 6 the object of his look is a new, enchanting environment in the form of an island used by Armida (representing evil, pagan forces) to distract him from his important social, warlike duties. It therefore functions as an obstacle to the Christian cause, in other words, to plot movement. The way Rinaldo looks around ('cupido e vagante') reveals the sensual part of his character to be dominant in this phase of his development. This facet of Rinaldo, namely his *id*, will be subjugated by his super-ego. For most characters in the poem, the actual locus of power-determined relationships which the act of looking helps to define is to be found on an interpersonal level. In the case of Rinaldo, however, it takes place not only interpersonally (with other people) but also intrapersonally (within himself), as discussed in the previous chapter. In example no. 7, it is on the interpersonal level that Rinaldo's second look around takes place. He looks for the most difficult point from which to attack Jerusalem in an attempt not only to prove his military superiority over the others by rejecting the *comuni vie* and an *onor plebeo*, but also to maintain a class difference between himself and the *vulgo*. There follows an account of the heroic exploits of this exemplary socio-military hero, whose central role in the defeat of the pagans is ordained by heaven and fostered throughout by both religious (Piero) and social (Ubaldo) patriarchs.

Another prominent Christian knight is the subject of nos. 5 and 8. Tancredi is also a *cavalier*, albeit, in no. 5, *giacente* and *stupido* because of his injuries. As he looks around him in an attempt to regain control over his environment, the first objects of his look to re-establish both his consciousness and his superior social position are his *servi*. Again in a supine state in no. 8, Tancredi looks around to find an opportunity to prove his superior position as a knight. He surveys the scene as the unprotected Raimondo is left abandoned and, despite his physical weakness, shouts a rebuke at the others who are running away, and then proceeds heroically to defend Raimondo himself.

The subject of the look around in no. 4, *il fer circasso* (Argante), maintains his position of strength (*fer*) and superiority by sending out an all-embracing look, even while at rest. The image of a lion suggests latent power and readiness for conflict; Argante's superiority throughout the poem is almost of an animal, rather than a military, nature. Because of this, although he is in a position of power among his own kind, when compared with the Christian Goffredo, his superiority is presented as being of a lower, less than human, degree.

The subjects of these examples of the look around, used to establish or maintain some form of superiority over the object of the look, are as follows: Goffredo, the Christian captain himself, who uses this look three times; Rinaldo and Tancredi, who each use it twice, and who are the most important Christian knights; and the pagan Argante, who uses it once, and then only as part of an animal metaphor. All these subjects of the look are of superior social/military rank (none is less than a *cavalier*), the majority belong to the 'superior' religion and all are male. Concomitantly, the objects of these looks are expressed in terms denoting inferiority to the possessor of the look. The look around can be considered instrumental in the imposition and maintenance of power and, as such, forms part of the body politics underpinning the existing power balance.

Another subdivision of the spatial group *directing the look* also fulfils this function. This is the look which is directed downwards, denoted by the adverbial *in giú, in giuso, da l'alto soglio, dal cielo* and *dal suo gran seggio*, in conjunction with the verbs *(ri)volgere gli occhi/i lumi/lo sguardo/il guardo*, or by implication when it is *il Padre eterno* looking at his earthly *schiere fedeli*. Instances of the downward look reveal the subject to be either God, who uses it four times, or Goffredo, the divinely ordained Christian captain, who uses it once, and then as part of a heaven-sent dream:

(1)   quando *da l'alto soglio* il Padre eterno,
        ch'è ne la parte piú del ciel sincera,
        e quanto è da le stelle al basso inferno,
        tanto è piú in su de la stellata spera,
        gli occhi in giú volse, e in un sol punto e in una
        vista mirò ciò ch'in sé il mondo aduna (I, 7, 3–8).

(2)   *Gli occhi* fra tanto a la battaglia rea
        dal suo gran seggio il Re del Ciel *volgea*.
        Sedea colà ... (IX, 55, 7–8; 56, 1).

(3)   Le accolse il Padre eterno, ed a le schiere
        fedeli sue *rivolse* il guardo pio (XIII, 72, 5–6).

(4)   sedeva al suo governo il Re del mondo, ...
        e *rivolgea dal Cielo* al franco duce
        lo sguardo favorevole e giocondo (XIV, 2, 4–6).

(5)   Cosí l'un [Ugone] disse; e l'altro [Goffredo] *in giuso i lumi*
        volse, quasi sdegnando, e ne sorrise,
        ché vide un punto sol, mar, terre e fiumi,
        che qui paion distinti in tante guise,
        ed ammirò che pur a l'ombre, a i fumi,
        la nostra folle umanità s'affise (XIV, 11, 1–6).

God is expressed twice in a way denoting the superior family member, and with a capital 'P' ('Padre'). He bears the *Nom-du-père* par excellence, never to be supplanted because he is *il Padre eterno*. In nos. 2 and 4, God is also given the superior social rank of *Re* (again with a capital letter). Example no. 1 emphasizes how high this supreme figure of God is above *il mondo*, thereby underlining the link between spatial difference, in terms both of distance and direction, and power itself. In no. 5, Goffredo (*l'altro*) is accorded the same vision as God, as they see the world *in un punto sol* and *in un sol punto*, respectively. Goffredo is God's supreme representative on earth, and it is his duty to carry out the orders of his Father and King in his role as *sommo capitano*. As power is transmitted down from God to Goffredo, the latter is raised temporarily to the level of God's vision, as his superior status over the other Christians is reinforced and he is given specific instructions on how to command them.

Unlike most instances of the freewheeling look, the object in these particular examples is unaware of being looked down upon, a factor which underlines the superior position of the looker. In addition, the object in nos. 1 and 5 is reduced to diminutive proportions by the look, as the entire world is seen as *un sol punto* and *un punto sol*. The notion of the superior subject/looker as possessor of the object recurs here in no. 3, when God looks down at 'le schiere fedeli *sue*', while submission and obedience, characteristic patterns in the behaviour of an inferior towards a superior, are suggested by the other qualifier (*fedeli*). Class difference is the criterion by which the superiority of the looker is determined in no. 4, where the subject, described as *Re*, looks down at the object, *duce*. The exact domain of power is also detailed in each case: the superior *Re* rules the whole world (*del mondo*), whereas the inferior *duce* has power only over the Franks (*franco duce*). Recognition of disobedience and revolt (the behaviour of an inferior attempting to reverse power positions) is revealed by the pejorative description of the object in no. 2 as 'la battaglia *rea*', as, in God's words, the outcast 'empia schiera d'Averno' challenges *his* (*mia*) obedient (*fedel*) flock. The critical expression 'la battaglia rea' is not spoken by God, but occurs in a passage of third-person narration, therefore constituting a direct judgement on the part of the poet as persona. This detail illustrates Tasso's not unexpected concordance with God's view, and his automatic identification with the Christian cause.

All the objects of the downward directed look are expressed so as to imply that spatial inferiority is indicative of inferiority in terms of power. Another aspect of the look which contributes to this polarization of power is the posture of the subject. In examples no. 1 and 4, and twice in no. 2, reference is made to the sitting position of God ('da l'alto soglio', 'dal suo gran seggio', 'Sedea colà', 'sedeva al suo governo'). Superiority is underlined by the relaxed, stationary position of the looker, before whose eyes the inferior object moves around, or even knowingly parades, as in the case of Goffredo and his troops: 'S'era egli *fermo*, e si vedea davanti / passar distinti i cavalieri e i fanti' (I, 35, 7–8). A similar case is the position of Armida in her temporarily superior status over the Christian knights whom she has successfully lured to her castle: 'ed in *eccelsa* parte Armida *siede*, onde senz'esser vista e ode e vede' (VII, 36, 7–8). The Egyptian king, too, sits high above his subjects:

> Egli in *sublime soglio*, a cui per cento
> gradi eburnei s'ascende, *altero siede* ...
> Cosí *sedea*, cosí scopria il tiranno
> d'*eccelsa* parte i popoli adunati;
> tutti *a' suoi piè* ... (XVII, 10, 1–2; 13, 5–7).

The look directed downwards can be categorized with the freewheeling look as one of the types of look used to establish or maintain power (look type A). Looking upwards at someone, conversely, is the look of an inferior to a superior (look type B) (denoted in the following examples by variations of *alzare il guardo*):

(1)   *Alzo* allor, bench'a pena, *il debil ciglio*
e veggio due vestiti in lungo manto
tener due faci, e dirmi sento: 'O figlio' (VIII, 27, 4–6).

(2)   Desto il Soldan *alza lo sguardo*, e vede
uom che d'età gravissima a i sembianti (X, 9, 1–2).

(3)   Vergognando tenean basse le fronti,
ch'era al cor picciol fallo amaro morso.
Al fin del re britanno il chiaro figlio
ruppe il silenzio, e disse *alzando il ciglio* (X, 59, 5–8).

(4)   S'offerse a gli occhi di Goffredo allora,
invisibile altrui, l'agnol Michele (XVIII, 92, 1–2).
'*Leva piú in su l'ardite luci*, e tutta
la grande oste del ciel congiunta guata'.
Egli *alzò il guardo*, e vide ... (96, 1–3).

(5)   Qui chinò vinti *i lumi* e gli *alzò* poi,
né lo spettacol grande ei piú rivide (XVIII, 97, 1–2).

(6)   ... ella rivenendo alzò la china
faccia, del non suo pianto or lagrimosa.
Tre volte *alzò le luci* e tre chinolle
dal caro oggetto, e rimirar no 'l volle (XX, 129, 5–8).

With the exception of no. 5, the upward look in these examples is not freely produced by the looker, but is prompted by the action or suggestion of another character. This is unlike examples of the downward directed look of the superior, in which only Goffredo looks down at Ugone's suggestion. God, however, looks down at will, unless responding to prayer. The latter case differs from the others in that the downward direction is not suggested adverbially, but is implicated by the earthly object. This is also the only example of God looking down in which no mention is made of his seated position.

The subject in the first example is inspired to look up when his attention is drawn to a light accompanied by whispering. Looking up, he sees two hermits, one heaven-sent, who is referred to as old (*il vecchio santo*, 34, 3; *il vecchio*, 40, 1; *dal santo vecchio*, 42, 7). This is a truly patriarchal character. As well as being aged and authorized in his position by the highest power, he imposes his authority by opening the conversation with an imperative. He also addresses Carlo as *figlio*, an inferior position in the social context of family hierarchy. By using this term, the hermit takes over the superior, correlative position of *padre*. In the second example, it is once more a character with the patriarchal attributes of authority (*voce severa*) and age (*d'età gravissima*) who causes another, in this case Solimano, to look up at him. This particular *uomo antico* is Ismeno. After an initially domineering reaction, Solimano becomes submissive and accepts an inferior, filial position (' "Padre", risponde' X, 13, 35).

Piety is one of the hallmarks of a superior person in the third example, in which it is *il pio Goffredo* who, in the company of the patriarchal instigator of the entire crusade, prompts another to look up at him. The element of superiority is underlined by the fact that the Christian leader is referred to by name, whereas the subject of the upward look bears only the *Nom-du-père* ('del re britanno il chiaro figlio'). The illustriousness of the father, and the positive attribute of *chiaro* given to his offspring, do not detract from the actual anonymity and inferiority, in patrilineal terms, of the son. If anything, the power of the father throws into greater relief the lesser status of the son. The fact that the poet does not feel the necessity to mention him by name at all in this episode (nor at XI, 42, 2) indicates that this manner of identification is considered to be sufficient, rather than simply the result of purely metrical dictates. The inferior subject of the upward look also emerges from a state of shame indicating subordination to another.

In no. 4, Goffredo is told to look up at the heavenly host, divine beings who are superior to all humans, by another divine figure, the archangel Michael. The relationship of inferior looking up at superior is further supported by the fact that the former is instructed where to look. When Goffredo looks up of his own volition in the following example, he does not, significantly, see what he expects. In example no. 6, Rinaldo's tears force Armida to look up at him, which she does, unwillingly. In all these examples of the upward look, the inferior looker is made to look up at a superior, an act which functions ideologically as a reiteration and consequent reacceptance of position (look type B).

Directing the look can also be used for the narrative effect of vividness, for example, to convey the intricacies of combat (with a notable parallelism in the following example between *colpi* and *guardi*): 'Cautamente ciascuno a i colpi *move* / la destra, a i guardi *l'occhio*' (VI, 42, 1–2). It can also form part of a larger narrative function, such as contributing to Armida's strategy for distracting the Christians from their activities against the pagans. This is initiated by her appearance in the Christian camp, which attracts all looks in her direction: 'A l'apparir de la beltà novella / nasce un bisbiglio e *'l guardo ognun v'intende*' (IV, 28, 3–4).

C. Staring

This group uses a similarly wide range of verbs and verbal phrases: *affissar(si)*, *(af)fissare lo sguardo, gli occhi, fissare la vista, affissare le ciglia, mirare fiso, tenere fisse le luci/il volto diritto, pendere dal volto di, non battere occhio/torcere la fronte da, affiggere in*, and *fermare il guardo intento*. The most frequently used verb is *(af)fissar(si)*, which occurs in 50 per cent of the examples.

Staring, like *directing the look*, is a variation of the standard type of look represented by the first group, *looking*, and can be described as a prolonged, intensified version. A certain type of *directing the look*, namely looking up at the sky, was seen earlier to have religious connotations. When this is accompanied by the intensity of the stare, religious devoutness is indicated. The first of the next two examples presages the second, as Clorinda sees Sofronia staring at the sky in an attitude that prefigures her own final, post-baptismal look: 'vede ... / e tacer lei *con gli occhi* al ciel sí *fisa*' (II, 42, 5, 7) and 'e *gli occhi* al ciel *affisa*' (XII, 69, 3).

The emphatic intensity of this type of look often has the effect of drawing particular attention to the object being looked at, a feature which makes it especially suitable as a vehicle for introducing narrative information. This can serve the function of presenting necessary background details for subsequent action, the narration of which can proceed without the encumbrance, for example, of character description. Background information to the entire Crusade is introduced in this way at the beginning of the poem by the prolonged stare of God. Having directed his all-seeing look at the whole world, he then focuses exclusively on the Christian Crusaders: '*s'affisò* poi ne' principi cristiani' (I, 8, 2). What is seen as a result of this stare provides an introduction to major Christian characters ('vede Goffredo ... Baldovin ... Tancredi ... Boemondo ... Rinaldo ... Guelfo'), and accompanies a succinct description of each.

The identity of the looker is important here in that it serves the additional function of ensuring verisimilitude, and not only in the Aristotelian sense. God is the ultimate Looker and, for him, to look is to know. Whatever he sees is indisputable and must be given credence. This applies not only to factual information, but extends also to what are in effect value judgements. Consequently the pagans are automatically and indisputably *empi*, and Tancredi's love *vano*. Acceptance of the total authority of the looker entails acceptance of an entire code in which *empio* and *vano* (relating to earthly rather than heavenly desires, as well as 'coming to naught'), also signify 'wrong'. This surplus signified constitutes the ideological kernel of the passage, and is conveyed covertly.

In addition to introducing narrative information providing a backcloth for action, the stare can also function in preparing the ground for subsequent action by drawing attention to the participants who are about to be involved. One such look is that of the pagan king who stares at Rinaldo ('n lui *fisa lo sguardo*' III, 37, 7). As well as providing yet another opportunity to emphasize the central importance of Rinaldo with hyperbolic praise of his prowess, this stare also introduces a description of Dudone and Gernando. This prepares the Reader for an important episode linking all three warriors which is to take place a few stanzas later, culminating in Rinaldo's departure from the Christian camp. This is a highly significant plot obstruction which is not removed until eleven cantos later. Rinaldo's return precipitates plot movement towards resolution as he removes perhaps the greatest obstacle to the Christian cause by disenchanting the wood.

On another level Aladino's stare, which is accompanied by Erminia's description of the status of each warrior, also forms part of an attempt to acquire knowledge about the enemy, an important prerequisite for any imposition of power. When an armed knight confronts Tancredi, the latter stares at him in a similar way. In this case, staring leads to recognition: '*S'affisa* a quel parlar Tancredi in lui / e riconosce l'arme' (VII, 33, 3–4). An element of aggression may be present in this stare of Tancredi, whose reply to Rambaldo is menacing ('empio fellon'). Goffredo's fixing of his opponent (Alete) with a stare is openly hostile, and is a clear attempt to assert power (look type A): 'Il capitan rivolse gli occhi in giro / e poi nel volto di colui gli *affisse* / ch'attendea la risposta' (II, 80, 5, 7–8).

Other examples of the stare used to gain knowledge are two of the three cases of *osservare* ('il fanciullo … / cauto *osserva* Argillan', IX, 83, 1, 5, and 'l'arti e gli ordini *osserva*', XIX, 60, 4). Both subjects of this stare (Argillan and Vafrino) do so unnoticed by the object (Lesbino and the Egyptian army respectively), and in both cases this leads to a superior position for the looker: Argillan slays Lesbino, and Vafrino uncovers the Egyptian plan to kill Goffredo. The subject of the third case of *osservare* (Armida), on the other hand, is known to be doing so. This kind of observing, which is not carried out from a superior position of secrecy, is used by an inferior to monitor the success or failure of a request to a superior, in this case Goffredo (look type B). Armida's two other stares at the Christian captain in the same passage are also those of a subordinate, and are accompanied by reactions of apprehension and fear ('ne teme e sospira'): 'la donna in lui *s'affisa*' (IV, 67, 3) and 'la donna … dal suo volto / intenta *pende*' (IV, 67, 3–4). Her position of inferiority (which is of course feigned) is reversed later when she notices that members of the pagan council are under her control because all have their eyes fixed on her: 'ella che vede / tutte le viste in sé *fisse ed intente*', XVII, 42, 1–2).

Other examples of the stare show a subject who is not in control of the look, but who is forced by the nature of the object to stare at it. This is indicated in some cases by the reaction to the object causing the stare (both the reaction and the verb of staring are italicized):

> l'altro, *attonito* quasi e *stupefatto*,
> pur là *s'affissa* e nulla udir ben mostra (VI, 28, 5–6)
> Io *non sapea da tal vista levarmi* (VIII, 39, 7)

> *Stupido* il cavalier le ciglia inarca,
> ed *increspa la fronte*, e *mira fiso*
> la nube e 'l carro ... (X, 17, 1–3).

In other cases the reason for the stare instigated in the subject appears in the description of the object. The following examples show an element of scopophilia as the beauty of the object excites a look that is prolonged because it is pleasurable:

> *Fisa* egli *tosto gli occhi* al *bel lavoro*
> del bianco marmo ... (XIV, 57, 7–8)

> ... 'n su la *vaga fronte*
> *pende* omai sí che par Narciso al fonte (XIV, 66, 7–8).

The following examples show, in the first case, the stare caused by pleasure in novelty, while in the second case an element of pleasure in dread is also present:

> il guerrier ... *affisa*
> a *maggior novitate* allor *le ciglia* (XVIII, 26, 1–2)

and:

> Questo popolo e quello incerto *pende*
> da sí *novo* spettacolo ed *atroce* (VI, 49, 1–2).

D. Spying

The feature of the unseen looker, present in some instances of the stare by a superior subject seeking information about an inferior object, recurs in some cases of *spying*. The purpose of this is specifically to acquire information (for example, '*spia* gli occulti disegni' XIX, 60, 6), and 'Da la concava nube il turco fero / non veduto rimira e *spia* d'intorno' X, 35, 1–2). The information sought is hidden, an indication of deliberate concealment on the part of an object on the defensive, portrayed by terms such as *occulti* (XIX, 60, 6), *secreti* (X, 18, 3; XVIII, 56, 8) and *celi* (XIV, 42, 6). An aggressive subject is clearly in evidence in the following examples using the metaphor of a wolf:

> Qual lupo predatore ...
> le chiuse mandre insidiando aggira,
> ... tale egli intorno *spia* (XIX, 35, 1–2, 5)

and:

cosí lupi notturni …
… per la nebbia oscura
vanno a le mandre e *spian* come in lor s'entre (XX, 44, 5–7).

E. *Looking and state of mind*

The look is sometimes used more obviously as an instrument of aggression in establishing dominance in cases of looking that reveal the state of mind of the looker. The herald reporting back to Argante says: 'mille i' vidi *minacciosi sguardi*' (VI, 20, 5) and Carlo, relating the fate of Sveno: 'Quando ecco furiando a lui s'aventa / uom grande, c'ha sembiante e *guardo atroce*' (VIII, 23, 5–6). This type of look is, not surprisingly, most typically found in a battle context. Other examples use vocabulary denoting heat: 'fuor de la visiera *escono ardenti* / *gli sguardi*' (VII, 42, 7–8), '*arde il feroce* / *sguardo*' (IX, 76, 1–2), and 'il vecchio accolto / … *drizza gli occhi accesi* a ciascun loco' (XX, 87, 2, 5).

The notion that the look reveals the looker's state of mind was by no means a novelty in the sixteenth century, particularly in view of the Neoplatonic idea that the eyes are the window of the soul. Other examples outside the context of battle appear in Erminia's admission to Vafrino of her love for Tancredi:

> e 'n vece forse della lingua, *il guardo*
> manifestava il foco onde tutt'ardo (XIX, 96, 7–8)

and, in conjunction with movements of the body:

> La fanciulla regal …
> … *nel moto de gli occhi* e de le membra
> non già di boschi abitatrice sembra (VII, 17, 5, 7–8)

and:

> … il sommo duce
> e *ne l'atto de gli occhi* e de le membra
> altro che mortal cosa egli rassembra (XX, 7, 1, 7–8).

F. *The woman's look as dangerous*

In connection with the look used as an instrument of aggression, there is one specific group that is openly regarded in the poem as particularly dangerous. This is the woman's look, especially that of Armida, of her likeness in the enchanted wood, and of her nymphs. This look is used as part of a pattern of behaviour designed to obstruct the progression of the plot by diverting the attention of the Christian knights. Guglielmo, their spokesman, relates how Armida's looks had rendered them powerless by controlling and intensifying their emotions: 'Nutrian gli amori e i nostri sdegni … / … guardi' (X, 60, 7–8). The intrinsic element of power assertion in her look is directly conveyed by a variety of power-related words. The metaphor of riding equipment, obvious instruments of control, is present (italicized) in the following examples:

> Or tien pudica il guardo in sé raccolto,
> Or lo rivolge cupido e vagante:
> la sferza in quegli, il freno adopra in questi (IV, 87, 5–7).

Signs of diffidence and refusal to accept dominance are countered by a look that functions like a spur:

> Se scorge alcun che dal suo amor ritiri
> l'alma, e i pensier per diffidenza affrene,
> gli apre un benigno riso, e in dolci giri
> volge le luci in lui liete e serene;
> e cosí i pigri e timidi desiri
> sprona (IV, 88, 1–6).

The look of Armida is used like a weapon, and is considered an arme (V, 65, 1). The dangerous potency of her look and that of her nymphs is not to be underestimated, as is indicated by the following patriarchal warnings: 'né beltà che soave o rida o guardi, / con tenere lusinghe il cor ti pieghi' (XVIII, 10, 6–7) and, regarding her donzelle infide, 'voi, gli sguardi … / sprezzando' (XIV, 75, 7–8). The 'wrongness' of the power inherent in un girar d'occhi is pinpointed in Rinaldo's realization:

> e miriam noi torbida luce e bruna
> ch'un girar d'occhi …
> scopre in breve confin di fragil viso (XVIII, 13, 6–8).

As the plot closes, Armida's weapons (both her look and her bow) are finally rendered powerless: 'Colpo d'occhio o di man non pote in lui' (XX, 66, 5).

Armida's look is one of the weapons used by evil forces supporting the pagan cause, and is openly integrated into the plot. However, her look is not restricted to Christians. It is in effect used to gain control over men, rather than simply over Christians as opposed to pagans. This would seem to indicate an area of conflict based on sexual dif-

ference which overrides the overt conflict based on religious difference. This coincides with a feature that emerges when examining the
woman both as subject and object of the look in this poem. Women
both see and look at men (47 and 63 times) as often as men see and
look at women (50 and 61 times). However, there is a difference in
the type of look used, the major discrepancy being that men are the
sole possessors of the look that penetrates and/or fragments.

G. *The penetrating/fragmenting look*

This look invariably has sexual connotations of an aggressive nature,
doubtless a response to fear of the woman's look or sexuality as dangerous (see Ch. 5). Since men are the sole proprietors of this look, of
which a woman is invariably the object, it seems clear that sexual conflict, in which men dominate, is very much present. This type of look
takes the form of an almost tactile penetration of the woman's body.
In the following example, the look-as-phallus corresponds directly to
desire (*occhi* = *amoroso pensier* = phallus) before its entry is described:

> ... invida vesta:
> invida, ma s'a gli occhi il varco chiude,
> l'amoroso pensier già non arresta,
> ché non ben pago di bellezza esterna
> ne gli occulti secreti anco s'interna (IV, 31, 4–8).

It penetrates: 'per entro il chiuso manto osa il pensiero / sí *penetrar* ne
la vietata parte'. Then it fragments:

> ... ivi contempla il vero
> di tante meraviglie *a parte a parte*;
> poscia al desio le narra e le descrive (IV, 32, 5–7).

In another example of this look, *desir* = *occhi cupidi* = *guardo* = phallus:

> Non lascia il desir vago a freno sciolto,
> ma gira gli occhi cupidi con arte:
> volge un guardo ... (XIX, 69, 3–5).

The look begins by fragmenting: 'volge un guardo a la mano, uno al
bel volto' and then penetrates:

> talora insidia piú guardata parte,
> e là s'interna ove mal cauto apria
> fra due mamme un bel vel secreta via (XIX, 69, 6–8).

The penetration of the city's defences is described in almost identical terms which place the battering ram in the same position of phallus:

> … aspro ariete,
> onde comincia omai …
> a discoprir *le interne vie secrete* (XI, 51, 2–4).

One symbol of power (Jerusalem) is aggressed by another (the battering ram), thereby underlining the essential *power* element implicit in
the phallus, as well as emphasizing the fact that sexual conflict is
power-related, rather than exclusively a matter of erotics.

The aggressive nature of this type of penetration is apparent in the
suggestively defensive vocabulary often used in the description of the
object, such as fleeing ('*s'invola* / … a gli sguardi', II, 14, 7–8), secret
(*secreti*, IV, 31, 8; *secreta via*, XIX, 69, 8), closed ('invida vesta: / … a
gli occhi il varco *chiude*', IV, 31, 4–5; *chiuso manto*, IV, 32, 3), forbidden (*vietata* parte, IV, 32, 4), guarded ('piú *guardata* parte', XIX, 69, 6)
and badly guarded ('*mal cauto apria* / … secreta via', XIX, 69, 7–8).
This look is thinly disguised in the following example by a metaphor
that ultimately has the effect of rendering the sexual connotations
even more explicit:

> Vergine era fra lor di già matura
> verginità …
> È il suo pregio maggior che tra le mura
> d'angusta casa asconde i suoi gran pregi (II, 14, 1–2, 5–6)

> Pur guardia esser non può ch'in tutto celi
> beltà degna ch'appaia e che s'ammiri;
> né tu il consenti, Amor, ma la riveli
> d'un giovenetto a i cupidi desiri.
> Amor, ch'or cieco, or Argo, or ne veli
> di benda gli occhi, or ce gli apri e giri,
> tu per mille custodie entro a i piú casti
> verginei alberghi il guardo altrui portasti (II, 15).

Here *guardo/desiri*/phallus penetrates *angusta casa/casti verginei alberghi*/
vagina. The metaphor of a house for Sofronia's body, and the dis-
placement of responsibility from Olindo to Amor, may be linked to
the high status of these two characters in the main plot, in which they
both figure as paragons of Christian virtue. Sexual conflict surfaces
nonetheless to counter the purportedly paramount theme of
Christians vs. pagans. As a result Sofronia and Olindo are placed on
opposite sides, thereby creating a Christian (man) vs. Christian
(woman) conflict.

Another form of attenuation can be seen in the example of what is essentially a fragmenting look by Tancredi at Clorinda:

> … il cavalier …
> né sí dal ferro a riguardarsi attende,
> come a guardar i begli occhi e le gote
> ond'Amor l'arco inevitabil tende (III, 24, 1–4).

Responsibility is once again taken away from a Christian character and given to Amor. The main area of disguise here is the use of a traditional mode of reference, namely love poetry, in relation to parts of the body that are not as overtly sexual as those objectified in the previous examples. This look occurs shortly after another traditional device, the topos of the sudden release of long hair from a displaced helmet to denote the unexpected revelation of a woman's presence on the battlefield (Shepherd 1981). In this case it is Tancredi who breaks the straps, with the result that 'parte nuda ella ne resta' (III, 21, 4). The attenuation of this dismembering look would seem to favour not only the Christian, male looker, but also the pagan, female object. There is no doubt that Clorinda's position as a woman is a privileged one, with her whiteness, despite her black mother, a sign of the poet's empathy with the character (Connelly 1977). However, this look still contains elements of the fragmenting look found in more extreme form elsewhere in the poem. In other words, the identity of the object determines *how* the look takes place, but it takes place all the same.

The different types of attenuation found in the case of Clorinda and Sofronia are notably absent when Armida is the object of this look. In the penetrating/fragmenting look analysed above (IV, 31–2), the subject is not even a named individual, but the entire Christian army. This look consequently takes on the character of a generic, male look. Given the fact that Armida's role in the plot is to distract Christian knights on behalf of pagan forces, it comes as no surprise that there is no attenuation in her case. In another example, it is not clear whether it is she and/or the other *donzelle* who are the object of Altamor's look:

> … Altamor, ch'in cerchio accolto
> fra le donzelle alquanto era in disparte.
> Non lascia il desir vago a freno sciolto,
> ma gira gli occhi …
> Alza alfin gli occhi Armida (XIX, 69, 1–4, 70, 1).

The object of the Altamor's look appears to be a de-personalized, de-individualized female body, or ultimately the female body itself (also pagan here). His look is therefore displaced from the main plot (pagan vs. Christian) into a purely sexual zone, and suggests another surfacing of sexual conflict into and across the overt zone of interest. One possible conclusion to be drawn from this is that Armida performs two functions in these examples. As well as being a significant obstruction to the Christian cause and the epitome of paganism and evil, she is also the epitome of Woman. In her latter function she encapsulates the female side of the sexual conflict in the poem, together with her diametrical opposite (in terms of the main plot), namely Sofronia.

Another dimension of this look reveals the extent of its permeation into the narrative. The penetrating/fragmenting look is not only invariably in male possession, but is sometimes also shared by other male characters watching the looker. For instance, the fragmenting look of Rinaldo is narrated and re-enacted in breathless, excitable, rhythmically repetitive detail ('quinci … quinci … quinci') by the Mago, a character of high social and religious status, to two other male characters, who thereby also become bearers of this look of sexual arousal:

> … là con gli occhi corse,
> e mover vide un'onda …
> e quinci alquanto d'un crin biondo uscio,
> e quinci di donzella un volto sorse,
> e quinci il petto e le mammelle, e de la
> sua forma infin dove vergogna cela (XIV, 60, 2–3, 5–8).

Another example is that of Vafrino looking at Altamor looking at women. The additional element of another, unseen, male looker who partakes of Rinaldo's and Altamor's stare reinforces the dominant position of the male look.

The heightened superiority of the voyeur is again found in the case of Carlo and Ubaldo, whose look suggestively penetrates first of all the plants, 'Ecco tra fronde e fronde il guardo inante / penetra' (XIV, 17, 5–6), and is then involved in an erotic interplay between seeing and not seeing, 'e vede, o pargli di vedere, / vede pur certo', before coming to rest on the *atti amorosi* of Armida and Rinaldo. Carlo and Ubaldo continue their observations from a hidden vantage point. The emphatic position of *ascosi*, after a full stop (an infrequent feature in the middle of a line) and at the end of a line, serves to underline the importance of the looker being hidden: 'Ascosi / mirano i duo guerrier gli atti amorosi' (XVI, 19, 7–8).

In the case of the unseen Carlo and Ubaldo looking at Armida and Rinaldo, and the unseen Vafrino watching Altamor looking at women, there is yet another person (also unseen) who shares the look of both hidden and non-hidden lookers. This is the Reader, who not only shares all looks from a hidden vantage point, but is moreover placed by the text in the position of the looker, rather than of the person being looked at. The Reader is thereby invited to play the part of a voyeur twice removed, as it were. This indicates that the point of view for and by which this part of the text was written is a male one. The poetic 'camera eye' is clearly that of the male spectator, while female vision is not shared. Indeed, Altamor's/the Reader's penetrating look is cut short when Armida looks up. His look takes place during the absence of Armida's, as does that of Adrasto and Tisaferno. The male look is permitted by her 'not looking', while she is 'romita e sospirosa', with her eyes cast down.

2. Not looking and not seeing

In this section there is a clearly distinguishable group of examples referring to women who specifically do not look. For reasons of a sexual nature, such as modesty, or shame, they look down at the ground rather than at the man. In the case of Armida, there are many instances when this is a deliberate act of false modesty, a simulation of the obsequious pose of the socially correct, virtuous woman, that forms part of her design to distract and gain control over men. This has the desired effect on Eustazio, for instance: 'e rimirar da presso i lumi volse / che dolcemente atto modesto inchina' (IV, 34, 3–4). She is able to induce 'timore e riverenza' when 'de' cari detti e de' begli occhi è parca' (IV, 89, 3, 4). This is described as an art: 'Usa ogn'arte la donna ... / Or tien pudica il guardo in sé raccolto' (IV, 87, 1, 5). Womanly shame and modesty are artfully displayed by *l'ingannatrice donna*: 'O pur le luci vergognose e chine / tenendo, d'onestà s'orna e colora' (IV, 94, 1–2).

In Erminia's case, however, the modesty and shame of her downcast eyes are not feigned: 'E qui si tacque, e di rossor si tinse / e chinò gli occhi ... / ... vergognando' (XIX, 90, 2–3, 6). Chastity is the particular form of modesty characterizing Sofronia, receiving six direct mentions in the space of thirty-three lines, beginning with: 'Vergine era fra lor di già matura / verginità' (II, 14, 1–2). She steps out into the crowd, keeping her eyes appropriately averted: 'raccolse gli occhi, andò nel vel ristretta' (II, 18, 3). There is further emphasis on her not looking a few lines later. Despite the fact that she herself is being looked at, she does not return the look: 'Mirata da ciascun passa, e non mira / l'altera donna' (II, 19, 1–2). When she does look at Olindo, it is in an unmistakably non-sexual manner: 'umanamente / con occhi di pietade in lui rimira' (II, 30, 1–2). She looks, significantly, from a position of powerlessness as 'la bella prigioniera' (II, 27, 5). This takes the form of violent sexual subjection:

> Presa è la bella donna ...
> Già 'l velo e 'l casto manto a lei rapito,
> stringon le molli braccia aspre ritorte (II, 26, 1, 3–4).

The veil in which she could remain *ristretta*, recalling the *mura d'angusta casa* within which she hid her *gran pregi*, is now forcefully taken away from her, together with her *casto manto*. Her look is now powerless. This serves to undermine her claim to a masculine degree of strength in reply to Olindo's remark: 'Non pensò, non ardí, né far potea / donna sola e inesperta opra cotanta' (II, 28, 3–4):

> Non son io dunque senza te possente
> a sostener ciò che d'un uom può l'ira?
> Ho petto anch'io (II, 30, 5–7).

Clorinda is never the subject of this type of looking away, but she too is rendered powerless in a way that is clearly sexually related, when her defeat in combat makes her *la trafitta / vergine* (XII, 65, 1–2). Although she is regarded as equal to a man in strength and valour, she has to resort to devious means in order to avoid appearing as a mere *donzella* among knights, a fate she considers unacceptable:

> Quanto me' fòra in monte od in foresta
> a le fère aventar dardi e quadrella,
> ch'ove il maschio valor si manifesta
> mostrarmi qui tra cavalier donzella! (XII, 4, 1–4).

So as to carry out her plan to burn the tower, she places herself in an 'inferior' female position, arguing that, as a 'mere' woman, she is dispensable: 'Pure io femina sono, e nulla riede / mia morte in danno a la città smarrita' (XII, 8, 5–6). She even gives Argante credit for the idea itself: 'Argante qui ... / quella machina eccelsa arder promette' (XII, 10,

1–2). She then defers to his masculine superiority by saying: 'io sarò seco'.

The price she pays for carrying out her subversive plan to show *maschio valor* is not only to remain in this inferior position (it is implied that Argante could have saved her in XII, 49), but to die shortly afterwards (XII, 68). That she is punished specifically for assuming an inappropriately masculine role is mirrored by the surface narrative. Her donning of a different set of clothes (they are masculine and unadorned: 'senza piuma o fregio') is labelled *infausto annunzio*, and not only alarms Arsete, but prevents Tancredi from recognizing her 'true' (gender) identity. This precipitates her death at his hands. It also echoes the forbidden nature of same-sex role-change epitomized by the unhappy predicament of Erminia wearing Clorinda's apparel.

The sexually oriented version of *not looking*, denoting stereotypically feminine modesty and shame, is synonymous with dutiful passivity, behaviour indicative of an inferior in the presence of a superior. As it is used exclusively by only one section of society, namely women, it may be regarded as a gender-specific means of reinforcing the inferior status of this particular group (look type B). Shame of a different sort is the reason for *not looking* or *looking down* when the subject of the look is male. This type of shame stems from guilt as a result of behaviour condemned as wrong by a social superior in military, religious and age hierarchies. It does not, in other words, stem directly from the actual sexuality of the subject, as in the case of the woman not looking. Thus Alcasto's reaction to not having been able to fulfil his boast to conquer the enchanted wood:

> di trista vergogna acceso e muto …
> … quella faccia alzar …
> ne la luce de gli uomini non osa (XIII, 29, 5, 7–8)

is judged a result of *diffetto e fuga* by his military superior, *il capitan* (XIII, 30, 5–6). Similarly, when Goffredo asks a group of knights to explain what he has condemned as 'de' vostri brevi errori il dubbio corso', their guilt and consequent shame are apparent: 'Vergognando tenean basse le fronti' (X, 59, 5). And when Ubaldo, sent as an emissary of society, begins his criticism of Rinaldo by placing a shield before his eyes, Rinaldo's guilty reaction means that he looks neither at himself in the shield, nor at Ubaldo:

> ma se stesso mirar già non sostiene;

> giú cade il guardo, e timido e dimesso,
> guardando a terra, la vergogna il tiene (XVI, 31, 4–6).

Ubaldo then proceeds to censure him verbally, urging him to confront and overcome his senses/Armida (XVI, 41). When she appears, Rinaldo does not look at her ('ei lei non mira'), and when he finally does so ('se pur mira'), it is once again with shame: 'il guardo / furtivo volge e vergognoso e tardo' (XVI, 42, 7–8). He behaves similarly after the rebuke of 'il mago veglio' (his social superior in terms of age): 'volgeva a terra e vergognoso il ciglio' (XVII, 64, 4).

Fear in the presence of a superior power is another motive for an inferior (both male and female) not looking:

> Ella pur fugge, e timida e smarrita
> non si volge a mirar s'anco è seguita (VII, 2, 7–8)

> Qual semplice bambin mirar non osa
> dove insolite larve abbia presenti ...
> cosí temean (XIII, 18, 1–2, 5)

> Ma nel Soldan feroce alzar non osa
> Orcano il volto, e 'l tien pensoso e basso (X, 56, 5–6).

Before Goffredo infused with divine wrath, the crowd 'non osa ... / fra timor e vergogna alzar la fronte' (VIII, 82, 5–6). Lowering of the eyes is also a sign of defeat. For instance, when Goffredo is overwhelmed by the sight of the heavenly army, 'chinò vinti i lumi' (XVIII, 97, 1). He is momentarily in a similarly weakened position of indecision with respect to Armida: 'Mentre ei cosí dubbioso a terra vòlto / lo sguardo tiene' (IV, 67, 1–2). Armida's reaction to Goffredo's negative response to her request is also to stare at the ground: 'A quel parlar chinò la donna e fisse / le luci a terra' (IV, 70, 1–2). There is also the conventional connotation of looking down as a deliberate gesture on the part of an inferior to communicate respect, either genuine, or, as is probably the case in the following example, feigned: 'Ma la destra si pose Alete al seno, / e chinò il capo, e piegò a terra i lumi' (II, 61, 1–2).

Not seeing also occurs in speech in the first person singular, when its function is often the basic rhetorical one of persuasion, rather than literally signifying vision, as in the lines: 'la vittoria però, però non vedo / liberate, o signor, le mura oppresse' (X, 44, 3–4).

3. Appearing and not appearing

In this section the subject of the look sees or looks at the object as a direct result of the appearance of the latter. The look of the subject may be deliberately instigated by the object, which is superior in some way. Alternatively, the object may have been forced to appear by the subject, and is expressed in terms denoting inferiority in relation to the subject. The particular categories of power relationship revealed by examples of the former type of appearance relate to superiority in terms of religion: the divine angel Gabriel places 'la sua forma' before mortal eyes ('al senso mortal la sottopose', I, 13, 3–4); military superiority: Goffredo as *duce* 'si mostra a i soldati' (I, 34, 1); and age: an old man appears (*appare*) before Carlo and Ubaldo (XIV, 33, 3–4). Carlo and Ubaldo, representing the superior status of social justice over a recalcitrant Rinaldo, appear before him: 'scoprirsi a lui pomposamente armati' (XVI, 27, 8). In this last example, the reaction of the subject to the appearance of the object underlines the looker's inferior status ('tutto si scosse').

In cases when the subject has forced the appearance of the object, the power relationship similarly concerns the military category, for instance, the superiority of a *duce* who can order a generic group, *il campo*, to appear before him (I, 34). The expression of the relationship of superiority vs. inferiority is progressively more attenuated the nearer the object is in status to the subject. Rinaldo, taking part in the same parade, is individualized by the mention of his Christian name, and his superiority in relation to the others emphasized in elevated social terms:

> Ma il fanciullo Rinaldo, e sovra questi
> e sovra quanti in mostra eran condutti,
> dolcemente feroce alzar vedresti
> la regal fronte, e in lui mirar sol tutti (I, 58, 1–4).

Tancredi, treated likewise, is identified by his Christian name and described using superlatives:

> Vien poi Tancredi, e non è alcun fra tanti
> (tranne Rinaldo) o feritor maggiore,
> o piú bel di maniere e di sembianti,
> o piú eccelso ed intrepido di core (I, 45, 1–4).

Similarly in the case of the pagan parade, those less inferior in military terms appear in individualized form (Adrasto, XVII, 28; Tisaferno, XVII, 31), whereas objects more distanced in status from the subject are expressed in terms of unindividualized nation groups (XVII, 13–15). On a narrative level, not only is variety of narration achieved by such attenuation, but relevant character information is also communicated to the Reader, before whom, as well as before each respective leader, the Christian and pagan armies parade.

Establishment rather than maintenance of power is served by object appearing to subject in another set of examples. This can take the form of appearing aggressively as part of an attempt to gain power through violence, and often occurs in conflict situations:

> Ivi solo discese, ivi *fermosse*
> in vista de' nemici il *fero* Argante (VI, 23, 1–2)

> Su 'l ponte intanto un cavaliero armato
> *con sembianza apparia fera* e sdegnosa (VII, 31, 5–6)

> E si mostra in quel lume *a i riguardanti*
> *formidabil* cosí l'empio Soldano (IX, 26, 1–2).

Appearing is also used to gain superiority through sexual means, for instance when Armida first arrives in the Christian camp: 'A *l'apparir* de la beltà novella / nasce un bisbiglio e 'l guardo ognun v'intende' (IV, 28, 3–4). Following her failure to win Goffredo over with words, Armida appears before him in a vast variety of ways: 'Tentò ella mil-l'arti, e in mille forme / quasi Proteo novel gli *apparse* inanti' (V, 63, 3–4). Similarly in her likeness which appears to Rinaldo in the wood: 'mille affetti in un guardo *appaion* misti' (XVIII, 31, 1–2). Her way of appearing also plays an important part in her subjugation of members of the pagan council. She appears last of all, suddenly, and sublimely: 'Nessun piú rimanea, quando improvisa / Armida *apparve* ... / Venia sublime' (XVII, 33, 1–3).

The description of her mood concludes with the lines: 'e cruda ed acerbetta / par che minacci e minacciando alletta' (XVII, 33, 7–8). The phrase *cruda ed acerbetta* recalls *acerbe e crude* in the description of her breasts when she first appears in the Christian camp: 'Parte *appar* de le mamme acerbe e crude, / parte altrui ne ricopre invida vesta' (IV, 31, 3–4). The explicitly sexual context of the earlier phrase is recalled by the later variation, thereby giving sexual resonance to a passage which is characterized by the marvellous rather than the overtly sexual. The sexual element is present nonetheless, in what could be considered a form of parody. The four unicorns pulling her chariot symbolize purity and chastity, according to Tasso himself, as well as in Christian interpretation, which includes the unicorn as an attribute of the Virgin Mary, St Justina of Padua and St Justina of Antioch.[3] The whiteness of the horses bearing her *donzelle* and *paggi* have the same symbolic value. However, Armida's unicorns are coupled, as well as unusually numerous. In paintings of the period, on the other hand, they always appear singly with a female figure, as in the representation of St Justina of Padua by artists of the Paduan and Venetian schools (Ferguson 1979, 128).

The section 'Parte appar de le mamme acerbe e crude, / parte altrui ne ricopre invida vesta' (IV, 31, 3–4) also denotes a specifically erotic type of sexual context. This example is one of many showing the interplay between appearing/not appearing, showing/not showing, which is responsible for the erotic element. In the first of his three essays on the theory of sexuality, 'The Sexual Aberrations' (1905), Freud links the sense of sight with that of touch ('Seeing—an activity that is ultimately derived from touching'), noting also that: 'The progressive concealment of the body which goes along with civilization keeps sexual curiosity awake. This curiosity seeks to complete the sexual object by revealing its hidden parts' (Freud 1984, 69). Armida's breasts partly appear (*parte appar*) to the *cupide turbe*, and partly are hidden and do not appear ('parte altrui ne ricopre invida vesta: / … a gli occhi il varco chiude', 31, 4–5).

On other occasions she hides her *tesori d'amore* from view, only to reveal them shortly afterwards (IV, 31, 1). Her cleavage is hidden (*secreta*) and at the same time revealed by her veil ('mal cauto apria / fra due mamme un bel vel', XIX, 69, 7–8). Her two 'donzelle garrule e lascive' reveal their heads and backs, having begun by concealing them: 'Si tuffano talor, e 'l capo e 'l dorso / *scoprono* alfin dopo il *celato* corso' (XV, 58, 7–8). One then proceeds to reveal:

---

[3] In his *Giudizio sovra la Gerusalemme Conquistata* Tasso refers to: 'la castità e l'innocenza della vita, figurata co 'l segno d'armellino e d'unicorno' (*Prose diverse*, 483). He also mentions the unicorn in *Il Conte overo de l'imprese*: 'De l'unicorno n'ho vedute alcune [imprese]: altri assai leggiadramente ha figurato l'unicorno fulminato sotto il lauro, forse per darci a divedere che gli amanti de le vergini non sono sicuri sotto l'ombra de la virginità e de la castità, perché gli unicorni, come dicono, rifuggendo a le vergini e nel lor grembo addormentandosi, son presi da' cacciatori; altri portò l'unicorno che purga la fonte dal veneno con la secreta virtù del suo corno, e vi aggiunse questo motto VENENA PELLO' (*Dialoghi*, ii. 1077). See also Ferguson 1979, 26.

>   ... le mammelle
>   e tutto ciò che piú la vista alletti
>   ... dal seno in suso, aperto al cielo (XV, 59, 5–7),

while at the same time *not* showing what is already revealed on the formal level by a euphemism: 'e 'l lago a l'altre membra era un bel velo' (XV, 59, 8). When, feigning shame, she conceals all, what has been shown and seen (*vago spettacolo*) is now no longer visible (*è lor tolto*) and is hidden ('da l'acque e da' capelli *ascosa*'). Armida's hair partly, and then completely, appears in view, mirroring the appearance/non-appearance of explicitly sexual areas of her body: 'la chioma ... or dal bianco velo / *traluce* involta, or *discoperta appare*' (IV, 29, 3–4). In the *carpe diem* birdsong, the metaphor of the rose (itself *modesta e verginella*) is used. The rose, half-open and half-closed, suggests the baring/concealing (opening/hiding) of female sexual parts (the vagina): 'mezzo aperta ancora e mezzo ascosa'. This interplay is considered highly effective: 'quanto si mostra men, tanto è piú bella' (XVI, 14, 3–4). Armida herself exercises immense sexual power for similar reasons: '*Veduta a pena* ... / invaghir può genti sí varie e tante' (XVII, 36, 5–6).

In Sofronia's case, there is an attempt to negate any such eroticism. However, the negation has the effect of actually introducing an erotic interplay into the text: 'non coprí sue bellezze, e non l'espose' (II, 18, 2). What the poet is in effect trying to negate is any responsibility on Sofronia's part for such an interplay. While it is part of Armida's role to use her art to such an end, Sofronia, presented as the ideal Christian woman, must be exculpated from any such behaviour. The fact that the poet fails significantly in this endeavour indicates a belief that all women are sexual temptresses. *Appearing/not appearing* and *showing/not showing* imply culpability on the part of the woman. It is she who is responsible for appearing and showing herself, thereby inviting and justifying the penetrating/fragmenting male look, together with all its aggression.

4. Directing the look of another

Related to examples of appearing in which a superior object appears to an inferior subject, thereby dictating the look of another, is the instigated look. This is found when one person, using the imperative, orders another to look at someone or something. Speech is usually the vehicle for commanding this look. However, there are a few non-verbal examples involving gestures such as pointing or showing. The subject of this look tends to be inferior in some way to the person who has ordered the look, in itself an act which commonly forms part of a pattern of behaviour designed to make the subject/inferior think or behave in a certain way.

This involves mostly the same categories of power relationship found in other sections. For instance, the superiority of divine over human beings, such as the now-divine Ugone speaking to Goffredo in a heaven-sent dream: ' "*China*" poi disse (e gli *additò* la terra) / "*gli occhi* a ciò che quel globo ultimo serra" ' (XIV, 9, 7–8) and the archangel Michael to Goffredo: ' "*Non chinar, non chinar gli occhi* smarriti; / *mira* con quante forze il Ciel t'aiti" ' (XVIII, 92, 7–8). In the case of the superiority of God in relation to Michael, a lesser divine being, there is an attenuated imperative (a negative interrogative with the force of an imperative), perhaps reflecting the harmony of life in heaven: ' "*Non vedi* or come s'armi / contra la mia fedel diletta greggia / l'empia schiera d'Averno?" ' (IX, 58, 5–7). The category of the supernatural vs. the human is also represented in the form of Fortuna vs. Carlo and Ubaldo: ' "*Mirate*", disse poi, "quell'alta mole / ch'a quel gran monte in su la cima siede" ' (XV, 44, 1–2). Aletto, taking on the shape of a treacherously slain Rinaldo, speaks to a fellow knight in a dream, also using the negative interrogative form: ' "Fuggi, Argillan; *non vedi* omai la luce?" ' (VIII, 60, 7).

Old age vs. youth is represented by the *vecchio santo* who addresses Carlo as *figlio* and gives him a command: ' "Ma *leva* omai *gli occhi* a le stelle, e *guata* / là splender quella, come un sol lucente" ' (VIII, 31, 5–6). Similarly *il venerabil Piero* says to Tancredi, using the negative interrogative form in keeping with the image of the humble *buon pastore* tending an *agnella inferma*: ' "Questa sciagura tua del Cielo è un messo; / *non vedi* lui?" ' (XII, 86, 5–6) and ' "pendi già cadente e prono / su 'l precipizio eterno: e tu *no 'l miri?*" ' (XII, 88, 5–6). In terms of military superiority, Goffredo urges his men on by telling them to look at the enemy: ' "Qual timor" grida "è questo? ove fuggite? / *Guardate* almen chi sia quel che vi caccia" ' (IX, 47, 3–4). Class superiority is present in Erminia's order to the squire: ' "Ben dessa i' son, ben dessa i' son; *riguarda*" ' (XIX, 82, 4). Lastly, human (Christian) forces beat animal (pagan) forces by directing the lion's look towards a magic wand and so dispelling its power (XV, 50, 2).

The same superior instigator of the directed look is also to be found explaining to the seeing inferior the exact nature of what is/has been/will be/should be/could be seen. This is particularly the case when superior knowledge is crucial to dominance. In the divine vs. the human category, the archangel Michael tells Goffredo: '"*vedrai* gli ignudi spirti in volto"' (XVIII, 93, 6), while in the category of the supernatural vs. the human, Fortuna explains to Carlo and Ubaldo:

> l'isole di Fortuna ora *vedete*,
> di cui gran fama a voi ma incerta giunge.
> Ben son elle feconde e vaghe e liete,
> ma pur molto di falso al ver s'aggiunge (XV, 37, 3–6).

In the age/wisdom vs. youth group, the *vecchio onesto* or *padre* explains to Carlo and Ubaldo what they will see: '"Vi scòrgo al mio palagio, il qual accenso / tosto *vedrete* di mirabil luce"' (XIV, 41, 5–6) and '"aprir la gran bocca orsi e leoni *vedrete*"' (XIV, 73, 4–5). Similarly *mago veglio* says to *figlio* (Rinaldo): '"ivi de' tuoi maggior l'opre *vedrai*" ' (XVII, 64, 8). With reference to what Rinaldo has seen, *veglio* says to *garzon*: '"*Veduto hai* tu de la tua stirpe altera / i rami e la vetusta alta radice"' (XVII, 86, 3–4); and, regarding what he could see, were the Mago to continue: '"cosí *potessi* ancor *scoprire a pieno* / ne' secoli avenire i tuoi nepoti"' (XVII, 87, 3–4) and '"ché de' futuri eroi già *non vedresti* / l'ordin men lungo, o pur men chiari i gesti"' (XVII, 87, 7–8). Finally, it is explained to Rinaldo (*il cavalier*) by *l'eremita santo* that what he has seen ('*hai scorso*') are 'Ben gran cose' (XVIII, 6, 7). In the realm of military superiority, this time on the pagan side, Solimano says to *le genti*: '"*Vedete* là di mille furti pieno / un campo piú famoso assai che forte"' (IX, 17, 1–2).

In a different set of examples, *vedere* is used, like *non vedere*, in a more non-literal, rhetorical way, to persuade or to threaten. In this case the person speaking is not necessarily a superior maintaining or reasserting a position of power. On the contrary, it can be someone in an inferior or equal position who is trying either to achieve a certain end, for which the assent of a person in a superior or equal position is necessary, or to gain the upper hand by telling the subject of the look what (s)he is/will be/has been seeing. As part of an attempt to persuade, using the present tense, Alete says to Goffredo: '"ben son le tue schiere or molto sceme / tra le guerre e i disagi, e tu te 'l *vedi*"' (II, 73, 5–6). Using the future tense, Guelfo says to Goffredo: '"Scoter le mura ed atterrar le porte / *vedrailo*, e salir solo a tutti inante"' (XIV, 23, 5–6) and, in the subjunctive governed by a future, Adrasto to Armida: '"assai tosto averrà che l'empia testa / di quel Rinaldo a piè tronca ti *veggia*"' (XIX, 71, 3–4). The negative future is used by Sofronia speaking to Aladino: '"quel [furto] *no 'l vedrai* in eterno"' (II, 24, 1) and the past by Orcano to Aladino: '"vi *fu mostro* / quanto potea maggiore il valor nostro" ' (X, 45, 7–8).

As part of an attempt to gain superiority by threat, Alete, having failed by persuasive means, says to Goffredo: '"*scorgerai*, ch'ove tu la guerra prenda, / hai di temer, non di sperar cagione"' (II, 70, 3–4). In like vein Argante says to Goffredo, also in the future tense: '"*Vedrai* ben tosto / come da me il tuo dono in uso è posto"' (II, 93, 7–8), and Tancredi to Argante: '"e che del mio indugiar non fu cagione / tema o viltà, *vedrai* co 'l paragone"' (XIX, 4, 7–8). The present tense is used in a similarly aggressive context by Argante to the Christians: '"*Vedete* là il sepolcro ove il figliuolo / di Maria giacque: or ché non gite avanti?"' (VII, 74, 5–6).

5. Seeming

The object of the look here appears to be something which it perhaps is not. This is a deliberate attempt to deceive and sabotage the look, and is part of a pattern of behaviour designed to gain an advantage. This is often conveyed by the verb *parere*, as in the description of Vafrino in the pagan camp: 'Vafrin vi guata e *par* ch'ad altro intenda' (XIX, 61, 7). On the level of narrative technique *parere* is used, frequently in the manner of a simile, to achieve vividness by means of litotes (the figure of intensification by understatement). In other words, something or someone 'seems to be' (rather than is). This creates the illusion of the dawning of a first impression, of something seen for the first time, as in the following examples: 'l'aria *par* di faville intorno avampi' (I, 73, 5), '*Parve* … 'l ferro un lampo' (V, 27, 1), '*par* senza governo in mar turbato, / rotte vele ed antenne, eccelsa nave' (VII, 98, 3–4).

Looking that is transformed into false vision by the deceiving object, mostly engineered by evil, pagan forces, is central to the plot of the poem. One important example is Rinaldo's mock death, and the 'false' *villanel*'s testimony, engineered by Armida. By creating discontent and disorder in the Christian camp, it functions in the narrative as a plot obstruction. The second major episode based on false vision is that of the wood (as perceived by Christian knights) and bewitched by Ismeno on behalf of pagan forces. This acts as a considerable, long-lasting plot obstacle, the overcoming of which, six cantos later, is crucial to plot resolution.

Another plot obstruction based on false appearances and distracting Rinaldo from his martial duty is Armida's garden:

> par che la dura quercia e 'l casto alloro
> e tutta la frondosa ampia famiglia,
> par che la terra e l'acqua e formi e spiri
> dolcissimi d'amor sensi e sospiri (XVI, 16, 5–8)

her nymphs:

> ... una ben pare
> di quelle che già presso a la tirrena
> piaggia abitàr l'insidioso mare (XIV, 61, 4–6),

and even the doors:

> D'oro fiammeggia l'onda, e par che tutto
> d'incendio marzial Leucate avampi (XVI, 4, 5–6).

The garden, like the wood, disappears, not being founded in Christian/social reality, but concerning only the 'unreal' (pagan and anti/ante-social) realm of outer, physical appearance which deceives the undisciplined/unsocialized individual eye.

That this type of deception can take place at all is due in part to the potential susceptibility of the looker in relation to the object. For instance, sight can be a source of suffering, as it is for Solimano catching sight of Lesbino slain on the battlefield: 'vede, ahi, dolor!, giacerne ucciso / il suo Lesbin' (IX, 85, 7–8). Likewise Tancredi, realizing he has killed Clorinda, exclaims: 'Ahi vista!' (XII, 67, 8). When he later thinks he sees her in the enchanted wood, he cannot bear to look: 'né può soffrir di rimirar quel sangue' (XIII, 45, 7). At the other extreme, looking can provide pleasure, as in the case of Tancredi gazing at Clorinda earlier in the poem: 'Sol di mirar s'appaga' (VI, 27, 7); or when he believes he will never see her again: 'ma di piú vago sol piú dolce vista, / misero! i' perdo' (VII, 49, 1–2).

6. Seeing as knowing

Knowing is one of several conventional connotations of sight that operate in the poem as an ideological reinforcement providing a network of stock associations as a backcloth against which to set other instances of looking. Verbs of seeing, such as *scorgere, accorgersi di, avedersi di,* and

vedere itself, already bear the dual meaning of cognitive as well as purely visual perception. In the following examples, the cognitive denota-
tion of knowing is uppermost in verbs of sight (italicized): 'Ma poi
ch'ebbe di questi e d'altri cori / *scòrti* gl'intimi sensi il Re del mondo'
(I, 11, 1–2), '*veggio* secure vie che tu vietarmi / il morir non potresti'
(XX, 133, 5–6), 'traggon tutti per *veder* chi sia / sí bella peregrina, e chi
l'invia' (IV, 28, 7–8), 'Ei molto per sé *vede*, e molto intese / del *preveduto* vostro alto viaggio / (già gran tempo ha) da me' (XIV, 31, 1–3).
Realization is implicit in the following instances of perception:
'riguardando d'ogni parte i suoi, / *scorge* che a tutti la vittoria arride'
(XVIII, 97, 3–4), 'che 'l possente Guelfo (e *se n'accorge* / questo popol
e quel) percosso cade' (XI, 59, 3–4), 'del gran rischio *s'accorge* ove ella
gía' (XII, 19, 4), '*s'avidero* i pagani (e ben turbàrsi) / che la torre non è
dove esser sole' (XVIII, 64, 3–4), and '*Vede* or che sotto il militar sembiante / ir tra feri nemici è gran follia' (VI, 98, 1–2).

Seeing in the sense of *knowing* brings social rewards. The superior
rank of *duce* is accorded to Dudone because he has seen (and done)
more than the others: 'ch'avea piú cose fatte e piú *vedute*' (I, 53, 4).
Carlo, also aspiring to superior status, wishes to inspire envy in the
others by seeing and knowing what is not yet known to his society.
He asks to be allowed to undertake an *alta impresa*:

> e *veder* questi inconosciuti lidi,
> *veder* le genti e 'l culto di lor fede
> e tutto quello ond'uom saggio m'invídi,
> quando mi gioverà narrar altrui
> le novità *vedute* e dir: 'Io fui!' (XV, 38, 4–8).

However, at the top of the hierarchy, a superior authority controls
and limits human knowledge and power. The ultimate inferiority of
ingegno umano to God, the ultimate Seer, in the realm of sight, is also
indicated in the reference by Fortuna to the Dantesque *folle volo* of
Ulysses, swallowed by *l'ocean vorace* as a result of being 'di *veder* vago
e di *saper*' (XV, 25, 8).

One type of sight as knowledge that is particularly significant in
the poem is that of foresight, expressed by verbs such as *prevedere*,
antivedere, *vedere lunge*, and *mirar da lunge*. The ability to see or know
ahead of time is highly prized. The Mago, for instance, considers
that *mirar da lunge* and *preveder gli estremi* 'de la matura età pregi men
degni / non fiano' (XVII, 92, 1–2). Eustazio credits Goffredo with
the same talent: 'Sí come a te conviensi, o capitano, / questa lenta

virtú che *lunge vede*' (V, 6, 3–4). The gift of foresight is similarly valued on the pagan side. Ismeno says to Aladino: 'Ben tu di re, di duce
hai tutte piene / le parti, e *lunge hai visto*' (II, 3, 5–6). This special
type of sight is in the almost exclusive possession of characters who
are superior in some way, the particular categories of difference
being those identified during the course of this analysis. The above
examples show the typical superiority of age over youth (*la matura
età*), military superiority (*capitano*), and the socio-military superiority of a *re* or *duce*.

Piero, instigator of the Crusade and the most important religious
patriarch in the poem, is a prominent possessor of foresight: 'Ecco
chiaro *vegg*'io, correndo gli anni' (X, 75, 3); ' "Ei molto per sé *vede*,
e molto intese / del *preveduto* vostro alto viaggio / (già gran tempo
ha) *da me*" ' (XIV, 31, 1–3). Interestingly, Armida is at one point
declared to have the power of foresight:

> 'Prese l'armi la maga, e in esse tosto
> un tronco busto avolse e poi l'espose;
> l'espose in ripa a un fiume ove doveva
> stuol de' Franchi arrivar, e 'l *prevedeva*.
> E questo *antiveder* potea ben ella' (XIV, 53, 5–8, 54, 1).

However, there are pejorative associations latent in the verb *antivedere*.
The prefix *anti* has a dual meaning: as well as signifying anteriority, it
can also denote hostility. *Antivedere* is used only in Armida's case by
the Mago (a Christian patriarch) and by the heroic Tancredi (a
Christian knight) in taunting Argante (XIX, 9, 7). The way in which
Armida's foresight is expressed would seem to indicate a negative and
inferior type of foresight. This surfaces in the more overt ' "*né potrà
pur, cotal virtú vi guida, / il giunger vostro antiveder* Armida" ' (XIV,
78, 7–8), once again spoken by the Mago. It is in his words, moreover,
rather than in those of Armida herself, that her foresight is 'contained',
so that it enters the narrative passively, as well as being limited.
Ismeno's powers of foresight are similarly curtailed. He can only see
dimly into the future: ' "Ma pur dirò, perché piacer ti debbia, / ciò che
oscuro vegg'io quasi per nebbia" ' (X, 21, 7–8). The pagan Armida and
Ismeno appear to be deprived of full powers of foresight, a faculty that
belongs exclusively to the highest of Christian patriarchs.

The faculty of sight in the poem also has other positive, traditional connotations, such as birth ('ove gli [occhi] apersi in prima', IV, 50,
8), light (the use of *lumi* and *luci* for eyes), and the association of light

with goodness and God (the angel is described 'a paro co 'l sol, ma
piú *lucente*', I, 15, 7). Heaven itself is a place of light: 'questi *lucidi*
alberghi e queste vive / fiamme che mente eterna informa e gira'
(XIV, 9, 3–4). Hell, evil and the Devil, on the other hand, are associated with lack of sight, and so with darkness and blindness:

> Ma quando parte il sol, qui tosto adombra
> notte, nube, caligine ed orrore
> che rassembra infernal, che gli occhi ingombra
> di cecità (XIII, 3, 1–4).

Evil can be in the form of 'bad' light, as in the case of Pluto's look:
'rosseggian gli occhi, e di veneno infetto / come infausta cometa il
guardo splende' (IV, 3–4). Lack of sight is also linked to death, as in
the phrase *chiuder gli occhi* (IV, 50, 8).

There is, therefore, a traditional system of sight-connotation in the
poem, a system whereby positive, power-related types of sight are in
the exclusive possession of those with superior status in the various
domains of power relationship (God vs. lesser divine beings, the
divine vs. the human, age vs. youth, social/religious/military/sexual/
superiority vs. inferiority). In another context, and as one might
expect from a text belonging to a genre whose surface narrative proceeds via actions (rather than, for instance, on the basis of stages in the
logic of contemplation), *seeing* is integrated into narrative progression.
This occurs in the many cases when the emphasis is not so much on
the seen object *per se*, but, rather, on what the object is seen to be
doing (italicized in the following examples): '*Pianger* lui *vede* … e *tacer*
lei' (II, 42, 5, 7), 'verso lei se 'n corse / il duce lor, ch'*a sé venir la vede*'
(III, 14, 5–6), 'Andianne ove quell'empio / *veggiam* ne' fuggitivi *insu-
perbire*' (IX, 28, 3–4) and 'Goffredo, ove *fuggir* l'impaurite / sue genti
vede, accorre e le minaccia' (IX, 47, 1–2).

This in turn may lead to an action on the part of the seeing
subject, thereby moving the narrative forwards. This is apparent
in the last three of the above examples, where seeing precipitates
the following actions or proposed actions respectively: *corse, andianne*, and *accorre* and *minaccia*. The same is true when the object
itself is non-human, such as an inanimate object, or the coming
of dawn:

> Ma come vede il ferro ostil che molle
> fuma del sangue ancor del giovenetto …
> Corre sovra Argillano (IX, 87, 1–2, 5)

and: 'Come vide spuntar l'aureo mattino, / mena fuori Goffredo il campo instrutto' (XX, 6, 1–2).

7. The Reader and the look

Sight is often manipulated by the text in such a way as to create a level of Reader involvement over and above the obvious one of reading the poem in the first place. As already indicated above, the Reader is made to participate, at times along with the characters, in the act of looking. This is achieved in a variety of ways, for instance, by means of certain inflections of *vedere* and *(ri)mirare*. For example, *vedresti* (conditional mood): 'Qui mille immonde Arpie *vedresti*' (IV, 5, 1), 'Ma il fanciullo Rinaldo ... dolcemente feroce alzar *vedresti* / la regal fronte' (I, 58, 1, 3–4) and 'in varia imago / vincitrice la Morte errar per tutto / *vedresti* ed ondeggiar di sangue un lago' (IX, 93, 2–4). This means 'you too would see' (if you were here). Similar use is made of *veggiam* (first person plural, present tense): 'qual ne l'ore piú fresche e matutine / del primo nascer suo *veggiam* l'aurora' (IV, 94, 5–6). The use of this person and tense of *vedere* includes the Reader, along with certain characters and the poet as persona, in a habitual act of seeing used to illustrate a point in the narrative.

Vedi (second person singular present indicative), meaning 'You see/are seeing', tells the Reader, with the force of an imperative, that (s)he is seeing something in particular; for example: '*Vedi* appresso spiegar l'alto vessillo' (I, 64, 1). Occasionally, *vedi* is preceded by *se*, and then followed by what would be seen (were the Reader to see it); in other words, what *is* seen by the Reader: 'se 'l *miri* fulminar ne l'arme avolto' (I, 58, 7). The adverb *ecco* has the effect of the imperative *see*, particularly in conjunction with a verb of looking, and is a direct exhortation to the Reader. For example, '*ecco* apparir Gierusalem *si vede*' (III, 3, 5) and '*Ecco* tra fronde e fronde *il guardo inante* / *penetra e vede, o pargli di vedere*' (XVI, 17, 5–6). *A vedello dirai* also has the force of an imperative. For example: 'a *vedello* / *dirai* che ringhi' (XVII, 69, 3–4). By describing what *you* (the Reader) *will* see (were you to see him), it follows that you see him. The infinitive of the verb *to see*, and a description of what is seen, has a similar effect: 'e le nascenti lagrime *a vederle* / erano a i rai del sol cristallo e perle' (IV, 74, 7–8).

The infinitive used as a noun, such as *nel rimirar* and *il vedere*, is an instance of an impersonalized form of looking and seeing that also assumes the Reader as the subject: ''l vincitor dal vinto / non ben saria *nel rimirar* distinto' (XIX, 28, 7–8) and 'Grande e mirabil cosa era *il vedere* / quando quel campo e questo a fronte venne' (XX, 28, 1–2). The same effect is achieved by the exclamatory use of the nouns *spettacolo* and *vista*: 'talché (strano *spettacolo* ed orrendo!) / ridea sforzato e si moria ridendo' (XX, 39, 7–8) and 'Mirabil *vista*! a un grande e fermo stuolo / resister può, sospeso in aria, un solo' (XVIII, 77, 7–8). The impersonal constructions *si vede* and *si mira* have the same effect of including the Reader as subject: 'Baldovin poscia in mostra addur *si vede*' (I, 40, 1) and 'Là giacere un cavallo, e girne errante / un altro là senza rettor *si mira*' (VII, 105, 3–4). In the following example, the Reader is involved, together with the persona of the poet as subject of a penetrating look, by use of the pronouns *ne* and *ci* which merge the Reader's identity with that of *altrui*:

> Amor, ch'or cieco, or Argo, ora *ne* veli
> di benda gli occhi, or *ce* gli apri e giri,
> tu per mille custodie entro a i piú casti
> verginei alberghi *il guardo altrui* portasti (II, 15, 5–8).

This example shows how the Reader is positioned by the text as superior (male) subject of the penetrating look, rather than as inferior object (see sect. 1(g)). Another instance of a privileged Reader position occurs when the Reader is accorded a look almost corresponding to that of God (a look shared only on one occasion by Goffredo):

> *Vedi* tosto inchinar giú le visiere,
> lentare i freni e por le lancie in resta,
> e *quasi in un sol punto* alcune schiere
> da quella parte moversi e da questa (VII, 104, 3–6).

On another level, this type of Reader involvement also serves the narrative function of vividness. Details of the narrative are made to appear as if happening before the eyes of the Reader, by virtue of the effect of the Reader 'being there'. Such heightening of narrative effect often occurs in action-dominated areas of the poem, such as scenes of battle or single combat, requiring an element of immediacy in narration (as at IX, 93). Detailed descriptions of works of art or craft (XVI, 6 and XVII, 69) are also made to seem more life-like. Rinaldo's reaction to the representations on the shield even echoes the actual theory of how vividness is supposed to function, both in terms of verisimilitude and visuality: 'pur, come sia presente e come vero / dinanti a gli occhi suoi vedere avisa' (XVII, 82, 5–6).

Syntax

In addition to the semantic categories of vision outlined above, syntax is also significant in determining the nature of the relationship between subject and object of the look. In terms of active as opposed to passive constructions, implications for subject and object can be located at the level of deep and surface structures. For example, deep and surface structures are very close in the following subject–verb–object construction:

il Padre eterno   mirò   tutte le cose (I, 7, 3; I, 8, 1)
        S   V   O

However, in the following passive verb–agent–subject construction:

mirata   da ciascun   l'altera donna (II, 19, 1, 2)
  Vp   A   S

the surface, passive form makes *altera donna* the subject of the action. This has the effect of moving *donna* from the original object position in which it is generated in the deep, active structure:

ciascun   mira   l'altera donna
    S   V   O

If this object position is in itself negatively valued, then the subject position of the passive form in the surface structure must also be considered to be in an inferior position. While passive constructions form only a small minority in the poem (twenty-two in all), their distribution, however, mirrors the system of power relations dominating the poem.

Interestingly, of these examples only three show Christian men (Goffredo, Rinaldo and *il popol franco*) and one (male) Christian angel, in the negative deep object/surface subject position. The remainder consist of six women (five pagan and one Christian, four instances of which take place in overtly sexual situations); two pagan men (Argante and Alete); and ten non-human objects (*spada* II, 93, *piaggie e montagne* III, 12, *spade* V, 28, *lampi* XIII, 74, *novità* XV, 38, *case e culture* XV, 41, *catapulte* XVIII, 64, *strage* XIX, 52, *spoglie* VI, 108, and *colomba*, XVIII, 49). Moreover, Goffredo deliberately places himself in the object position. He does so in order to be seen by his men who believe him to be badly injured, and thereby hopes to improve their morale: 'ascendendo in un leggier cavallo, / giunger non può che non sia visto al vallo' (XI, 56, 7–8). The example involving Rinaldo is not quite straightforward either. Although he is being watched by

Armida, it is perhaps not coincidental that her look embodies the two anti-social aspects/manifestations of Rinaldo's *id* that were suppressed by social reprimand: 'egli è da lei mirato / con occhi d'*ira* e di *desio* tremanti' (XX, 61, 5–6) (see Ch. 5).

It can be concluded that the look, both in terms of semantics and syntax, is used in the *Gerusalemme liberata* as a system of body language that correlates with dominant power positions. The look functions to reinforce the social hierarchies of gender, age, religion and the military, as represented by the poem. This can only be partly explained by factors such as the context of the Counter-Reformation within which the *Gerusalemme liberata* was composed, or the psychological characteristics of Tasso himself. Twentieth-century theories on the workings of power are still governed by hegemonic ideologies and cultures in terms of hierarchies of dominance and subordination.[4] As a consequence body language, in conjunction with other forms of communication, continues to contribute to strategies of reinforcement of the status quo.[5]

---

[4] For a discussion of theories of power in relation to another Renaissance text, Machiavelli's *Il principe*, see Günsberg 1995.

[5] For a discussion of body language in a theatrical context, see 'Behind the Veil: Body Politics in *Sei personaggi in cerca d'autore*', in Günsberg 1994, 164–91.

BIBLIOGRAPHY

Primary sources

ARISTOTLE, *The 'Art' of Rhetoric*, trans. J. H. Freese (London: Heinemann, 1959).

—— *Metaphysics*, trans. H. Tredennick (London: Heinemann, 1933).

—— *Physics*, trans. P. H. Wicksteed and F. M. Cornford (London: Heinemann, 1929).

—— *Poetics*, in *Aristotle, Horace, Longinus: Classical Literary Criticism*, trans. T. S. Dorsch (Harmondsworth: Penguin, 1965).

—— *Poetics*, in *Aristotle: The Poetics; 'Longinus': On the Sublime; Demetrius: On Style*, trans. W. Hamilton Fyfe (London: Heinemann, 1927).

—— *The Rhetoric of Aristotle*, trans. C. Jebb (Cambridge: Cambridge University Press, 1909).

Aristotle, Horace, Longinus: Classical Literary Criticism, trans. T. S. Dorsch (Harmondsworth: Penguin, 1965).

Aristotle: The Poetics; 'Longinus': On the Sublime; Demetrius: On Style, trans. W. Hamilton Fyfe (London: Heinemann, 1927).

CAMPANELLA, T., 'Poetica italiana' (1596), in Bolzoni (ed.), *Opere letterarie di Tommaso Campanella*, 337–456.

CASTELVETRO, L., *Poetica d'Aristotele vulgarizzata et sposta*, (1570; repr. Munich: Wilhelm Fink Verlag, 1968).

CICERO, *Brutus*, trans. G. L. Hendrickson (London: Heinemann, 1939).

—— *De inventione*, trans. H. M. Hubbell (London: Heinemann, 1960).

—— *De optimo genere oratorum*, trans. H. M. Hubbell (London: Heinemann, 1949).

—— *De oratore*, trans. H. Rackham and E. W. Sutton, 2 vols. (London: Heinemann, 1942).

—— *De partitione oratoria*, trans. H. Rackham (London: Heinemann, 1942).

—— *Orator*, trans. H. M. Hubbell (London: Heinemann, 1939).

DEMETRIUS, *De elocutione*, in *Aristotle: The Poetics; 'Longinus': On the Sublime; Demetrius: On Style*, trans. W. Hamilton Fyfe (London: Heinemann, 1927).

GEOFFROI DE VINSAUF, 'Poetria Nova', trans. in Gallo 1971, 14–128.

GILIO DA FABRIANO, G. A., *Topica poetica* (1580; repr. Munich: Wilhelm Fink Verlag, 1970).

GIRALDI, G. B., *Discorso intorno al comporre delle comedie e delle tragedie* (1554), ed. C. Guerrieri Crocetti (Milan: Marzorati, 1973).

HORACE, *Ars poetica*, trans. H. Rushton Fairclough (London: Heinemann, 1955).

—— *Q. Horatius Flaccus, Briefe*, commentary by A. Kiessling, ed. R. Heinze (Berlin: Weidmannsche Verlagsbuchhandlung, 1957).

MAGGI, V., and LOMBARDI, B., *In Aristotelis librum de poetica communes explanationes* (1550; repr. Munich: Wilhelm Fink Verlag, 1969).

MINTURNO, A. S., *L'arte poetica* (1564; repr. Munich: Wilhelm Fink Verlag, 1971).

PLATO, *Gorgias*, trans. W. R. M. Lamb (London: Heinemann, 1961).

—— *Phaedrus*, trans. H. N. Fowler (London: Heinemann, 1960).

QUINTILIAN, *Institutio oratoria*, trans. H. E. Butler, 4 vols. (London: Heinemann, 1959–63).

Rhetorica ad Herennium, trans. H. Caplan (London: Heinemann, 1954).

RICCOBONI, A., *Compendium artis poeticae Aristotelis* (1591; repr. Munich: Wilhelm Fink Verlag, 1970).

—— *Poetica Aristotelis latine conversa* (1587; repr. Munich: Wilhelm Fink Verlag, 1970).

ROBERT OF BASEVORN, 'Forma praedicandi', trans. L. Krul, in Murphy 1971, 109–215.

ROBORTELLO, F., *In librum Aristotelis de arte poetica explicationes* (1548; repr. Munich: Wilhelm Fink Verlag, 1968).

RUSSELL, D. A., and WINTERBOTTOM, M. (eds.), *Ancient Literary Criticism: The Principal Texts in New Translations* (Oxford: Clarendon Press, 1978).

TASSO, B., 'Ragionamento della poesia' (1562), in Weinberg 1970–4, ii. 567–84.

TASSO, T., *Allegoria della Gerusalemme liberata* (1581), in *Prose diverse*, ed. Guasti, i. 297–308.

—— *Apologia in difesa della Gerusalemme liberata* (1585), in *Prose*, ed. Mazzali, 411–86.

—— *Apologia in difesa della sua Gierusalemme liberata. Con alcune altre opere, parte in accusa, parte in difesa dell'Orlando Furioso dell'Ariosto, della Gierusalemme istessa e dell'Amadigi del Tasso padre* (Ferrara: G. C. Cagnacini, 1585).

—— *Il Cataneo overo de le conclusioni amorose* (1590), in *Prose*, ed. Mazzali, 257–95.

—— *La cavaletta overo de la poesia toscana* (1584), in *Dialoghi*, ed. Guasti, iii. 61–114.

—— *Le conclusioni amorose* (1570), in *Prose*, ed. Mazzali, 296–302.

—— *Il Conte overo de l'imprese* (1594), in *Dialoghi*, ed. Raimondi, ii. 1029–124.

Dialoghi, ed. C. Guasti, 3 vols. (Florence: Le Monnier, 1858).

—— *Dialoghi*, ed. E. Raimondi, 2 vols. (Florence: Sansoni, 1958).

—— *Discorsi dell'arte poetica e del poema eroico*, ed. L. Poma (Bari: Laterza, 1964).

—— *Discorsi dell'arte poetica* (written 1561–2, published 1587), in *Discorsi*, ed. Poma, 3–58.

—— *Discorsi del poema eroico* (1594), in *Discorsi*, ed. Poma, 59–262.

—— *Discourses on the Heroic Poem*, trans. M. Cavalchini and I. Samuel (Oxford: Clarendon Press, 1973).

—— *La Gerusalemme liberata* (1581), ed. L. Caretti (Turin: Einaudi, 1971).

—— *Giudizio sovra la Gerusalemme conquistata* (1594), in *Prose diverse*, ed. Guasti, i. 443–547.

—— *Le lettere di Torquato Tasso*, ed. C. Guasti, 5 vols. (Florence: Le Monnier, 1852–5).

—— *Prose*, ed. E. Mazzali (Milan and Naples: Riccardo Ricciardi, 1959).

—— *Prose diverse*, ed. C. Guasti, 2 vols. (Florence: Le Monnier, 1875).

THOMAS OF ERFURT, *Grammatica speculativa*, trans. and commentary by G. L. Bursill-Hall (London: Longman, 1972).

VETTORI, P., *Commentarii in primum librum Aristotelis de arte poetarum* (1560; repr. München: Wilhelm Fink Verlag, 1967).

Secondary sources

ARBUSOW, L., *Colores rhetorici* (Göttingen: Vandenhoeck and Ruprecht, 1963) (first published 1948).

BALDASSARI, G., 'Inferno' e 'cielo': tipologia e funzione del 'meraviglioso' nella 'Liberata' (Rome: Bulzoni, 1977).

BALLERINI, C., *Il blocco della guerra e il suo dissolversi nella 'Gerusalemme liberata'* (Bologna: Pàtron, 1979).

—— (ed.), *Atti del Convegno di Nimega sul Tasso, 25–27 ottobre 1977* (Bologna: Pàtron, 1978).

BARTHES, R., *Le Plaisir du texte* (Paris: Seuil, 1973).

BATTAGLIA, S. (ed.), *Grande dizionario della lingua italiana* (Turin: UTET, 1975).

BIRD, O., 'The Canzone d'Amore of Cavalcanti according to the Commentary of Dino del Garbo', *Mediaeval Studies*, 2 (1940), 150–74, and 3 (1941), 117–60.

BOLZONI, L. (ed.), *Opere letterarie di Tommaso Campanella* (Turin: UTET, 1977).

BRAGHIERI, P., *Il testo come soluzione rituale: La Gerusalemme liberata* (Bologna: Pàtron, 1978).

BRANCA, V., et al. (eds.), *Il Rinascimento: aspetti e problemi attuali* (Florence: Olschki, 1982).

—— 'Torquato Tasso e l'"oscurità"', *Studi secenteschi*, 3 (1962), 27–43.

BRAND, C. P., 'Stylistic trends in the *Gerusalemme conquistata*', in C. P. Brand,

K. Foster, and U. Limentani (eds.), *Italian Studies presented to E. R. Vincent* (Cambridge: W. Heffer & Sons. Ltd., 1962) (1962a), 136–53.

—— *Torquato Tasso: A Study of the Poet and of his Contribution to English Literature* (Cambridge: Cambridge University Press, 1965).

BRECHT, B., *Brecht on Theatre*, ed. and trans. J. Willett (London: Methuen, 1986).

BROOKS, P., *Reading for the Plot: Design and Intention in Narrative* (Cambridge, Mass.: Harvard University Press, 1995).

BROWN, H., *The Venetian Printing Press 1469–1800: An Historical Study Based upon Documents for the most Part hitherto Unpublished* (Amsterdam: Gerard Th. van Heusden, 1969) (first published 1891).

BROWN, P. M., 'The Historical Significance of the Polemics over Tasso's *Gerusalemme Liberata*', *Studi secenteschi*, 11 (1970), 3–323.

BRUSCAGLI, R., 'Il campo cristiano nella *Liberata*', in G. Papagno and A. Quondam (eds.), *La corte e lo spazio* (Roma: Bulzoni, 1982), ii. 783–819.

CATALLO, E., 'Aspetti del montaggio cinematografico nella tecnica narrativa del Tasso', in Branca *et al.* (eds.), *Il Rinascimento*, 251–8.

CERMOLACCE, J., 'La Nuit dans la *Gerusalemme Liberata*', *Revue des études italiennes*, 19 (1973), 244–59.

CHATMAN, S., *Story and Discourse* (Ithaca, NY: Cornell University Press, 1979).

CHIAPPELLI, F., *Studi sul linguaggio del Tasso epico* (Florence: Le Monnier, 1957).

—— 'Struttura inventiva e struttura espressiva nella *Gerusalemme Liberata*', *Studi Tassiani*, 14–15 (1964–5), 5–33.

—— *Il conoscitore del caos: una 'vis abdita' nel linguaggio tassesco* (Rome: Bulzoni, 1981).

CHOMSKY, N., *Syntactic Structures* (The Hague: Mouton, 1969).

CLARK, D. L., *Rhetoric and Poetry in the Renaissance* (New York: Columbia University Press, 1922).

COHAN, S., and HARK, I. R. (eds.), *Screening the Male: Exploring Masculinities in Hollywood Cinema* (London: Routledge, 1993).

CONNELLY, J. P., 'The Moslem Enemy in Renaissance Epics: Ariosto, Tasso and Camoens', *Yale Italian Studies*, 1 (1977), 162–70.

CORRIGAN, B., 'The Opposing Mirrors', *Italica*, 33 (1956), 165–79.

—— 'Erminia and Tancredi: The Happy Ending', *Italica*, 15 (1963), 325–33.

CORTI, M., *La felicità mentale* (Turin: Einaudi, 1983).

COYLE, M. (ed.), *Niccolò Machiavelli's* The Prince*: New Interdisciplinary Essays* (Manchester: Manchester University Press, 1995).

CURTIUS, E. R., 'Über die altfranzösische Epik' *Zeitschrift für romanische Philologie*, 64 (1944), 233–320.

DOANE, M. A., *Femmes fatales: Feminism, Film Theory, Psychoanalysis* (London: Routledge, 1991).

DONADONI, E., *Torquato Tasso* (Florence: La Nuova Italia, 1967) (first publ. 1920–1).

ECO, U., *Opera aperta* (Milan: Bompiani, 1967).

—— *The Role of the Reader* (London: Hutchinson, 1981).

—— *Trattato di semiotica generale* (Milan: Bompiani, 1982).

EISENSTEIN, E. L., *The Printing Press as an Agent of Change* (Cambridge: Cambridge University Press, 1972).

FARAL, E., *Les Arts poétiques du XIIe et du XIIIe siècle* (Paris: Librairie Honoré Champion, 1962) (first published 1923).

FERGUSON, G., *Signs and Symbols in Christian Art* (Oxford: Oxford University Press, 1979).

FIRETTO, G., *Torquato Tasso e la Controriforma* (Palermo: Sandron, 1933).

FREGE, G., 'Die Verneinung: Eine logische Untersuchung', *Beiträge zur Philosophie des deutschen Idealismus*, 1 (1918–19), 143–57.

FREUD, S., 'The Sexual Aberrations' (1905), in *On Sexuality: Three Essays on the Theory of Sexuality*, ed. A. Richards and J. Strachey (Harmondsworth: Penguin, 1984), 45–87.

—— *The Standard Edition of the Complete Psychological Works*, ed. J. Strachey, 24 vols. (London: Hogarth Press, 1953–74). Cited as Freud *SE*.

—— 'Group Psychology and the Analysis of the Ego' (1921), *SE*, xviii. 69.

—— 'Negation' (1925), *SE*, xix. 235.

FUBINI, M., 'Osservazioni sul lessico e sulla metrica del Tasso' (1945), in *Studi sulla letteratura del Rinascimento* (Florence: La Nuova Italia, 1971), 216–40.

GALLO, E., *The Poetria Nova and its Sources in Early Rhetorical Doctrine* (The Hague: Mouton, 1971).

—— 'The Poetria Nova of Geoffrey of Vinsauf', in Murphy 1978, 68–84.

GARIN, E., *Science and Civil Life in the Italian Renaissance*, trans. P. Munz (New York, 1969).

GREENE, J., 'The Semantic Function of Negatives and Passives', *British Journal of Psychology*, 61 (1970), 17–22.

GRENDLER, P. F., 'The Roman Inquisition and the Venetian Press, 1540–1605, *Journal of Modern History*, 47 (Mar. 1975), 48–65.

—— *The Roman Inquisition and the Venetian Press 1540–1605* (Princeton: Princeton University Press, 1977).

GÜNSBERG, M., *Patriarchal Representations: Gender and Discourse in Pirandello's Theatre* (Oxford: Berg, 1994).

—— 'The End Justifies the Means: End-Orientation and the Discourses of Power', in Coyle 1995, 115–50.

HALM, C., *Rhetores latini minores* (Leipzig: Teubner, 1863).

HASELL, E. J., *Tasso* (Edinburgh and London: William Blackwood and Sons, 1882).

HAUPT, H., *Bild- und Anschauungswelt Torquato Tassos* (Munich: Wilhelm

Fink Verlag, 1974).

HERRICK, M. T., *The Fusion of Horatian and Aristotelian Literary Criticism 1531–1535* (Urbana: University of Illinois Press, 1946).

HERRICK, M. T., *Comic Theory in the Sixteenth Century* (Urbana: University of Illinois Press, 1950).

IOVINE, F., *La 'licenza del fingere'* (Rome: Bulzoni, 1981).

JENNINGS, M., 'The *Ars componendi sermones* by Ranulph Higden', in Murphy 1978, 112–26.

JONARD, N., 'Le Temps dans la *Jérusalem Délivrée*', *Studi Tassiani*, 24 (1974), 7–22.

KELLY, D., 'The Scope of the Treatment of Composition in the Twelfth-and Thirteenth-Century Arts of Poetry', *Speculum*, 41 (1966), 261–78.

KUHN, A., *Women's Pictures: Feminism and Cinema* (London: Routledge and Kegan Paul, 1982).

LACAN, J., 'Le Stade du miroir comme formateur de la fonction du "je" ' (1936), in *Écrits 1* (Paris: Seuil, 1966), 89–97, trans. as 'The Mirror Stage as Formative of the Function of the *I*' by A. Sheridan, in *Écrits* (London: Tavistock, 1985), 1–7.

LAUSBERG, H., *Handbuch der literarischen Rhetorik*, 2 vols. (Munich: Max Hueber Verlag, 1960).

LEMON, L. T., and REIS, M. J., *Russian Formalist Criticism: Four Essays* (London: University of Nebraska Press, 1965).

LEO, U., *Torquato Tasso: Studien zur Vorgeschichte des Secentismo* (Bern: Francke, 1951.

LEPSCHY, A. L., 'Appunti su antitesi e anafora nella *Gerusalemme Liberata*', in *Umanesimo e rinascimento a Firenze e a Venezia*, vol. iii of *Miscellanea di studi in onore di Vittore Branca* (Florence: Olschki, 1983), 799–802.

MARTINELLI, A., *La demiurgia della scrittura poetica* (Florence: Olschki, 1983).

MATEJKA, L., and POMORSKA, K. (eds.), *Readings in Russian Poetics: Formalist and Structuralist Views* (Cambridge, Mass.: MIT Press, 1971).

MOLHO, A., and TEDESCHI, J. (eds.), *Renaissance Studies in Honour of Hans Baron* (De Kalb: Northern Illinois University Press, 1971).

MOMIGLIANO, A., 'I motivi del poema del Tasso', in *Introduzione ai poeti* (Rome: Tumminelli, 1946), 79–100.

MULVEY, L., *Visual and Other Pleasures* (London: Macmillan, 1989).

MURPHY, J., *Rhetoric in the Middle Ages* (Berkeley: University of California Press, 1974).

—— *Medieval Eloquence* (Berkeley: University of California Press, 1978).

—— (ed.), *The Three Medieval Rhetorical Arts* (Berkeley: University of California Press, 1971).

NEALE, S., 'Masculinity as Spectacle: Reflections on Men and Mainstream Cinema', *Screen*, 24/6 (Nov./Dec. 1983), 2–16.

NOERO, C., 'Il notturno nella Gerusalemme Liberata', *Studi Tassiani*, 14–15

(1964–5), 35–40.

NORDEN, E., *Die antike Kunstprosa vom VI. Jahrhundert v. Chr. bis in die Zeit der Renaissance* (Leipzig: Teubner, 1909).

PAPAGNO, G., and QUONDAM, A. (eds.), *La corte e lo spazio*, 3 vols. (Rome: Bulzoni, 1982).

PERELMAN, C., and OLBRECHTS-TYTECA, L., *Trattato dell'argomentazione. La nuova retorica*, 2 vols. (Turin: Einaudi, 1966) (first publ. as *Traité de l'argumentation. La nouvelle rhétorique* (Paris: Presses Universitaires de France, 1958)).

PETERS, F. E., *Aristotle and the Arabs: The Aristotelian Tradition in Islam* (New York: New York University Press, 1968).

PROPP, V., *Morphology of the Folktale* (1928), trans. L. Scott (Austin: University of Texas Press, 1979).

RAIMONDI, E., *Poesia come retorica* (Florence: Olschki, 1980).

RANK, O., *The Double* (1914) (New York: New American Library, 1979).

RENAN, E., 'Averroës et l'Averroisme' (1852), in *Œuvres complètes*, ed. H. Psichari, 3 vols. (Paris: Calmann-Lévy, 1947), iii. 11–365.

RICOEUR, P., *Temps et récit* (Paris: Éditions du Seuil, 1983).

RUGGIERI, R. M., 'Latinismi, forme etimologiche e forme "significanti" nella *Gerusalemme Liberata*' (1946), in *Saggi di linguistica italiana e italo romanza* (Florence: Olschki, 1962), 197–212.

SALVIATI, L., 'Degli Accademici della Crusca Difesa dell'Orlando Furioso dell'Ariosto contra 'l Dialogo dell'epica poesia di Camillo Pellegrino, Stacciata Prima', in Tasso, *Apologia*.

SAPIR, E., 'The Unconscious Patterning of Behavior in Society', in *The Unconscious: A Symposium* (New York: Knopf, 1927), 114–42, repr. in *Selected Writings of Edward Sapir*, ed. D. G. Mandelbaum (Berkeley: University of California Press, 1958), 544–59.

SCAGLIONE, A., *The Classical Theory of Composition from its Origins to the Present: A Historical Survey* (Chapel Hill: University of North Carolina Press, 1972).

SCHOLES, R., *Structuralism in Literature* (New Haven: Yale University Press, 1974).

SCRIVANO, R., 'Letteratura e immagini del Tasso', in *La norma e lo scarto* (Rome: Bonacci, 1980), 249–66.

SEMPOUX, A., 'Armida allo specchio', in Ballerini 1978, 307–29.

SHEPHERD, S., *Amazons and Warrior Women* (Brighton: Harvester Press, 1981).

ŠKLOVSKIJ, V., *Teoria della prosa* (1925), trans. G. C. De Michelis and R. Oliva (Turin: Einaudi, 1976).

SOLERTI, A., *Vita di Torquato Tasso*, 3 vols. (Turin: Loescher, 1895).

SOZZI, B. T., *Studi sul Tasso* (Pisa: Nistri-Lischi, 1954).

TEDESCHI, J., 'Florentine Documents for a History of the "Index of

Prohibited Books"', in A. Molho and J. Tedeschi, *Renaissance Studies* (1971), 579–605.

Thesaurus linguae latinae, editus auctoritate et consilio Academiarium quinque Germanicarum Berolinensis, Gottingensis, Lipsiensis, Monacensis, Vindobonensis (Leipzig: Teubner, 1900–).

TODOROV, T. (ed.), *I formalisti russi* (Turin: Einaudi, 1968).

ULIVI, F., *Il Manierismo del Tasso e altri studi* (Florence: Olschki, 1966).

WEINBERG, B., *A History of Literary Criticism in the Italian Renaissance*, 2 vols. (Chicago: University of Chicago Press, 1961).

—— (ed.), *Trattati di poetica e retorica del Cinquecento*, 4 vols. (Bari: Laterza, 1970–4).

ZATTI, S., *L'uniforme cristiano e il multiforme pagano: saggio sulla Gerusalemme Liberata* (Milan: Il Saggiatore, 1983).

INDEX OF NAMES AND TEXTS

SUBJECT INDEX